PUBLIC
TRIALS

PUBLIC TRIALS

*Burke, Zola, Arendt, and the
Politics of Lost Causes*

LIDA MAXWELL

OXFORD
UNIVERSITY PRESS

OXFORD
UNIVERSITY PRESS

Oxford University Press is a department of the University of Oxford.
It furthers the University's objective of excellence in research, scholarship,
and education by publishing worldwide.

Oxford   New York

Auckland   Cape Town   Dar es Salaam   Hong Kong   Karachi
Kuala Lumpur   Madrid   Melbourne   Mexico City   Nairobi
New Delhi   Shanghai   Taipei   Toronto

With offices in

Argentina   Austria   Brazil   Chile   Czech Republic   France   Greece
Guatemala   Hungary   Italy   Japan   Poland   Portugal   Singapore
South Korea   Switzerland   Thailand   Turkey   Ukraine   Vietnam

Oxford is a registered trademark of Oxford University Press
in the UK and certain other countries.

Published in the United States of America by
Oxford University Press
198 Madison Avenue, New York, NY 10016

Library of Congress Cataloging-in-Publication Data
Maxwell, Lida.
Public trials : Burke, Zola, Arendt, and the politics of lost causes / Lida Maxwell.
pages cm
Includes bibliographical references and index.
ISBN 978-0-19-938374-0 (hardback)
1. Democracy—Philosophy.   2. Justice, Administration of—Philosophy.   3. Hastings,
Warren, 1732–1818—Trials, litigation, etc.   4. Burke, Edmund, 1729-1797.   5. Dreyfus,
Alfred, 1859-1935—Trials, litigation, etc.   6. Zola, Emile, 1840–1902.   7. Eichmann, Adolf,
1906-1962—Trials, litigation, etc.   8. Arendt, Hannah, 1906–1975. I. Title.
JC423.M3786 2014
320.01'1—dc23
2014014575

135798642
Printed in the United States of America
on acid-free paper

FOR MY PARENTS,

Carol Maxwell and Phil Maxwell

Many Theresas have been born who found for themselves no epic life wherein there was a constant unfolding of far-resonant action; perhaps only a life of mistakes, the offspring of a certain spiritual grandeur ill-matched with the meanness of opportunity; perhaps a tragic failure which found no sacred poet and sank unwept into oblivion.. . . Here and there is born a Saint Theresa, foundress of nothing, whose loving heart-beats and sobs after an unattained goodness tremble off and are dispersed among hindrances, instead of centring in some long-recognizable deed.

—George Eliot, "Prelude" to *Middlemarch*

CONTENTS

ACKNOWLEDGMENTS

Hannah Arendt says that our supposedly solitary process of thought is deeply shaped and sparked by our conversations and interactions in the world. Happily, that is surely the case with this book. It is a pleasure to acknowledge here the individuals and institutions that have offered varied forms of support, advice, criticism, and thoughts during the conception and writing of this book.

I can say in all truthfulness that I never would have become a political theorist were it not for Roxanne Euben. In the last semester of my senior year at Wellesley College, while finishing up my Religion major, I took a seminar in "Feminist Political Theory" with Roxanne. I was so blown away by that class that I decided not to go to law school and to apply to graduate programs in political theory instead. Thanks to Roxanne for opening my eyes to what theory is and could be, and for her continuing enthusiasm for and support of my work.

This book has its origins in my doctoral dissertation at Northwestern University. At Northwestern, Bonnie Honig, Linda Zerilli, Sara Monoson, and Miguel Vatter were supportive and encouraging advisors, and they created a stimulating environment in which to study political theory. In particular, Linda Zerilli encouraged me to pursue my idiosyncratic thoughts from the outset and spent countless hours with me in her office, talking about Benjamin, Burke, Arendt, Montesquieu, Rousseau, and all the other thinkers I was enamored of. Linda's early support of me, and these long conversations, helped me to figure out how and why I love doing political theory. I am tremendously grateful for this, and for her continued support.

As my dissertation advisor and beyond, Bonnie Honig has given incredible support to me and my work—more than I could describe or

ACKNOWLEDGMENTS

thank her for here. Looking through my files as I finish this project, I see the tangible remnants of this support—restaurant napkins with scribbled notes from lunch discussions, notes from long phone conversations, and her comments written on (countless) drafts of chapters and papers. As these artifacts attest, Bonnie has been incredibly generous with her time and thoughts—sharing her keen insight, pithy phrases, and intellectual imagination with me at every step of this way. The conversations that I have had with her about democratic agency, law, and Arendt form important threads running through this book. I am indebted to her for that, but I am also indebted to her for the intellectual example she provides. Her intellectual generosity, frankness, good humor, and relentless attention to the political stakes of arguments have provided me with a model that it is a pleasure to be guided by. I am also grateful to Bonnie for saying, "the book is done."

I developed many of the core ideas of this book while a Mellon Postdoctoral Fellow at Cornell, where Susan Buck-Morss, Burke Hendrix, Isaac Kramnick, Diane Rubenstein, Anna-Marie Smith, and, especially, Jason Frank made me feel a part of the Political Theory community. I am grateful for the insights I gained into my project in the Mellon Interdisciplinary Faculty Seminars in which I participated, and I thank the participants in 2006–2007 and 2007–2008 for what they have added to my thinking and to this project. I also benefited from conversations with Katherine Biers, Rebecca Givan, Cary Howie, Katherine Lieber, Alison McQueen, and Robert Travers. Ithaca and Cornell provided a wonderful first academic home after graduate school. My thinking was challenged, transformed, and clarified in all the best ways.

Ike Balbus, Steve Engelmann, and Norma Moruzzi were similarly supportive of me and my work at the University of Illinois, Chicago. Dick Simpson created a welcoming environment for me in the department. I also learned from conversations with the graduate students in my Democratic Theory course, especially Clifford Deaton, Abe Singer, and Alan Ward.

I have found a wonderful academic home at Trinity College. I couldn't ask for better, more supportive colleagues, both in and outside my department. In the Political Science Department, Sonia Cardenas, Stefanie Chambers, Diana Evans, Andy Flibbert, Isaac Kamola, Kevin McMahon, Tony Messina, Reo Matsuzaki, Gitte Schulz, and Abby

Fisher Williamson are terrific interlocutors. They are also just lovely, interesting, and intellectually engaging people to be around, which makes Trinity a pretty great place to go to work. All the members of my department at Trinity, as well as Zayde Antrim, Rob Corber, Christopher van Ginhoeven Rey, Chris Hager, Sara Kippur, and Vijay Prashad, workshopped and gave me great feedback on an early version of my chapter on Burke. I am especially grateful to Sara Kippur for her insight not only on the Burke chapter, but on the project as a whole (and for her help with French). My students at Trinity—especially students in my Political Trials classes—have productively challenged and aided my thinking about the book.

In the broader academic world, I am grateful to those who have read parts of the manuscript, or with whom I've had important conversations about it: Crina Archer, Lawrie Balfour, Katherine Biers, Japonica Brown-Saracino, Sonali Chakravarti, Roxanne Euben, Burke Hendrix, Adriene Hill, Bonnie Honig, Ayten Gundogdu, Demetra Kasimis, Isaac Kramnick, Sharon Krause, Lori Marso, Alison McQueen, Ella Myers, Andy Schaap, Rebekah Sterling, Elizabeth Wingrove, Linda Zerilli, and Karen Zivi. Jason Frank offered terrific feedback on the entire manuscript, as did an anonymous press reader. Laura Ephraim also read most of the manuscript and offered characteristically smart feedback and hard questions. Laura's thinking and ideas always refresh my own, and her friendship has sustained me, intellectually and personally. I am extremely grateful for it.

A version of Chapter 4 was previously published in *Contemporary Political Theory* as "Toward an Agonistic Understanding of Law: Law and Politics in Hannah Arendt's *Eichmann in Jerusalem*" (11[2012]: 88–108). I thank the reviewers of that article for their comments. Portions of this essay are reproduced here with the permission of Palgrave Macmillan. I also presented versions of Chapters 3 and 4 at the American Political Science Association Conference and a version of Chapter 4 at the Conference of the Association for the Study of Law, Culture, and the Humanities. While I was at Northwestern, the American Bar Foundation and the Alice Berline Kaplan Humanities Center provided supportive and intellectually vibrant atmospheres in which to write my dissertation. I am also grateful to Wellesley College for the support of a Vida Dutton Scudder Fellowship.

The extended Maxwell and Cunha families have been sources of support, laughter, and great discussions. I would like to especially acknowledge my grandmother, Ruth Cunha, and my late grandfather, Cliff Cunha. My grandfather, a master of the pun, showed me the value of jokes and laughter in creating community. My grandmother, an expert spinner of tales, continues to show me the value of storytelling and narration in making meaning out of life—a debt I don't know if I can ever repay. I also appreciate the support of Alex, Jami, and Walker Maxwell, who remind me to have fun, and I am thankful for the love and support of the larger Brown-Saracino clans—especially Pam Brown, Annie Garvey, Mike Saracino, Maggie Saracino, Jocelyn Brown-Saracino, Dave Nelson, and Brooke Brown-Saracino. I am grateful to Sara Kippur, Josh Lambert, Asher Lambert, and the Lambert-to-come for providing a home away from home in West Hartford—and excellent conversation and hugs from small children, to boot.

I owe more to Japonica Brown-Saracino than I can say—but I will try to say a little. I am tremendously grateful for the insight, honesty, and sheer intelligence that Japonica shares with me in discussions of my work and, really, of everything. Our conversations, debates—and, yes, arguments—about politics and theory and the world have deeply shaped the way I think, and have left significant traces throughout this manuscript. Japonica has also endured (mostly with good humor) my bouts of spaciness when I've been caught up in the book, made me laugh in moments of frustration, kicked me out the door to go running when I've hit a moment of writer's block, and—most important—convinced me to stop working from time to time and get out into the world with her. In what often feels like our whirlwind life together, Japonica has also helped give me the space and time to do the actual, practical writing of this book, which I am deeply grateful for. In sum, being with Japonica has made my life (and work) better, fuller, and more meaningful—and I am profoundly thankful for it.

Louisa Maxwell arrived as I was really getting serious about this book. Happily, she has ensured that I do not take myself *too* seriously, and that I keep a healthy balance between playing (especially playing Uno) and working. I also appreciate the boost to my self-esteem from Louisa's continued insistence that I am the biggest one in our house.

When I was in the fourth or fifth grade, my parents took me out to dinner and told me that from now on, they were not going to bother me about my grades. I had to get at least C's, but the rest was in my court. I have dedicated this book to my parents, Carol Maxwell and Phil Maxwell, in part because, as this anecdote suggests, they were and are great parents. I've also dedicated it to them, though, because as this anecdote also suggests, they encouraged me not to be captured by conventional standards of success and failure, and to find meaning in experiences, desires, and ideas that do not fit within them. As an aspiring leftist, intellectual feminist growing up in a conservative and often anti-intellectual town, I was pretty lucky to have such parents. I was also lucky to have them when I decided to be a Religion major, and go on a Tibetan Studies abroad program, and to turn down law school so that I could study political theory. Thanks, Mom and Dad, for supporting me in everything. You will never know how much it has meant to me.

PUBLIC
TRIALS

PUBLIC TRIALS AND LOST CAUSES

The Politics of Democratic Failure

On November 25, 1897, the popular French novelist Emile Zola published his first article defending the innocence of a Jewish army captain convicted of treason—Alfred Dreyfus. As the army and the government continued to insist on Dreyfus's guilt, Zola and other Dreyfusard intellectuals filled the press with their claims that Dreyfus's conviction had been based on fraudulent evidence, and that the public and official refusal to recognize the injustice done to Dreyfus was the work of anti-Semitism. Yet Zola also insisted in his writings that "truth is on the march!" and that the public would ultimately see the truth of Dreyfus's innocence and restore France's commitment to justice. Zola's most potent appeal to the public came in "J'Accuse!" in which he indicted members of the government and the army for intentionally deceiving the public. In "J'Accuse!" Zola wrote, "I am confident and I repeat, more vehemently even than before, the truth is on the march and nothing shall stop it."[1] Yet the public response to "J'Accuse!" was not what Zola had hoped for. After its publication in January 1898, the Dreyfus case truly became the Dreyfus *Affair*: riots broke out from Paris to Algiers—with Zola and Dreyfus being hung in effigy—and Zola was put on trial for libel, a trial that he ultimately lost.

In July 1898, after several appeals and proceedings, Zola fled to England to avoid having the sentence (a large fine) served on him. In a letter to his wife, Alexandrine, written in October of the same year, Zola spoke of his misgivings about the future of the Dreyfus Affair. In stark contrast to his repeated proclamations in his essays published prior to his exile—"Truth is on the march! And nothing can stop it!"—and to his published claim that France "will always reawaken" and "will always triumph amid truth and justice!"[2] Zola writes in this letter:

> For the sake of my peace of mind, I wish I could recover the faith I have lost. You remember how serenely I used to proclaim, even during the darkest days of my trial, that the truth would triumph over everything. Now as we are drawing near our goal I no longer dare believe that the triumph of truth is inevitable, because what is going on is such a sorry sight that it has destroyed all the hope I once had in men's reason and decency. I know of nothing more dreadful. To think that they are keeping Picquart in prison, that all of Paris did not rise up at the idea that Dreyfus is innocent, that France continues to be accomplice to so many crimes! That means we can expect the worst kinds of infamy, to hide so many other infamies that have already been committed. That is why I continue to be so pessimistic. Until the very last day, the authorities will do everything they can to make the innocent pay the debts of the guilty. Never has a country gone through a more dreadful period. And I will go so far as to say that, even when Dreyfus has been acquitted, you'll see, they will continue to call us traitors and say we've sold out.[3]

Zola's letter bespeaks a deep disappointment with the actions of the legal authorities in Dreyfus's case: they have imprisoned Picquart, the military officer who proclaimed Dreyfus's innocence in opposition to his superiors' claims of Dreyfus's guilt. Further, a military court-martial acquitted Esterhazy (the actual spy). Law here has not safeguarded justice, but has been used as a tool of *injustice*. Yet here Zola is focused not only on the failure of law. His letter also reveals a deep disappointment in the people of France, who "continue. . . to be accomplice to so many crimes!" Zola expresses shock and disappointment, almost a year after writing "J'Accuse!" that "all of Paris did not rise up at the idea that Dreyfus is innocent." Not only the law, but also the people, have failed to assure justice—and Zola foresees (correctly) that even if Dreyfus is legally rehabilitated, popular and governmental sentiment will not uniformly support it and may still proclaim Dreyfus's guilt.

Zola's writings on the Dreyfus Affair portray it as an instance of what I call "democratic failure": a moment when both law and the people fail to assure justice. While some stories of democracy stay with us because they appear as almost miraculous instances of democratic achievement and inspiration—the American founding, the French Revolution, the American civil rights movement—stories of democratic failure, such as Zola's narrative of the Dreyfus Affair, stay with us for a different reason: they haunt us with the specter of the people betraying their own ideals—sanctioning injustice, inequality, and oppression rather than seeking justice, equality, and freedom.

In this book, I examine three narratives of democratic failure: Zola's writings on the Dreyfus Affair in late nineteenth-century France; Edmund Burke's writings on the impeachment and trial of the governor-general of the East India Company, Warren Hastings, in late eighteenth-century Britain; and Hannah Arendt's writings on the Adolf Eichmann trial in 1960s Israel (Eichmann was a former Nazi who was kidnapped in Argentina by Israeli agents in 1960 and was brought to Jerusalem to stand trial). These writers all claim that law and legal officials failed to do full justice to the crimes they confronted: Hastings's imperial oppression of Indians, the French government's "crime against society" (Zola defines this as the crime of misleading the French people about Dreyfus's guilt), and Eichmann's "crimes against humanity." These writers also argue, however, that this legal failure was enabled by broad public complicity in the national myths that made injustice (or incomplete justice) appear to be "justice." If the theatrical spectacle of each of these trials served as a kind of funhouse mirror for the nations in which they took place, these writers argue, in each case, that the public bought into a false image of itself that distorted its sense of justice.

As we will see, Burke's, Zola's, and Arendt's claims of democratic failure are by no means uncontested. Many others viewing the same events saw them as achievements of justice. These writers' narrations of these events *as* democratic failures thus function not only as attempts to offer true facts, but also as political claims that contest their contemporaries' rival narratives of justice done. These claims diagnose failures to assure justice that involve, but also exceed, the formal verdict. In particular, their narratives of democratic failure address how court judgments reflect and deepen broader political and social injustices. For example, Arendt argues that the Jerusalem Court was right to find Eichmann guilty for his role in the mass killing of Jews by the Nazis (Eichmann had been in charge of deporting European Jews to extermination camps). However, she also argues that the Court failed to do full justice when it portrayed Eichmann's crimes primarily as "crimes against the Jewish people," rather than as "crimes against humanity." For Arendt, the Court's judgment inadequately attended to how crimes like Eichmann's harm humanity as a whole and how they could be perpetrated against any people in the future, not only the Jews. The failure of justice here is less a failure of justice *to Eichmann* and more a failure to adequately identify, repair, and set a future precedent for protecting the community harmed by his crimes—a community that Arendt claims is humanity itself. This failure of repair is not only a failure of the Court, but also of the public(s) which failed to call for international justice. Arendt's claim of democratic failure in *Eichmann in Jerusalem* thus challenges Israel's claim of justice done, but not because she believes the verdict is wrong. Rather, her claim interrupts nationalistic, state-based, and popularly sanctioned understandings of justice, which she sees as masking a failure to do full justice to Eichmann's unprecedented crimes against humanity.

By saying that these narratives work as political *claims* of democratic failure, I foreground how they do not reflect an empirical reality (indeed, the nature of that reality is contested), but instead *solicit* a public that would affirm, respond to, and act on behalf of them. In other words, these narratives do not throw out the funhouse mirror with which the public identifies in favor of an unmediated reality. Rather, they provide a new or "counter-mirror" with which the public might identify. The "counter-mirrors" offered by Burke, Zola, and Arendt reflect a harsh, jolting image of the public and the justice it supposedly has pursued—revealing a purportedly just national identity as an ugly pretext for exclusion and scapegoating, and the imagined impartiality of the rule of law as an excuse for ignoring crimes and wrongdoing that do not fit within its parameters.

Yet these writers' narratives also attempt to *rework* or *repurpose* this ugly picture of the public's and law's complicity in injustice (or incomplete justice) by showing this complicity to be contingent and, thus, to suggest that things could have been—and still might be—otherwise. I call this kind of narrative—in which writers repurpose democratic failure on behalf of future democratic possibilities—a "lost cause narrative." While we usually associate the term "lost cause" with a cause that has no chance of success, I choose it here to describe narratives that insist on a cause being irrevocably lost while at the same time insisting on the democratic agency of loss—that is, that democratic support was the enabling condition of injustice. Through foregrounding the agency of loss, lost cause narratives operate in a temporality of "not yet." They encourage their audiences to grapple with popular responsibility for and complicity in injustice and at the same time to imagine how things could have been (and might yet be) otherwise. For example, Zola's narrative of the Dreyfus Affair portrays the people as possible seekers of justice who have bought into the mythological, nationalistic thinking proffered by the army, rather than developing the "taste for truth" that would have allowed them to seek justice. This "could have been" narrative does not lie solely in the realm of imagination. Zola's narrative is buttressed by his depiction and affirmation of Dreyfusard collective action on behalf of justice that persists beyond the Affair. Zola's lost cause narrative, like the other lost cause narratives I examine here, thus works in a double register: on the one hand, to diagnose the irrevocability of democratic failure and, on the other hand, to trace an outline of persistent democratic possibility—an outline that can itself be seen in the actions of Zola and other Dreyfusards.

By showing that democratic action could have made a difference in the past, lost cause narratives call for a public to challenge and redress injustice in the present. Zola's "could have been" narrative, for example, calls to a public of the future that would continue to contest the exclusionary, nationalistic self-understandings that hindered the public from seeking full justice in the Dreyfus Affair. While such contestation can never remedy the injustice done to Dreyfus, it can continue to resist the forms of popular myth and identity that enabled the French public's scapegoating of Dreyfus. Zola's call does not demand that the public begin *ex nihilo*, but rather to continue and maintain a politics already begun during the Affair. Lost cause narratives thus make claims of democratic failure, but never portray failure as *just* failure. They also highlight the (actual and possible) seeds of democratic resistance and political action contained therein—seeds that may be cultivated and maintained by future democratic action.

This book argues for the importance of conceiving democratic failure as such a site of democratic ambivalence and explores the democratic productivity, stakes, and dilemmas of this "politics of lost causes."

DEMOCRATIC FAILURE OR THE FAILURE OF DEMOCRACY? TWO NARRATIVES

My focus on lost cause narratives of democratic failure stands in contrast to another, more dominant way of narrating democratic failure in political theory and practice: a mode of narration that I call "fatalistic." Fatalistic narratives generalize from particular instances of democratic failure to suggest that democratic self-governance is itself (or may be) a failure—for example, because of the essential irrationality or self-interestedness of the demos. Fatalistic narratives do not call for further democratic action on behalf of justice, but point toward the need for regulation of the demos by experts and/or law.

Lost cause and fatalistic narratives may be easily confused, and for good reason. Both may point to the need for better laws and institutions, or for the replacement of some officials with others. Both also may indict the public for their failure to seek justice. In this sense, one often seems to have the shadow of the other. Yet these narratives are politically distinct. Fatalistic narratives' portrayal of democratic failure as revealing the failure of democracy interpolates citizens into a deferential relation to law and technocracy—positioning citizens as dependent on rules and experts (rather than themselves) for the survival of democracy. The people are simply and always a disappointment. In contrast, lost cause narratives position democratic citizens as agents responsible for, and able to address, their own failures, as well as the failings of laws and experts. In lost cause narratives, democracy is not in danger of falling apart due to the people's irrationality, but has been deadened or corrupted by the people's willingness to defer to expert, elite, and/or legal judgments. In short, the two forms of narrating democratic failure yield radically distinct politics. Fatalistic narratives locate proper democratic agency in actions and speech that are def-erential to rules and experts and that solidify hierarchy and barriers to participation. In contrast, lost cause narratives claim that agency is much more broadly shared and proclaim the importance of resisting (legal and other) restrictions on democratic action.

A fatalistic narrative of democratic failure stands at the origin of the Western tradition of political thought and may radiate throughout it. In Plato's *Apology*, Socrates defends himself against charges of impiety and corrupting youth. Yet we readers know (as does Socrates by the end of the *Apology*) that he will be unjustly convicted and sentenced to death. His only crime, Socrates argues, is challenging democratic norms in Athens on behalf of justice. Plato's *Apology* narrates a particu-lar moment of democratic failure: that both law and the people failed to do justice to Socrates during his trial. Yet Socrates' speeches also nar-rate this particular moment of democratic failure as caused by the fact that democracy *is* a failure—that is, that the people, when unguided by philosophers, will almost always act irrationally, favoring pleasure over wisdom, wealth over virtue, the will of the stronger over justice. Indeed, Socrates suggests that it was inevitable that he would be killed by the demos: "no human being will preserve his life if he genuinely opposes either you or any other multitude and prevents many unjust and unlawful things from happening in the city."[4] When the demos governs itself, it will inevitably fall victim to its passions and, conse-quently, sanction injustice.[5]

The foremost modern thinker of democracy—Jean-Jacques Rousseau—repudiates Plato's distrust of democracy while propagating his fatalistic narrative in new form. Whereas Plato's diagnosis of democ-racy's inevitable failure to assure justice leads him to reject democ-racy altogether in favor of the rule of experts (philosophers), Rousseau defends popular sovereignty as the necessary condition of individual freedom. Like Plato, however, Rousseau sees popular self-governance as inevitably prone to failure because of individuals' love of particular interest—a love that leads them to will against their true, collective interest. Consequently, Rousseau argues that the demos is inhabited by a tension between the "will of all" (particular interest) and the "general will" (the public interest). Yet where Plato sees the demos's tendency to will injustice as offering reason to reject democracy alto-gether, Rousseau—who sees popular sovereignty as the condition of

freedom—argues that the demos's tendency toward failure reveals the
need to properly *guide* the demos in forming its will. In particular,
Rousseau argues that the people "often does not know what it wants,
because it seldom knows what is good for it"[6] and, consequently, that
it should be guided by a lawgiver who will enable the demos to will
its will *correctly*. The supervision of the lawgiver, and the laws he gives,
assure the survival of democracy by leading the people to understand
and will its true interest.

Many contemporary liberal and deliberative democratic thinkers
reiterate the Rousseauian narration of democratic failure as the inevitable tendency of the people to will particular interest ("the will of all")
over the public interest ("the general will"). Consequently, they also,
like Rousseau, turn to outside agents as necessary constraints on democratic self-governance. Liberals such as Stephen Holmes, for example,
argue that the tendency of the demos to will the "will of all" means
that democracy, to be legitimate and respectful of individual rights,
must bind its hands in advance via constitutional rules and procedures
on behalf of assuring its allegiance to its ideals.[7] Deliberative democrats see popular sovereignty as more important than liberals to maintaining democratic ideals of freedom and equality, but like Rousseau,
they see the persistent problem of "the will of all"—which poses, in
Seyla Benhabib's words, the problem of the "hiatus between rationality
and legitimacy"[8]—as pointing toward the importance of democratic
proceduralism. Specifically, they argue for channeling democratic
deliberation through legitimate procedures that can assure legitimate
outcomes.[9] By passing the anarchic discussions of the public sphere
through the "sluices" and "funnels" of law and formal democratic
deliberation guided by legitimate procedures,[10] the inevitable failure
of the demos is forestalled and the narrative of democracy becomes,
through the guidance offered by laws and procedures, one of inevitable
progress and improvement.[11]

Of course, Rousseau's own framing of his lawgiver is more ambiguous than the turn to law by liberal and deliberative democratic theorists. Rousseau's lawgiver, after all, turns out to be chosen by the very
demos he also characterizes as a "blind multitude."[12] His fatalistic narrative thus suggests that laws and expertise are vulnerable to the problem of particular interest they are supposed to resolve. Consequently,
the demos's tendency to betray its own desires and values appears as an

intractable problem of democracy that can be addressed through laws and expert guidance, but never fully resolved. In this sense, Rousseau's framing foreshadows the lost cause narratives I focus on here, which not only diagnose the failure of the people to do justice, but also portray legal failure as entwined with and enabled by popular failure. Yet Rousseau's framing of democratic failure as inevitable also downplays the contingency and contestability of instances of democratic failure because he obscures (1) how a particular moment of democratic failure may be due not only to love of particular interest, but also to particular circumstances, conditions, and demotic self-understandings that could have been otherwise; and (2) the contested character of his own claim of democratic failure.

Focusing on lost cause narratives allows us to attend to the contestability and contingency of democratic failure that fatalistic narratives obscure. Specifically, lost cause narratives draw attention—in their practice of narration, as well as in their content—to their own character as a *claim* of democratic failure on behalf of a particular vision of the demos and its laws and, consequently, to the fact that the demos does not speak with one voice. Lost cause narratives also draw attention to how democratic failure is enabled by particular conditions and particular demotic self-understandings that could have been otherwise. Lost cause narratives, in other words, narrate and enact democratic failure as a contested *part* of democratic politics, rather than as the harbinger of democratic death that must be remedied by laws and expert guidance for democracy to survive.

This might seem like a small distinction, but the stakes are large. When fatalistic narratives portray democratic failure as possibly ushering in (or revealing) the death of democracy, they use the blackmail of emergency politics to press citizens into deference.[13] This is how, for example, Jeffrey Toobin has recently portrayed Edward Snowden's leaking of National Security Agency (NSA) documents to the press. In his essay, "Edward Snowden Is No Hero," Toobin disputes characterizations of Snowden as a "hero" who revealed unjust governmental wrongdoing and argues instead that he should be seen as a criminal: "These were legally authorized programs.... So he wasn't blowing the whistle on anything illegal; he was exposing something that failed to meet his own standards of propriety." Toobin thus claims that public admiration of Snowden should be seen as a democratic failure—a moment of failing to bring a criminal to justice and misguidedly seeing his actions as just. Yet implicit in this narration is the worry that this particular democratic failure could usher in the failure of democracy as such. If Snowden's acts are admired and imitated, Toobin suggests that the government would fall apart and fail to function. He asks, for example, "whether the government can function when all of its employees (and contractors) can take it upon themselves to sabotage the programs they don't like."[14] Toobin's claim that we are failing democratically when we admire Snowden thus has the double valence of fatalistic narratives: not only is the demos failing now, but its failure represents a broader failure of democracy. Not surprisingly, Toobin uses this threat of chaos to undergird his argument on behalf of deference: that is, that government officials and experts are better than ordinary citizens like Snowden at assuring justice, freedom, and equality and, hence, that we should defer to their judgments of what is legal and what is not, rather than exercising our own.

In contrast, lost cause narratives defuse emergency-based arguments for deference by emphasizing the dangers of deference, as well as the complex character of democratic failure: that it is inhabited by resistance to, not just complicity with, failure. Steven Johnston's narrative of Snowden's leaking falls into this camp. Johnston's essay on Snowden places him in a long tradition of democratic citizens responding to governmental (and public) failures through illegal and/or democratically disruptive actions—from vandalizing royal tax collectors during the time of the American founding to protest revenue policies, to the refusal of Boston residents in the nineteenth century to allow Anthony Burns to be returned to slavery in the South (a refusal that resulted in killing the marshal charged with returning him to the South), to the whistleblowing of Daniel Ellsberg and the truth-telling of Chelsea Manning.[15] By placing Snowden's leaking in this chain of other actions, Johnston positions him—and us—as participants in a tradition of responding to the failures of democracy (perpetrated by the law, officials, and people) through democratic action itself. Such democratic action is crucial not only in its concrete resistance to state and popular failures to assure justice. It is also crucial in challenging citizens' attachments to habits of deference and in inviting them to understand their citizenship differently—as calling for their judgments, action, and participation, rather than for their deference. As

Johnston says, "[w]hat really matters to the Obama Administration and other governments is Snowden's audacity—that he would take it upon himself, as a citizen, to force a conversation on not just transparency but also on democracy itself."[16] Within the context of a tradition of popular resistance, the democratic failure of the Snowden controversy appears not in the public's admiration for Snowden, but rather in the public's deference to a government that treats a dissident whistleblower as an ordinary criminal—in particular, the public's failure to actively contest the Obama administration's decision to level charges against Snowden, and the public's concomitant failure to press lawmakers to adequately address the injustices that Snowden revealed. Johnston's depiction of Snowden's acts is a lost cause narrative. On the one hand, Johnston emphasizes the ineradicable failure of the public (and law) to rally on behalf of justice in Snowden's case while, on the other hand, lauding the resistance to deference exemplified in Snowden's acts and those of his supporters, and finally—and, in the context of this book, most important—calling the public to build on and respond in a certain way to Snowden's acts in the future.

Lost cause narratives like Johnston's decenter the question of the survival of democracy, which stands at the heart of fatalistic narratives, and instead foreground the question of the *character* of democratic practice and life—appealing to democratic actors to identify with and engage in more sympathetic (Burke), literary (Zola), comedic (Arendt), or diffuse and contestatory (Johnston) democratic practices. To use Bonnie Honig's recent terminology, they sideline the supposed problem of "mere life" (or survival)—a problem that leads to authority-deferent behaviors—and focus instead on the problem of "more life," of the dilemmas and promise of the character of democratic life, of its tastes, its practices, its self-understandings.[17] To put the point differently, if fatalistic narratives paint democratic failure as revelatory of the failure of democracy as such that calls for external regulation and hierarchical forms of guidance, lost cause narratives portray democratic failure as a contested and contestable part of democratic politics that calls for re-examination and enrichment of demotic self-understandings, tastes, and appetites for action.

By turning to lost cause narratives in this book, and the dilemmas they open up, I aim to challenge the sway that fatalistic narratives of democratic failure exercise on our political imagination and practices.

However, I do not mean to say that we should discard fatalistic narratives. Indeed, the claim of the essential corruption or failure of the demos—while it can be turned to anti-democratic ends—can also draw our attention (as it does in Rousseau's work) to the deep persistence of failure and thus deflate problematic progress narratives or aspirations to democratic perfection. Rather, I focus on lost cause narratives on behalf of pluralizing our narratives of democratic failure. Through such pluralization, we may be better equipped to see claims of failure *as* narratives and, in turn, to see the practice of telling alternative stories about democratic failure as one important democratic practice of, in James Tully's words, "speaking and acting differently"[18]—that is, one way in which democratic actors challenge democratic norms, recode the meaning of democratic action for future actors, and valorize new political precedents and forms of engagement that may be narrated as outlandish or untenable in our present moment, but may also inspire future political action.[19] For example, Johnston's portrayal of Snowden's independent action as a source of *strength* for democracy—rather than posing a danger to its existence—recodes such practices of contestation as enabling precedents for future democratic actors.

Thus, like fatalistic narrators of democratic failure, I assume that there is no way out of democratic failure—the failure of law and people to assure justice recurs, and recurs. Yet unlike them, I do not frame this recurrence as the result of an inevitable fatal flaw of the demos. Instead, I examine particular claims of democratic failure in the context of broader democratic practices of contestation and claims-making and I ask after the stakes of narrating that failure differently. One important implication of attending to lost cause narratives' repurposing of democratic failure, as I will suggest in the next section, is the possibility of engendering a democratically robust attunement to possible "failures," or political blockages, in our own moment, revealing them as occasions for democratic responsiveness rather than expert or legal guidance.

THE BELATED PUBLIC: A POLITICS OF RESPONSIVENESS

As I suggested earlier, lost cause narratives recast democratic failure as a call for more democratic action, in part by insisting that failure is never *just* failure. Zola's late writings on the Dreyfus Affair diagnose the overall democratic failure to assure justice while also focusing on the important political solidarities created through resistance to the Affair. Similarly, and as we will see in later chapters, both Burke and Arendt suggest that the failures of justice in the Hastings and Eichmann trials are inhabited by promising practices of resistance that provide enabling precedents for future action. Burke's, Zola's, and Arendt's "could have been" narratives, in other words, solicit future publics that would address injustice not by starting all over again, but that would build on and respond to the calls for, and practices on behalf of, justice that Burke, Zola, and Arendt claim were present during these democratic failures.

Following Patchen Markell, I call the form of democratic action called for by lost cause narratives "responsiveness" so as to highlight how lost cause narratives portray democratic failure as an irrevocably lost cause *and* as an occasion for political action. As Markell argues (via a distinctive reading of Arendt), our association of democracy with *either* rule or interruption has blinded us to how events may appear as both endings (an irrevocable event) and, at the same time (and consequently), as potential beginnings—occasions to respond, to act. Markell suggests that our capacity for responsiveness turns on having an attunement to events through which we can see them in this double valence: where they appear as both a past event, yet also as occasions for response, as sites from which we can begin to act. For him, such an attunement is cultivated through our enmeshment in contexts of acting and doing, in which events appear as demanding action and response. Such contexts include "[t]he contours of the built environment; the aesthetics of print, televisual, and electronic media; the discursive forms through which events are distinguished, measured, scaled, organized, and presented."[20] Lost cause narratives similarly create such a context by generating a trans-temporal web of narratives of resistance and calls for democratic action—a web that display past failures as themselves *already* a site of resistance (enacted in the narrative itself) that nonetheless stand in need of further response. This web of narratives reveals democratic action and resistance as possible where it might not have appeared so before. In this sense, we may think of lost cause narratives as altering our political vision, or effecting, in Aletta Norval's words, "aspect changes" in the way we see the world.[21]

I call the kind of democratic agency enabled by responsiveness to lost cause narratives the figure of the "belated public"—that is, a public which, through attunement to past failure as an occasion for response, seeks justice for the past and in its present. Calls to a belated public form an important part of the fabric of democratic life—as when, for instance, dissenting Supreme Court opinions on behalf of a lost cause (as in *Korematsu v. United States*) serve as enabling precedents for future struggles for justice and reparations, or when John Brown becomes an enabling precedent for contemporary thinking on racial inequality,[22] or when feminist work and writings on behalf of the 1970's "wages for housework" movement offer potent resources for thinking about gender equality today.[23]

Such calls to a belated public are not calls for the fulfillment of true popular sovereignty or the true general will, but instead calls that emphasize the *non*-sovereignty of democratic agency. Indeed, calls to a belated public work to solicit public responsiveness to circumstances that the public did not create and is not fully responsible for, and they demand that the public do justice in a cause that has already been lost. Examples of such politics could include demands for reparation that aim to redress the persistence of past injustice in the present—as in demands for reparations for slavery in the United States, or for Japanese internment.[24] They could also include theatrical political claims-making that contests dominant groups' attempts to re-narrate past injustice as justice—for instance, early twentieth-century Suffragettes' dramatic public actions (in Congress, outside the White House, etc.) that contested male political figures' portrayals of Susan B. Anthony's earlier attempts to pass a suffrage amendment as misguided. The Suffragettes insisted in their public acts, in contrast, that Anthony's actions served as a call for justice to which they were responding.[25] Another form of belated public action could consist in politicizing present injustice through reference to past lost causes. We can see this, for example, in protests of the recent George Zimmerman trial that referenced past unjust trials in the South where white men who shot black men were acquitted. Such political protests and action claim authorization, and political significance, in the present by responding to past injustices that they can never fully remedy. They do so knowing that passive acceptance of the past creates active roads toward the future that they want to disown or redirect.

Implicit in lost cause narratives' call for a belated public is an alternative economy of political meaning. For the belated public, the meaningfulness of political action lies not only in outcomes—indeed, full justice can never be achieved for past wrongs—but also in how responsiveness to democratic failure (in the form of action, speech, and writing) creates alternative democratic goods: solidarity that may persist into the future and the creation of narratives and other traces that place claims on, and enable, future belated publics. Such an alternative understanding of political meaning is particularly well-suited to our contemporary context where, as Lauren Berlant and Ann Cvetkovich have argued, political actors often feel overwhelmed and "stuck" when faced with the large-scale and seemingly intractable nature of the political problems facing us today (global warming, structural racial and gender inequality, the oppression of non-Western nations by Western nations, etc.).[26] Fatalistic narratives encourage deference to authority and law as a response to this apparent intractability, rather than political action or solidarity. Narratives of democratic action based in experiences of democratic achievement or triumph (the Civil Rights movement, the American founding, etc.), on the other hand, encourage rather than loosen this feeling of "stuckness" by offering a fantasy of overcoming-of-failure that feels practically unattainable to contemporary political actors. In contrast, the politics of lost causes emphasizes the significance of democratic action *even when it is belated*, when it does not achieve full justice, but does achieve goods unrelated to, or in excess of, full success: solidarity, changes in public climate, partial justice in the case at hand, and the creation of enabling precedents for the future.

In *Rights at Work*, Michael McCann offers such a narrative of the comparable worth movement (or equal pay for equal work movement) of the 1980s. He notes that the movement was, in the legal arena, ultimately a failure: despite a promising Supreme Court ruling, the movement failed to win "a single direct judicial endorsement of the movement's basic comparable worth theory that survived appellate review."[27] Yet McCann shows that participants felt more politically and socially empowered as a result of their participation in it. Specifically, participants felt that their failure to achieve justice in the courts and in law-making were not *only* failures because their political action on behalf of equal pay also sparked a sense of democratic possibility in them—a sense that they were not powerless cogs in a machine, but democratic agents whose actions matter. This had real political implications. For example, McCann notes that in the late 1960s, nurses in Denver had "discussed and registered complaints about low salaries," but it was only when they filed a legal complaint with the Equal Employment Opportunity Commission (EEOC) in 1975 and pursued a Title VII lawsuit that a "concerted collective campaign develop[ed]."[28] While this lawsuit was "ultimately unsuccessful in court," "the political campaign it helped to generate continued for years with great success at the bargaining table."[29] McCann also suggests that these failures in the courts and legislative arena produced a successful call for a belated public: "[e]arly dramatic advances. . . played a key role in publicizing the issue and raising activist hopes, *while the limited nature of such advances amidst an overall discouraging judicial legacy emphasized from the start the need for action outside of the courts.*"[30] McCann's own recounting of the animating power of this democratic failure itself serves as an invocation to more such belated publics in the future—publics that will see the impossibility of full justice not as a blockage, but as an invitation to democratic action.

Examining the democratic significance and meaningfulness of such "belated" public action may enliven and revivify democratic possibilities for action in times of democratic failure and de-politicization. In addition, we gain a fuller understanding of the import, problems, and promise of non-sovereign democratic action—that is, of democratic action that builds on past resistance that is not its own work, responds to injustices that it did not create and cannot fully redress, and creates democratic goods that are not captured by their success or failure in achieving their aims.

PUBLIC TRIALS

The writings on lost causes that I examine are all made on behalf of justice in the context of a trial or trials. I call these trials "public trials" so as to evoke the double sense of the term: first, the idea of a trial being driven and defined not only by law, but also by public opinion and action; and second, the idea of the public, as well as law, being on trial. The term is also, however, meant to situate these trials in the ongoing conversation and contestation of the public sphere—where even "failures" of justice continue to be given meaning and import through the "incessant talk" and writing of people communicating with and calling to each other through and across temporal divides.

It is not surprising that Burke, Zola, and Arendt were spurred to examine and diagnose the double failure of people and law in the context of criminal trials. Indeed, as scholars of trials have often noted, trials tend to sharpen, heighten, and make more meaningful broader social and political conflicts for the public.[31] Zola notes in his early essay "Morality" that a trial has a narrative arc very similar to that of the "experimental novel" (of which Zola claimed to be the originator): "A lawsuit is simply an experimental novel, which unrolls itself before the public. Two temperaments are brought forward, and the experiment takes place, under the influence of exterior circumstances. This is the truth; a true drama brings sharply out into broad daylight the true mechanism of life."[32] The theatrical and antagonistic dimensions of trials, in other words, publicly reveal conflicts and political problems that we may face in ordinary life, but that we are not called to attend to with the same public urgency. And just as we are more affectively offended when the ending of a good novel is unsatisfying than we are when we confront similar dissatisfactions on a daily basis (staying in an unsatisfying relationship, bowing to the wishes of others rather than pursuing our own wishes, etc.), so, too, do we tend to be more offended and filled with a sense of injustice when a criminal trial appears to have an unjust ending than when we confront such injustices in our everyday lives. An unjust guilty verdict that seems to be based in racism, for example, has a much stronger affective impact, at least in the short term, than the racial injustices that exist around us in the workplace, the city, and the school. Contained as such an injustice is within the narrative arc of a story with great human stakes (Dreyfus's freedom or imprisonment), it sparks deeper and broader attention, indignation, and discussion among members of the public. Such public attention only increases when criminal trials, like the ones involved in the Dreyfus Affair, deal with "scandalous" issues like treason, involve mystical communications about Dreyfus's innocence from a woman in a black veil, and draw their primary characters from elites and high society.

Yet while trials—especially trials that, in Lynn Chancer's words, have "become vehicles for crystallizing, debating, and attempting to resolve

contemporary social problems"[33]—may generate popular response that
might otherwise remain latent, it is not clear that such trials are for that
reason fecund sites through which democratic theorists might seek to
understand the relationship between law, democracy, and democratic
failure. Indeed, despite the ubiquity of books and articles in democratic
theory on the relationship between law and democracy, very few democratic theorists have paid sustained attention to trials as an important
dimension of democratic life.[34] Those who do discuss criminal trials,
such as those who examine Burke's writings on Hastings's impeachment or Arendt's writings on the Eichmann trial, tend to downplay
the fact that those writings take place in the context of a trial. When
Uday Mehta offers his brilliant reading of Burke's views on empire
in *Liberalism and Empire*, for example, he barely mentions that Burke's
views on the relationship between Britons and Indians come in the
context of a *trial* of Hastings.[35] Seyla Benhabib is more attentive to
the courtroom context of Hannah Arendt's writings on the Eichmann
trial, but she nonetheless suggests that what is important in Arendt's
writings on the trial is her response to the tension between "the universal and the particular, the ideal of humanity and the fact of human
particularity and diversity" that Benhabib finds there[36]—a conflict that
Arendt, if she did intend to outline, could have done in any form of
writing, not necessarily in the context of trial writings. In other words,
these readers of Burke's and Arendt's trial writings treat them as any
piece of intellectual work—expressing a general viewpoint on topics
in political theory (sentiments versus reason, universal versus particular)—rather than examining the main topic of these writings: the writer's concern with the trials themselves. While these readings by Mehta
and Benhabib have value in their own right, and while the tensions
they identify may play a part in these trial writings, they nonetheless
sidestep what is, for Burke and Arendt, the central issues in these writings: the trial, its problems, and its political and legal implications for a
belated or disappointing public.

Why have democratic theorists, for the most part, shied away from
examining and discussing trials, even when written about by important thinkers like Burke and Arendt? I suspect there are three primary
reasons. First, trials (especially public trials) appear as deeply particular
events, each exceptional in its own way, that do not have an easily
identifiable general rule or principle that they illustrate or challenge.

Unlike constitutional cases and reasoning (especially by the Supreme Court), which obviously refer back to and reflect upon "first principles" that undergird American democracy—and thus are frequently cited by deliberative democrats and liberals alike as exemplary of "public reason"[37]—criminal trials deal with particular circumstances and individual lives that seem to have little bearing on general questions of law and democracy. While trials might *illustrate* a particular theoretical tension (for Benhabib, the tension between the universal and the particular), they do not, as it were, reveal general rules in their own right because they are always irreducibly particular.

Second, theorists also may have avoided studying trials because they appear to be an inappropriate site for the people (or the "general will") to appear and exert itself—and hence an uncomfortable site for democratic theorists to explore as a location of democratic agency. Indeed, our broader understanding of legitimate democracy suggests that trials can be legitimate and just only if the political will of the people is *not* exercised during the proceedings. This is because trials deal with particulars—individuals—and are not legislative in nature. Whereas, as Rousseau said, law "should spring from all for it to apply for all,"[38] a trial represents a particular *application* of that law. If the people as a whole intervened in a trial, its will would no longer be general—it would only apply to an individual—and hence would represent an illegitimate use of its power, which should always be applied fairly (to all). If only a portion of the people intervened in the trial, that intervention would also be illegitimate, since it would be interfering in the application of legitimately enacted law. Since trials appear as important to legitimacy only insofar as they do not appear as an object of democratic politics or will, theorists may have assumed from the outset that they have little to teach us about *proper* democratic agency.

Finally, some political theorists likely do not attend to trials because they think law is de-politicizing. Theorists such as Wendy Brown, for example, argue that law exerts a normalizing and disciplinary effect on political action and claims-making. As Brown argues in *States of Injury*, when marginalized groups make demands for equal rights, they seek inclusion within the norm rather than challenging it: they "count every potentially subversive rejection of culturally enforced norms as themselves normal, as normalizable, and as normativizable through law."[39] From this perspective, looking to trials as exemplary sites of democratic politics would likely give us a distorted, normalized picture of politics—that is, of democratic action as filtered through techno-cratic and legalistic depictions of equality and freedom.[40]

Trials as Revealing the Limits of Rule-Governed Behavior

These very blockages to studying trials as sites for democratic theo-rizing are what, for me, make them interesting and important, and I discuss each in turn. First, the very particularity that may make trials appear unsuitable for democratic theorizing concerned with standards of legitimacy or right may render trials a fertile site from which to cull lessons for a democratic theory concerned not only with law's incontrovertible successes, but also with the limits and problems of rule-governed behavior—or, we might say, with law as a failing insti-tution. Such limits become apparent even in "ordinary" criminal tri-als, where the limits of general rules to address or capture individual actions can become more apparent than in other legal settings, like the legislature or the voting booth. One need only think of the shortcom-ings of sentencing guidelines to capture and address individual crimes and/or to capture the varying degrees of damage to the community done by different crimes.

The limits of law are revealed even more acutely in public trials like the ones I examine here, where existing law appears not only unable to capture the novelty of a crime altogether, but also where legal offi-cials' rule-bound ethos leads them to ignore how following the rules may hinder rather than enable justice. Arendt argues, for example, that while the rule-bound ethos of the Jerusalem Court that tried Eichmann aided justice when it led the judges to resist the prosecution's attempt to use the trial on behalf of state-building, it hindered justice when it led them to judge Eichmann's unprecedented "crimes against human-ity" according to national laws and rules that hid the full truth from view. While these trial writings do not, then, offer a general rule about the rule of law or about the relationship between law and democracy, they reveal an *insufficiency* of such general rules and rule-bound ethoi to address the wrongs at issue.

Thinkers of transitional justice also focus on the insufficiency of legal rules—and especially trials—to do justice in situations where great wrongs seem to exceed the narrow categories of law. Most often, they do so in order to explore other forums through which justice and healing can be pursued. For example, Sonali Chakravarti has recently argued compellingly for the democratic importance of the emotion of anger, as displayed in truth commission proceedings, for doing justice and reconstructing the public/private distinction after mass violence.[41] My aim in attending to the insufficiencies of general rules and rule-following revealed in exceptional instances builds on the work of transitional justice scholars, but has a different aim: to suggest that these insufficiencies may reveal a general democratic predicament of persistent (but not inevitable) failures, insufficiencies, and shortcomings of law to address political and legal problems. This is why I choose not to use the label of "political trials" to describe the trials I study—a label that assumes from the outset a sharp distinction from trials in which "politics" interferes with law and those in which law operates "properly," without such interference. Indeed, most scholars of political trials study them with the aim of articulating criteria by which we can call some political trials "acceptable" (conforming to the rule of law) and others "unacceptable" (not so conforming). [42] The effect of these approaches to political trials is to wall off moments of legal shortcomings and insufficiencies from ordinary legal practice and consequently shore up the distinction between the "ordinary" rule of law and "political" corruption or intervention into law. While these scholars have done important work in revealing the political work that can be done by trials (supposedly captured by the legal arena), they nonetheless do not seriously entertain the possibility that I pursue here: that trials that reveal the limits of law in a particular case may also reveal, more generally, problems with rule-deferent or rule-governed behavior and ethoi, as well as with theoretical approaches that take rule-deferent behavior as the exemplary practice of democratic citizens.

Two thinkers who *have* usefully argued that high-profile, or "political," trials reveal the insufficiency of rule-governed approaches are Michael Walzer and Judith Shklar in their examinations of the trial of Louis XVI and the Nuremberg trials, respectively. Both thinkers argue that the novelty of the crimes in these trials reveals the need to abandon pretense of what Shklar famously calls "legalism": "the ethical attitude that holds moral conduct to be a matter of rule following, and moral relationships to consist of duties and rights determined by rules."[43] In both trials, the pretense that these novel crimes could be addressed through rule-following (when in fact no rules applied) rendered them vulnerable to the criticism that they were "political trials"—or as Shklar puts it, that they were "farce from beginning to end."[44] Consequently, both Shklar and Walzer argue that a better approach to these trials would focus not on whether or not rules were being followed, but instead on what kind of political *values* are being furthered by the trials. Shklar argues that we should view law as "one form of political action among others"[45] and judge trials like Nuremberg based on whether they pursue "the politics of persecution" or "liberal ends."[46] Similarly, Walzer argues that we should judge the trial of Louis XVI by the criteria of how well it furthers the values of the rule of law: "[r]evolutionary justice is defensible whenever it points the way to everyday justice" and this, ultimately, is the difference between "morally legitimate trials" and "proscription and terror."[47]

Both Walzer and Shklar thus suggest that legalism—a procedural approach to the rule of law—is itself necessarily the result of and dependent on non-legalistic, political acts that affirm its principles. Consequently, for them, a legalistic defense of political trials is insufficient—that is, because it does not explore the more important question of the *values* and *ends* served by trials. Yet Walzer and Shklar are also both very clear that such breaks with the ordinary rule of law are only appropriate in exceptional, or emergency, moments and that to pursue them in ordinary moments would betray the political values of tolerance and fairness on behalf of which both Shklar and Walzer argue. Shklar affirms deviation from the rule of law in Nuremberg only because it is an exceptional instance dealing with novel crimes; she sees such compromises as inappropriate in ordinary domestic trials where the rule of law is well established.[48] Similarly, Walzer only affirms the irregular trial of Louis because the revolutionaries faced an exceptional moment and an unprecedented crime. Put another way, both Walzer and Shklar see appeals to supplements to law (morality, "political ends," popular sovereignty) as only defensible in situations where the rule of law is not well established. Thus, while Walzer and Shklar importantly reveal the insufficiency of rule-governed, "legalistic" approaches to political and legal problems, they also quarantine non-legal, political responses to the problem of legal insufficiency to extraordinary moments when existing law has dramatically broken down.

The problem with this strategy of quarantining moments of legal failure that require popular, political response to exceptional situations is that it does not allow us to hear the voices of those actors within the very trials they study that view the insufficiencies of law in the trial as having *general* rather than exceptional implications. And in the events that Shklar and Walzer study, some actors do precisely that. For example, in the trial of Louis XVI, Maihle and Vergniaud—leading members of the Gironde—do not claim that supplementing rules on behalf of popular voice is an exceptional form of justice, but rather portray themselves as acting according to a general view of law that sees it as dependent on the people's actual voice (not just that of their representatives) and on the ability of that people to express the nature of justice, even when it is not so expressed in formal law.[49] Without that actual voice, Maihle and especially Vergniaud argue, representatives and others who claim to speak in the people's name—such as judges in courtrooms—may tend toward tyranny rather than representation. Read in this way, the Gironde's affirmation of Louis's trial does not offer a response to an exceptional dilemma that only has relevance in similarly exceptional situations, but rather exemplifies a practice of responsiveness to a problem that is broader than the trial, itself: the necessary dependence of law on the actual exercise and supplement of popular sovereignty for its efficacy and life.

My examination of public trials attends to the ways in which spectators and writers of trials narrate the democratic failures contained within them as having precisely this broader significance—namely, as having an *exemplarity* for more general understandings of and responses to juridico-political problems. Examples, as Aletta Norval argues, offer "alternative imaginary horizons" to orient democratic politics.[50] Such "alternative imaginaries" do not determine or offer rules for democratic action in advance, but instead offer precedents that "ha[ve] to be taken in a certain way" by political actors.[51] Examples also may allow democratic actors to grasp a problem, or to understand novel political claims, in ways that a rule or a rational justification may not. As Linda Zerilli has argued, the example can "*exhibit* connections that cannot be rationally deduced from given premises."[52] Examples, in other words, offer guidance and precedents that enable and offer models for action and thought without constraining that action in advance. By reading the trial writings that I examine here as having this exemplary power, I thus do not claim that their diagnosis of the insufficiency of rule-governed approaches to justice and trials offers a *rule* for democratic politics, but instead that they may change our way of seeing the possibilities and problems of rule-governed ethoi, or in Shklar's words, "legalism."

Trials as a Site of Contention over "Proper" Democratic Agency

As I suggested above, the emergence of and contention over a figure of democratic agency—"the public"—in a site where it is supposedly not legitimately allowed (the trial) may also make public trials appear as an inappropriate site to theorize democratic agency. However, this same apparent inappropriateness makes public trials an important site for democratic theorists concerned with showing that contention over democratic agency—and not just the exercise of already authorized agency—is itself an important aspect of democratic politics. Building on the work of Jacques Rancière, I argue that we may read Burke's, Zola's, and Arendt's writings as attempts to contest the image of "the people" as defined within what Rancière calls "the police" order—that is, as Rancière puts it, "the order of bodies that defines the alloca-tion of ways of doing, ways of being, and ways of saying."[53] In the trial writings that I examine here, the writers all contest the ways in which a particular, dominant understanding of "the people" renders certain things visible and invisible. For example, Burke contests how the national identity of Britons renders the oppressions and violence done to Indians invisible to them, rather than appearing as a matter of concern. Similarly, Zola argues that the French public's identification with the "honor" of the army renders the army's abuses of its power invisible.

I also suggest that we can read these trial writings as attempts to inaugurate an alternative image of "the people" or "the public" that will render new forms of speech sayable and certain forms of oppression and injustice visible. In other words, I read these writings as themselves enacting political claims, in Rancière's sense: "[p]olitical activity is whatever shifts a body from the place assigned to it or changes a place's destination. It makes visible what had no business being seen, and makes heard a discourse where once there was only place for noise."[54] Thus, while from a proceduralist perspective, calls for the public to intervene in and influence trial proceedings on behalf of justice may appear as a form of *in*justice—corrupting the fairness and impartiality of the proceedings—I argue here for seeing such claims as important exemplars of democratic politics, understood in two ways: (1) as inaugurating a dispute over the nature of "fair proceedings" as such; and (2) as an activity of expanding the realm of the sayable and visible on behalf of justice, equality, and freedom.

I identify two primary scenes of contention over the figure of "the public" in the trial writings I examine here. First, the writers I examine call to a public to influence a trial on behalf of justice—a trial which, to do justice, is supposed to exclude that very public influence. Second, these same writers—once confronted with the failure of the public to respond to their first call—reach out to the future to diverse figures of "the belated public": that is, to a public that always comes too late to exercise sovereign agency over the circumstances it confronts, and thus must practice responsiveness to the failures in which it finds itself enmeshed.

The scenes of contention over "the public" that I identify are different in kind from the kind of contention over "the public" identified by its most famous and one of its most astute thinkers, Jürgen Habermas. Habermas's story about the emergence of the public sphere in late eighteenth-century Britain portrays public opinion as constituted increasingly through rational-critical debate (conducted via the press and in-person conversation) and serving as the proper legitimator of legislative outcomes.[55] For Habermas, in the one perfect—or at least almost perfect—moment of this lively, vital form of the public sphere in late eighteenth-century Britain (around the time when Burke is impeaching Hastings),[56] contestation appears as essential to the rational character of the public sphere. For Habermas, if the outcome of rational-critical debate is to be legitimate and lend legitimacy to formal legislative outcomes, all arguments and all participants must in principle be admitted into the discussion. Yet I find in Burke's writings on the Hastings trial—as well as in Zola's and Arendt's writings—a portrayal of contestation over the nature of "the public" that is not part of Habermas's account. Specifically, I find contention over the nature of the public that disputes the dominant *image* of the public as the legitimator of the decisions of state institutions and aesthetically solicits an alternative, contestatory public to orient public opinion, action, and judgment. This kind of contestation is aimed not primarily at inclusion within the existing discussion, but at challenging the forms of identification that structure what is invisible and visible, how certain issues emerge as matters of concern and others do not, to participants in public discussion.

My discussions of contention over the nature of the public in these moments is deeply indebted to Michael Warner's approach to "the public" (which also harkens to Arendt's work), which focuses on the importance of *poesis*, or world-making, in constituting publics, rather than on the character of the debate that happens within them. Warner's approach to publics reveals them not as bearers of universal values, but as "constitutive of a social imaginary" that exists only "by virtue of being addressed"—an address which itself has no guarantee of being taken up by others.[57] As Warner says, "Public discourse says not only 'Let a public exist' but 'Let it have this character, speak this way, see the world in this way.' It then goes in search of confirmation that such a public exists, with greater or lesser success—success being further attempts to cite, circulate, and realize the world understanding it artic- ulates. *Run it up the flagpole and see who salutes. Put on a show and see who shows up.*"[58] By attending to the rhetorically and aesthetically inflected forms of public speech that seek to solicit and inaugurate publics, we can see how the scenes of contention over "the public" that I find in these trial writings are not *only* part of an exchange of arguments, but also aimed at effecting changes in public vision and identification.

Further, however, by attending to contestation over the nature of "the public" in the trial writings I examine here, we may also recognize tri- als as important sites of this contingent contention over "the public" and the forms of democratic agency that invocations of "the public" enables. Trials, in other words, are revealed as sites that do not just serve as appli- cation of rules derived from an interplay between legislature and the public sphere, but also as sites where that supposedly legitimate interplay is revealed and contested as part of a hegemonic image of proper public agency.

Law as an Ambiguous Resource for Democratic Politics

Finally, as I noted earlier, some theorists also may not write about trials because they think law is normalizing and de-politicizing. These think- ers offer an important critical perspective on the relationship between politics and law: showing how law can homogenize, normalize, and de-politicize what could have been radical democratic impulses. However, *Public Trials* suggests that the "turn to law" may itself be more open to democratic iteration and agency than these thinkers sometimes acknowledge—that this turn may be enacted deferentially, in a fatalistic register that encourages normalization and de-politicization, *and/or* via the politics of lost causes, in the register of contestatory enactments of or calls to law (think of Zola demanding justice for a "crime against society" that has no place in the law books). In this sense, and following diverse thinkers such as Jennifer Culbert, Lawrence Douglas, Michael McCann, Bonnie Honig, Jason Frank, Karen Zivi, and Leonard Feldman, *Public Trials* shifts the question of *whether* democratic actors turn to law to the question of *how* they do so.[59] By attending, in the trial writings I examine here, to how democratic actors' turn to law may not only deaden, but also enliven democratic agency and challenge rule-governed approaches to law, *Public Trials* suggests that law is an ambivalent site of democratic agency: one that may exert normalizing and de-politicizing force on democratic actors, but which may also provide an important, meaningful, and even radical site for democratic action and solicitations of publics on behalf of justice.

Public Trials thus follows popular constitutionalists such as Larry Kramer in suggesting that the realm of law is not opposed to democratic politics, but rather intimately and contentiously linked together. Yet in contrast to Kramer's focus on ("popular constitutionalist") moments when the people's action and resistance works as a necessary supplement to (failing) law and legal officials, I focus on political narrations of *democratic* failure—that is, narrations that claim not only that law has failed, but that the people has also been actively complicit in injustice. In other words, where Kramer's approach imagines a resistant people waiting to be called into action once the failures of law are revealed, *Public Trials* examines blockages to such resistance—especially popular complicity—and asks how democratic (popular *and* legal) failure, and not just legal failure, may be addressed.[60] By focusing on democratic, not just legal, failure, we are better able to see that the people's main obstacle to action may not be official oppression, seizure of authority, or hoodwinking, but the people's own view and enactment of their role and identity vis-à-vis law.

FROM LIBERAL TO DEMOCRATIC JUSTICE

By examining the persistence of democratic failure and the import of democratic political response to such failure, *Public Trials* calls for shifting our understanding of justice from a liberal conception focused

on implementing impartial rules and procedures, to a democratic conception focused on contesting ongoing *in*justice, as well as collective
self-understandings that can hide injustice from view. Or to put the
point differently, *Public Trials* calls for an understanding of justice as a
problem *for* democratic politics, rather than as the institutional precon-
dition of proper politics, which has been the dominant way of viewing
the relationship between justice and politics in the Western tradition.[61]

Indeed, as Rancière argues, beginning with Plato, justice in politics
has consistently been defined as consisting in "the order that deter-
mines the partition of what is common."[62] Rancière argues that this
attempt to portray justice as marking the *end* of the need for political
conflict (the order that Rancière calls "the police") obscures how justice itself always enshrines a "wrong" in its count—for example, the
count of the Athenian poor as having "freedom" even though actually
they have nothing—that in turn inscribes the possibility of a politics of
equality and dispute. Specifically, this miscount enables political *claims*
that inaugurate a dispute in the polity over the nature and bounds of
equality. As Rancière puts it, politics occurs when "egalitarian contingency disrupts the natural pecking order as the 'freedom' of the
people" and when this disruption produces "the setting-up of one part
as equal to the whole in the name of a 'property' that is not its own,
and of a 'common' that is the community of a dispute."[63] Justice is
inevitably a problem for and of democratic politics, even as it pretends
to regulate democracy.

Like Rancière in his argument about justice as a whole, I argue here
that justice in trials—which is supposed to depend on an absence of
politics—should be seen as a problem of and for democratic politics. Yet
where Rancière portrays justice as the project of ordering, and thus of
the police—not of politics—I suggest that the "doing" of justice may
also be construed as a site of politics and political claims-making. Put
differently, when Rancière portrays justice as the project of ordering the
polity, he misses or does not choose to elaborate on how the transformative egalitarian claims that he highlights as *disruptive* of the order of
justice may *also* be viewed as part of justice—that is, insofar as they reveal
the shortcomings of the existing order as a supposed representative of
justice on behalf of a more infinite, expansive idea of justice.

I find an ally in this approach to justice in Jacques Derrida, especially
in his seminal essay "The Force of Law: The Mystical Foundations of

Authority." There, Derrida characterizes justice in terms of a "double movement." The first movement acknowledges the demand of an "infinite" justice without limits and thus reveals the inevitable shortcomings of worldly institutions of justice,[64] while the second movement appeals for justice to be done now, even though it is imperfect: that is, through "the demand for an increase in or supplement to justice, and so in the experience of an inadequation or an incalculable disproportion."[65] These two movements propel each other because, on the one hand, it is only through demanding that we pursue justice beyond its existing parameters that we are led to interrogate the sufficiency of our institutions of justice—revealing them to be insufficient and indeterminate. And on the other hand, only through revealing the existing parameters of justice to be insufficient can we find the "motivation"[66] to demand that justice be done beyond them. Derrida thus offers a conceptualization of justice that is productively attuned to its doubled character: as a practice of ordering *and* disordering, of appealing to a justice beyond law *and* pursuing justice through supplements to law, of showing law to be insufficient to do justice *and* pressing law to do better justice in inevitably compromised institutions.

Derrida attends to this dual movement of justice in the formal structure of philosophical paradox. *Public Trials* extends and de-formalizes Derrida's approach by focusing on the Janus-faced character of justice in what Jason Frank calls the contested and contestatory political realm of "micropolitical enactments."[67] Specifically, I look at the practice of soliciting publics, contesting rule-bound ethoi, and rendering "the public" an object of contention on behalf of justice as exhibiting to various degrees the dual movement Derrida describes: as expressing an infinite demand for justice that reveals the insufficiency of existing institutions and, on the other hand, seeking nonetheless to do justice to the other (Indian imperial subjects, Dreyfus, humanity) through institutions that will of course be imperfect and insufficient. Yet "justice" is itself a contested term throughout *Public Trials* in ways that a formal depiction of the problem (which presumes a singular, defining tension) like the one offered by Derrida sometimes obscures. Indeed, Arendt, for example, will not define justice as the infinite demand of the other that is *compromised* by its institutionalization, but as a fundamentally worldly project of human laws, discursive contest, and political action. In *Public Trials*, then, justice is not a problem for democracy primarily

or only because of a single, defining paradox, but because its inevitable dependence on political action and contestation for its continued extension renders it what William Connolly calls, following W. B.
Gallie, an "essentially contested concept."[68]

Consequently, this book gestures toward the importance not only of
an agonistic understanding of law[69]—where law always depends for its
efficacy on risky political contestation and the solicitation of publics, or
on what Tully has called "the free agonistic activities of participation
themselves"[70]—but also of an agonistic, democratic understanding of
justice, where justice is shown to be dependent on and a fertile ground
for the agonistic, contestatory realm of politics that it is supposed to
regulate.

WRITING LOST CAUSES

Public Trials pays particular attention to writing and narrativization as
ways of rendering events available for democratic response. I do so in
order to suggest that the practice of writing events—or, in Arendt's
terms, the practice of turning a jumble of particular facts into a *story* of
the pursuit of a "lost cause"[71]—is a uniquely important part of democratic life. This is not only or primarily because these stories reveal
the truth of events. Indeed, these trial writings—even Arendt's "trial
report"—are not "objective" in the sense of depicting the "two sides"
in the story without offering judgment about who is right. Zola and
Arendt both heavily criticize such a view of "impartiality" as a refusal
to recognize the facts and judge. Rather, their stories are judgments—
written in diverse fashions and genres—about the meaning, import,
and failures of these trials that solicit a particular reaction from the
public that all these thinkers see as the ultimate safeguard of justice
and law.

As the chapters of this book unfold, I will suggest that such writing is democratically important because it shapes future public vision
and imagination of events, as well as the political precedents, possibilities, and solidarities that they enable and thwart. As Shoshana Felman
rightly says in her analysis of Arendt, it was Arendt's book on the
Eichmann trial—and not the trial itself—that "at once proves and seals
the impact of the trial as a true event."[72] Felman's point is not that

Arendt's judgment of the trial crowded out all other interpretations (indeed, Felman takes issue with it), but rather that Arendt's writings revealed Eichmann's trial as an important occasion for debate, response, and political action. Arendt's book is a major reason that we still talk about that trial today during debates over proper legal responses to the Holocaust, human rights, Israel, and international tribunals. Arendt will likely never "win" the ongoing public debate about the Eichmann trial and its implications; nor will her book likely solicit the public she hoped it would. Yet her book has enshrined the Eichmann trial (and, in her judgment, its failures) as an occasion for response: that is, as an event that calls for us to think, debate, act, and engage with each other about its meaning and import. Put differently, her narration of the trial creates a space between the events of Eichmann's trial and their official recording in newspapers and legal documents, between an experience of failure and the turn to existing categories of success—a space of judgment and response that calls on us to respond, as well.

It may be especially important for us to attend to these exemplary trial writings and their solicitations to belated publics in our particular moment, that is, in our moment of what Hannah Arendt calls, following Brecht, "dark times": times where "the function of the public realm to throw light on the affairs of men" is perverted and betrayed by "speech that does not disclose what is but sweeps it under the carpet, by exhortations, moral and otherwise, that, under the pretext of upholding old truths, degrade all truth to meaningless triviality."[73] Like Arendt's "men in dark times," who in their practices may "kindle" an "uncertain, flickering, and often weak light,"[74] the exemplars here offer us precedents and intimations of en-lightening practices that may shed some small light into the world by loosening the hold of fatalistic narratives on our democratic imagination—revealing democratic failure not as reason to defer to experts and rules, but as part of a chain of democratic failures that are never *just* failures, that provide precedents and calls to act collectively to remedy the injustices of our own time.

I build my argument for the importance of these trial writings and their thematization of democratic failure and responsiveness in the next four chapters. In Chapters 2, 3, and 4, I offer readings of Burke's, Zola's, and Arendt's trial writings that examine the lessons about democratic failure, action, and resistance that emerge out of their encounter with law's and the people's failure to assure justice in

particular circumstances. In Chapter 2, I read Burke's writings on the
Hastings impeachment as a diagnosis of democratic failure. I argue that
Burke claims that existing law fails to capture Hastings's novel imperial crimes *and* criticizes elites' and the public's failure to demand that
law do justice to Hastings anyway. Yet I show that Burke offers a "lost
cause narrative" about this dual failure that refigures it as a missed
opportunity for a particular form of democratic action: namely, for the
British public to cultivate *sympathy* with Indians. For Burke, cultivation of sympathy would have re-established the correct line between
right and wrong and pressed elites to do justice. I suggest that Burke's
"could have been" narrative about the Hastings trial may reveal possibilities for sympathetic responsiveness by a belated public to oppressive
transnational relationships.

However, there are also limits to Burkean sympathy. Specifically,
Burke's appeal to sympathy conjures a fantasy of connection across cultural boundaries that obscures the hierarchical oppression he seeks to
remedy, figuring the Indians as partners in a sympathetic conversation
between equals that he in fact dictates and ventriloquizes. I suggest,
though, that we can find a lost cause narrative of the impeachment
trial that encourages attentiveness to this problem in a letter that Burke
writes late in his life to French Laurence. There, he asks that a history of the Hastings trial serve as his "monument"—that is, as his
funeral monument. Through examination of late eighteenth-century
understandings of funeral monuments, I argue that this letter may gesture toward an alternative form of responsiveness to democratic failure: namely, a figure of a belated public of sympathy that mourns its
inability to achieve full sympathy and, in so doing, is freed, maybe, to
pursue a partial, always incomplete sympathy on behalf of justice.

In Chapter 3, I explore Zola's failure to fully distinguish between
true and false forms of writing (true and false forms of communicating
truth) in his attempt to call a truthful public to do justice to the French
government's "crime against society" during the Dreyfus Affair—that
is, the government's systematic attempt to mislead the public about
Dreyfus's guilt. For Zola, the public's ability to do justice is dependent
on their truthfulness—on their ability to distinguish governmental lies
from the truth. However, for Zola, as for Rousseau and contemporary democratic theorists such as Habermas and Joshua Cohen, public
truthfulness is intimately linked to autonomy: only a public that is

capable of discerning truth can be free from manipulation, and vice versa. I thus argue that Zola's attempt to enlighten the public—to teach them the truth and how to discern it—leads him to replay the problem he seeks to resolve: namely, the public's dependence on an authority to tell them the truth and, hence, the public's ongoing susceptibility to falsehood.

Rather than seeking to escape this problem (an attempt that I suggest is an impossible venture in any case), I argue for reconceiving truth-telling in politics as a practice of responding to its own risks and persistent failures. I find the beginnings of such a reconception in what I argue is Zola's lost cause narrative of the Affair, where he solicits a belated public that could do "poetic justice" to a cause that has been sentenced to formal *in*justice in court: namely, by offering re-narrations of the Affair as a cause that demands further remedy. The practice of "poetic justice" may enable a pursuit of transparency that disregards the need for plural perspectives—a danger that I argue is evident in Zola's own attempt to rewrite the Dreyfus Affair in his posthumously published *Vérité*. However, Zola's call for "poetic justice" as a necessary supplement to legal proceedings may nonetheless call a belated public to write and act on behalf of alternative stories about supposedly settled narratives of (in)justice.

Arendt's description of the Adolf Eichmann trial in *Eichmann in Jerusalem* is often taken to be exemplary of the kind of approach criticized by Burke and Zola—that is, narrowly legalistic and in favor of rule-following as ensuring justice. I argue in Chapter 4 for a different reading of that text: namely, as a narrative of democratic failure, where Arendt portrays the Jerusalem Court judges' legalistic approach to the trial as part of what enables their failure to adequately address, and do justice to, Eichmann's unprecedented "crimes against humanity." Yet I also claim that Arendt re-narrates this democratic failure as a "lost cause" in her depiction of the spectatorship and theatricality of the courtroom audience—which turns out to be capable of revealing and shining light on the truth where the judges' juridical approach obfuscates. I argue that Arendt's emphasis on the importance of political contestation of law on behalf of justice gestures toward a broader agonistic understanding of law inherent in *Eichmann in Jerusalem*—that is, an understanding of law as dependent on contestatory political practices for its inauguration and sustenance. Indeed, this is how I read her turn to an international tribunal—namely, as a political solicitation of a world public that would press for (even if not fully achieve) full justice to be done to crimes against humanity through the creation of such a court.

Yet in her response to the controversy over her book (where the public that Arendt solicited failed to appear), Arendt retreats from her embrace of risky contestation in *Eichmann in Jerusalem* by assessing the controversy over it in juridical fashion: by making claims about the distinction between proper contestation (the public of "public spirit," consisting of those who agree with her) and improper contestation (the rule of "public opinion," which influences those who contest her position). This retreat obscures the complexity of democratic failure that Arendt reveals in *Eichmann in Jerusalem*: that the people and law, even when they seek justice, may fail to do justice; or, to put the point differently, that the public of "public spirit" may become the public of "public opinion" and vice versa. I find a more promising approach to the problem of "public opinion," perhaps surprisingly, in Arendt's 1964 review of the fiction of Nathalie Sarraute, which she reads as a meditation on the problem of conformity. Specifically, I argue that Arendt's affirmation of Sarraute's comedic rendering of "the they" gestures toward how comedy and laughter may engender attunement to the oppressive character of the conformity of "public opinion" and make room for cultivating an alternative plural "we" in response.

In Chapter 5, I build on my analyses of these trial writings to further develop the democratic approach to justice that I have begun to outline in this introductory chapter. I do so, first, by more deeply exploring the figure of "the belated public" and the kind of democratic politics that it opens up. I suggest that calls to a belated public are, in part, calls to redress the persistence of past injustice in the present and, in part, calls to more generally embrace an agonistic sensibility to dominant narratives of failure and to failure itself. I then, second, discuss how this agonistic political sensibility offers an alternative perspective on what I argue is a contemporary public trials moment: namely, the trial of Khalid Sheikh Mohammed, as well as the trials (or lack thereof) for other alleged terrorists. Analyzing the debates over the Mohammed trial from this agonistic perspective, I highlight the insufficiency of the dominant "law versus exigency" framing to capture the problem of justice in the trial, especially the injustice of the American use of torture, and I argue for opening up alternative possibilities for democratic responsiveness—possibilities that some contemporary public intellectuals, such as David Cole and Slavoj Zizek, are already exploring. However, I ultimately argue on behalf of the lost cause narrative of the Mohammed trial that I find, perhaps surprisingly, in Kathryn Bigelow's *Zero Dark Thirty*. While many critics of *Zero Dark Thirty* contend that the film depicts torture as something that "works," I suggest that *Zero Dark Thirty* instead—in its "documentarizing" portrayal of war, torture, and the narrow mindset of government and public— reveals the ultimate emptiness of the instrumental logic of torture and may solicit (whether or not it succeeds in doing so) a public interested in experimenting with the non-instrumental value of justice.

However, even this portrayal of the "lost cause" is, like the others I examine in the book, vulnerable to the reaction (or lack thereof) of the public it solicits. In other words, the politics of lost causes does not resolve the problems of democratic failure; it restages them, gesturing toward the importance of an ongoing politics of responsiveness that is itself vulnerable to the double failure of law and people to which it seeks to respond. Consequently, in the final part of the conclusion, I frame the outlines of what I call the "art of losing causes." Such an art might help democratic actors respond to the predicament of ongoing failure while resisting the temptation to lose hope in democracy altogether.

JUSTICE, SYMPATHY, AND MOURNING IN BURKE'S IMPEACHMENT OF WARREN HASTINGS

From the late 1770s through the early 1790s, Edmund Burke waged what was at times a one-man battle in the British Parliament against the abuses of the East India Company. This battle culminated in Burke's successful impeachment of its governor-general, Warren Hastings, in the House of Commons in 1786, and Burke's speech opening Hastings's trial in the House of Lords was one of the premier social events in London in 1788. Despite waning public attention and his ultimate loss in Hastings's trial, Burke continued to devote much of his energy to the prosecution for the next seven years and retired from the House of Commons only after the conclusion of the trial. The large body of texts produced by Burke in his crusade against Hastings and the East India Company reveals a remarkable and searing critique of the British Empire in India that stands alone in the late eighteenth century in its deep concern for Indian culture and well-being, as well as in its pursuit of justice for imperial subjects. As Jennifer Pitts has shown,[1] there were other prominent critics of empire in the late eighteenth century, but none of them carried their critique to such a high and prominent pitch as Burke did—all the way to the bar of the House of Lords in an impassioned demand for justice.

Many scholars have recently turned to Burke's writings on the Hastings trial to assess what he offers us in grappling with the imperial heritage implicit within Western thought, or alternatively in addressing the rise of a potentially new "empire" in contemporary politics. This turn to Burke has produced a debate that, mirroring long-standing debates in scholarship on Burke,[2] largely swirls around the question of which kind of law Burke seeks to vindicate in the trial—universal/ natural law or local law/traditions. The stakes of this debate are large. If Burke's writings appeal to universal or natural law, then he may stand as an exemplar of opposition to imperial abuses based in natural law that transcends local laws[3] or, as Pitts has argued, as a defender of a "peculiar" universalism that harmonizes local and universal laws.[4] On the other hand, if he indicts Hastings as a defender of local law and tradition, then perhaps Burke offers an exemplary defense, as Uday Mehta argues, of both Indian and British rootedness and cultural connectedness over and against the imperial uprooting of those traditions on behalf of greed.[5] Or perhaps Burke emerges in a more sinister vein, as Nicholas Dirks has recently argued, as a defender of the British imperial order, hierarchy, and laws (or lawlessness), who attempts to save that empire by scapegoating Hastings.[6]

These debates have illuminated important facets of Burke's thought and generated a productive conversation about the diversity of late eighteenth-century comportments toward empire, as well as about what kind of exemplar best serves counter- or anti-imperial thinking today. However, in portraying Burke's critique of Hastings and the East India Company as necessarily connected to a defense of a particular kind of law or lawfulness, these debates have also obscured an alternative story to be told about Burke's writings on the Hastings impeachment: namely, a story about the insufficiency of rule-bound approaches in general to address Hastings's novel crimes. That is the story that I tell in this chapter. Focusing on Burke's diagnosis of the failure of *all* laws to capture Hastings's wrongs, I argue that Burke's writings on the trial do not reveal adherence to one set of laws or another, but rather a practice of dynamic reflective judgment that takes into account, but does not defer to, rules that do not capture Hastings's crimes. This reading sounds a note of caution about claiming Burke as an advocate of *either* universal *or* local laws, and suggests that imperial (or neo-imperial) oppression may demand more than rigorous adherence to law—it may also demand judgment that exceeds or is not captured by law. Further, however, in directing attention to the insufficiency of the rules and laws most often seen to be at the heart of Burke's approach to Hastings, this reading suggests that Burke's appeals to those rules and laws is only part of the story of his pursuit of justice in the trial.

I will argue that the other important part of the story can be found in Burke's ambivalent relationship with "the publick." Specifically, I will suggest that Burke stages his own practice of reflective judgment in the trial as a model not only for the Lords who stood in judgment of Hastings, but also for the public that he viewed as the last (if also uncertain) safeguard of justice in the trial. Burke's view of the public in Hastings's trial, I will argue—in part through a detour on Burke's broader understanding of the role of the public in politics—is deeply ambivalent. On the one hand, Burke sees the public, due to its members' enmeshment in sentimental networks of care, as more capable than elites of judging the true nature of the public good in moments of legal (and elite) failure. However, he also views the public in this case as troublingly indifferent to the sufferings of Indians, largely due to their desire for riches from the East India Company—a desire that has corrupted their (and elites') ability to distinguish between the public good and private interest. For Burke, not only law, but also the public has failed to assure justice.

I discuss Burke's diagnosis of this democratic failure of Hastings's trial in the first half of the chapter. In the rest of the chapter, I turn to what I argue is Burke's response to this failure: namely, his diverse invocations, stagings, and solicitations of a sympathetic public on behalf of justice. Burke solicits a public of sympathy to assure justice in the trial because sympathy, on his account, re-orients the public to the proper line between right and wrong, between the public good and private interest. Other readers of Burke have lauded his turn to sympathy as a solution to the problem of empire (as in Mehta's "cosmopolitanism of sentiments"[7]). However, putting Burke's writings in dialogue with contemporary (late eighteenth-century) critiques of the trial, I argue that Burkean sympathy is itself a site of problematic tension between

the public good and private interest. Specifically, I will suggest that
sympathy for the pain of the other may turn out not to re-instantiate
the true line between public good and private interest (as Burke hopes),
but instead to offer a fantasy of connection that serves as cover for the
pursuit of one's own interest and satisfaction of one's own desires. The
sympathetic public solicited by Burke appears not only as a solution to
the problem of justice, but also as itself a problem.

Read in this way, Burke's writings on the Hastings trial resist putting the question of whether universal or local laws are more important
to freedom and justice center stage. Instead, they press us to address the
importance and insufficiencies for justice of both sets of laws, as well
as sympathetic connections across boundaries. In particular, Burke's
writings on the Hastings trial call us, on the one hand, to acknowledge
the ways in which sympathy with the suffering of others is a necessary supplement to general laws that do not adequately grasp concrete
imperial oppression and, on the other hand, to grapple with the fact
that such sympathy can turn out to be simply a fantasy, a projection of
our own interests and images of connection rather than meaningful
connection with the other.

However, in the last section of the chapter, I will argue that in a letter to French Laurence toward the end of his life, Burke refigures the
Hastings impeachment as a "lost cause" that might spark a different
kind of sympathetic public in the future—one that acknowledges its
own insufficiencies. I make this claim by attending to Burke's request
in the letter that a history of the Hastings impeachment serve as his
monument—his *funeral* monument. I suggest that this request may gesture toward a sympathetic public comportment that enables the pursuit
of justice through mourning the loss of perfect sympathy—a form of
sympathy that I call "chastened sympathy." Where the sympathy that
Burke solicits during the trial threatens to obscure the inequalities and
abuses that he seeks to address, chastened sympathy seeks to remedy
wrongs across cultural and national boundaries that are not captured
by existing law, while at the same time remaining attentive to its own
shortcomings and blind spots.

Overall, the chapter makes a case for reading Burke's writings on
empire in the context of his relationship to an uncertain public—a
context that reveals (perhaps surprising) *democratic* implications of his
attempt (and ultimate failure) to bring Hastings to justice. While Burke

may have seen elites as most capable of good governance, the concrete circumstances of the Hastings trial (and other moments of persistent elite failure) pressed Burke to turn to an unruly public and grapple with its failures and unpredictabilities. The chapter suggests that closely examining Burke's diagnosis of, and responsiveness to, democratic failure in the Hastings trial generates insights and lessons for contemporary democratic theorists and actors in a similar position—that is, for democratic actors who must turn to an unpredictable, possibly failing public on behalf of doing justice to wrongs (like empire) that cross national boundaries and exceed existing laws.

I will discuss this in more depth at the end of the chapter. First, however, I will discuss the historical and legislative context for Burke's impeachment of Hastings, Burke's understanding of the despotism of the East India Company as novel and unprecedented, and his reasons for turning to impeachment to address that despotism.

THE TURN TO IMPEACHMENT

In 1773, Parliament passed the Regulating Act. The dual aim of the Act was to better supervise the East India Company's exercise of power in India and to make the Company profitable again. One way that the Act attempted to accomplish this was by doing away with local governorships (of Madras and Bengal, for example) that appeared inefficient and prone to graft and replacing them with the position of a single governor-general. The first appointee to this position was the former governor of Bengal, Warren Hastings. The governor-general was supposed to check the power of lower officials in India and, in general, to enforce new rules (also created by the Act) that prohibited Company servants from accepting bribes and presents. At the same time, however, the Act attempted to place a check on the power of the governor-general, himself, by rendering him accountable not only to the Court of Directors (elected by shareholders), but also to a four-man Council stationed in India. The Council would have veto power over the governor's actions.[8]

In 1773, Burke opposed the Regulating Act, arguing that it gave too much power to the Crown, rather than allowing commerce to check the Crown's power. However, as his involvement in Indian affairs deepened in the late 1770s (due to various personal and political factors) and he served as an important member of the Select Committee on Indian Affairs, Burke came to believe that the Company was not accountable *enough* to Parliament and that this lack of accountability allowed deep abuses and oppressions of Indians. Burke was especially concerned about the continued practice of bribe-taking (despite legislative prohibition), the use of war to secure profits, and the degradation of traditional structures of Indian governance in favor of appointing local officials who could be easily controlled by the Company. Burke viewed these practices as oppressive to Indians *and* as detrimental to the long-term profitability and stability of the Company.[9]

During the late 1770s and the early 1780s, Burke delved into Indian history and culture and developed a detailed knowledge of the East India Company's policies and behavior in India. His primary goal in this period was legislative reform, and he got the chance to propose a sweeping program of reform when the Rockingham Whigs were briefly allowed to form a government in the early 1780s. The bill crafted by Burke, known as "Fox's East India Bill," would have divided the economic and political administration of India into governance by two commissions, both of which would have been directly accountable to Parliament instead of to the shareholders of the East India Company. Shareholders and others raised a great outcry against the bill, making the argument that it threatened the rights of all corporations. While the bill passed the House of Commons, it was defeated in the House of Lords (after the king made clear he was against it) and it raised public sentiment against the Rockingham Whigs, who were turned out of office soon thereafter. It was at this point, in the mid-1780s, that Burke turned his focus from broad reform of the Company to a specific targeting of Hastings and, in particular, that he began threatening impeachment.

Burke turned to impeachment in part because he believed that continuing to participate in the oppression of the East India Company, now that his attempt at legislative reform had failed, would constitute an injustice. As Burke says in his opening speech of the impeachment, "[t]o have forborne any longer would not have been patience, but collusion—a participation in guilt and almost party with the Criminal."[10] Yet Burke also actively advocated *against* pursuing further legislative reform of the Company. Burke wrote in a November 23, 1785, letter to

Philip Francis, for example, that he would not support the Opposition pursuing broad legislative reform for Indian affairs. Burke said that his vote "will be given to Justice in the first place"—that is, to impeachment—and "in the next to you and Mr. Fox."[11] Burke, in other words, turned to impeachment in part out of practical necessity—because roads to legislative reform were completely cut off—but also because he came to believe that impeachment offered a superior approach to Hastings's and the Company's crimes.

Burke viewed impeachment as a superior approach because it offered a way of holding Hastings and the Company as a whole accountable for crimes that he increasingly believed could not be addressed by ordinary courts or ordinary practices of legislative reform. On Burke's account, these crimes presented a twofold novelty that resisted judgment according to existing categories and standards. Hastings's crimes are novel, first, because they were committed as part of an unprecedented political regime, where the profit motive directs the exercise of public power and overshadows and distorts concern with the public good.[12] In India, "the rapacity of a foreign hand" on behalf of profit has uprooted "the paternal, lenient, protecting arm of a native government" and thus renders insecure traditional local checks on power (WS 6:305).[13] At the same time, by making "money the medium of social and political circulation and order," in Uday Mehta's words, the British also undermined "the traditional and historically appropriate foundations" of their own checks on power, thus undermining their own ability to correct such crimes through traditional legal or political means.[14]

Hastings's crimes were also novel because of the novel field of their scope and application. That is, these crimes were perpetrated on a people "separated from *Great Britain* by a very great Part of the Globe; separated by Manners, by Principles of Religion, and of inveterate Habits as strong as Nature itself, still more than by the Circumstances of local Distance" (WS 7:153). If the Managers had tried Hastings in an ordinary court, "their Rule would be formed naturally upon their ordinary Experience, and the Exigencies of the Cases which in ordinary Course come before them" (WS 7:153). Yet this inquiry "touches many points, in many places, which are wholly removed from the ordinary beaten orbit of our English business" (WS 6:280). While in English affairs, "every allusion immediately meets its point of reference," in this case, they are caught "as it were into another world" (*WS* 6:280). Correctly judging the Company's crimes not only demanded a rule that did not exist in ordinary courts, but also a not yet existent practice of judgment that involved a willingness to travel in cultural and geographical perspective.

Burke also viewed legislative reform as inadequate to address Hastings's crimes because such reform was consistently rendered useless by a Company culture that resisted legal checks at all turns, as well as by a public and elites complicit in that culture. Burke argues that all legal regulations made by Parliament "were despised" in India because profit motive trumped all else. In general, "legal authority seemed to skulk and conceal its head like outlawed guilt" (*WS* 6:273).[15] The broad disregard for law in favor of commercial gain is, Burke argues, "perfectly uniform" within the Company (*WS* 5:394). Just as for Hastings, on Burke's account, "money is the beginning, the middle and the end of every kind of act" (*WS* 6:377) and thus overtook all concerns with local laws or customs, so, too, were all other servants of the Company guided by this "great principle of corruption" (*WS* 6:382)—essentially turning "bribery" into a "system of government" (*WS* 5:433). As Stephen White puts it, "in the figures of Hastings and his lieutenants Burke saw a phenomenon of human willfulness that was not adequately comprehended by the traditional categories of tyranny or despotism."[16]

Burke further argues that members of Parliament, other elites, and the British public are enmeshed in this *esprit du corp*—pursuing their private interest at the expense of the public good—and thus acquiesce in these crimes rather than seek to remedy them. Burke famously describes the young men of the Company as "birds of prey" (*WS* 5:402) and argues that their "prey" are not primarily Indians, but rather are "lodged in England" (*WS* 5:403). In part, Burke means to suggest that "birds of prey" who practice despotism in India (and make a fortune from it) will bring this despotism back to Britain. Yet Burke also suggests that the British public is no passive party here, corrupted by a rapacious East India Company. Rather, the public on Burke's account enables the Company's continued disregard for law due to their desire for the wealth and riches brought to them by the Company: returned "birds of prey" "ease your estates by loans; they raise their value by demand; they cherish and protect your relations which lie heavy on your patronage" (*WS* 5:403). The entwinement of desire by British public and elites for ill-begotten wealth with the corrupt, illegal practices necessary to procure it results in public support for an unaccountable East India Company. Burke argues, for example, that stockholders in the Company aim "to cover and support, against justice, some man of power who has made an obnoxious fortune in India. . . and to avail themselves in return of his patronage, that he may shower the spoils of the East, 'barbaric pearl and gold,' on them, their families, and dependents" (*WS* 5:437). More generally, Burke worries that this influx of money has a seductive effect on the British public, rendering the public and Parliament eager to avoid reform of the East India Company: "there is scarcely an house in the kingdom that does not feel some concern and interest that makes all reform of our eastern government appear officious and disgusting; and, on the whole, a most discouraging attempt" (*WS* 5:403).

Burke believed that impeachment could address these problems better than ordinary legislative reform for three primary reasons. First, Burke believed that the Lords could judge Hastings's crimes without recourse to existing precedent and laws. The Lords, Burke argues, have "boundless power" to judge Hastings (*WS* 6:277). In his view (which was contested), the Lords are not bound by common law or any other precedents in their judgment, except the "limits of justice" (*WS* 6:277); they are judges of "Law and Fact" (*WS* 7:118). Second, as we will see in more detail in a later section, Burke saw the theatrical spectacle of the impeachment proceedings (especially the trial) as a platform through which the public and the Lords could be shaken free of their enmeshment in the East India Company's wealth-driven mindset. Finally, Burke believed that by judging Hastings's crimes accurately, the Lords could create an important *example* of justice that would serve as an empowering precedent for the future: "You do not decide the Case only; you fix the rule" (*WS* 6:270–271). Burke's position here anticipates contemporary scholarship on transitional justice: he is suggesting that future justice and lawfulness in India depends on the Lords' willingness to make unprecedented judgments in the present.

Burke's fellow Whigs supported bringing impeachment proceedings against Hastings in the House of Commons, but it was a surprise to almost everyone when William Pitt gave his support to impeachment and thus assured that they would gain broad support in the House.[17]

Following the House of Commons' support of impeachment charges against Hastings, the case was moved to the House of Lords for trial, where Burke became the lead prosecutor. In the following sections, I discuss Burke's (ultimately insufficient) attempts to procure justice in the trial, and the tensions that inhabit them.

JUSTICE BEYOND LAW

While Burke's turn to impeachment was motivated by the need (on his account) to judge Hastings's crimes without recourse to existing precedents, his speeches and writings during the impeachment trial sometimes reflect the opposite approach: namely, an attempt to have Hastings's crimes judged by *all* existing laws and precedents. In particular, Burke calls at different times in his speeches for the Lords to judge Hastings according to natural law, the "law of nations," British law, and Indian law and customs (among others). In this section, I examine the tensions between Burke's calls for judgment *beyond* law and his calls for judgment *according* to law, as well as the tension between his dual appeals to natural law and to national, local laws. While it is tempting to reconcile these diverse claims into some version of universalism, localism, or pragmatism, I will argue for reading Burke's sometimes contradictory, and often conflictual, appeals to these diverse sets of laws as a dynamic practice of reflective judgment about the unprecedented that stands as a model for the Lords and public he hoped to engage on behalf of justice.[18]

Burke's speeches and writings on the impeachment have most often been read as reflecting a turn to a "natural law" approach to justice—and for good reason.[19] Burke argues in his speech opening the impeachment, for example, that Hastings must be judged by the rules of "natural, immutable, and substantial justice" (*WS* 6:276), or by "that law of common justice which cements them to us and us to them" (*WS* 6:279; cf. *WS* 6:275, 6:367). Similarly, he argues in his closing speech that the Lords must judge by "the Law of Nature and of Nations" (*WS* 7:280), which is the "birthright of us all" (*WS* 7:292).

Burke's appeals to natural law reflect his sense that national laws have been insufficient to address the crimes of the East India Company. On Burke's account, Britons' attachments to national laws and worldviews have often blinded them to abuses happening (in their name, and with their support) elsewhere. Burke's appeal to natural law also allows him to combat Hastings's argument that, while in India, he was governed by no laws at all because customarily, India was ruled through arbitrary power, and that he had to use his discretion in any case for the sake of saving the East India Company in dire circumstances. Hastings, on Burke's account, thinks that arbitrary power is the "constitution of Asia" (*WS* 6:349; cf. 7:283). Burke dubs this Hastings's "Geographical Morality" (*WS* 6:345) and argues against it that "*the laws of morality are the same every where*, and. . . there is no action which would pass for an action of extortion, of peculation, of bribery and of oppression in England, that is not an act of extortion, of peculation, of bribery and of oppression in Europe, Asia, Africa, and all the world over" (my emphasis, *WS* 6:346). By showing that Hastings is bound by law no matter where he is on the globe—"I know of no people excused from the Law" (*WS* 7:280)—Burke suggests that any claim on Hastings's part to have the authority or exigency to act without regard to law is specious.

Yet readings that focus on Burke's appeals to "natural law" often neglect the tension between these appeals and his appeals to national/ local laws in the same speeches and writings. Indeed, throughout his writings on the impeachment, Burke argues that Hastings must be judged not only by natural law, but also by British *and* Indian laws, customs, and standards. Burke appeals to British law, in part, simply through pursuing the particularly British procedure of impeachment, which he says provides "that great circulation of responsibility, by which, excepting the Supreme power, no man in any condition can escape *his responsibility to the laws of his Country*" (my emphasis, *WS* 6:272). Similarly, Burke says that the impeachment brings "the justice of the Nation" to bear on Hastings (*WS* 6:273) and that "this Country will force him to be tried by its laws" (*WS* 6:345).

Burke also consistently suggests that Hastings is responsible to Indian laws and customs. Burke says, for example, that "if we must govern such a Country, [we] must govern them upon their own principles and maxims and not upon ours" (*WS* 6:302). To do otherwise is to remove the checks on power inherent in traditional systems of governance in India. Where Hastings believes, on Burke's account, that India will only be useful to England if they make it "a uniform and compact body by one grand and systematic arrangement" (*WS* 6:348), Burke argues that the prosperity and well-being of Britain and India can only be assured through respecting and adhering to local customs and laws. By virtue of the treaty made with the Grand Mogul, Burke argues that British rulers "bound themselves as securities for their [Indian] subjects, to preserve the people in all rights, laws and liberties, which their natural original Sovereign was bound to enforce, if he had been in a condition to enforce it" (*WS* 6:282). If the Company fails to preserve these laws, Burke argues that the consequence can only be broad dissatisfaction and unrest: "every person exercising authority in any Country shall be subject to the laws of that Country, or he breaks the very covenant by which we hold our power there" (*WS* 7:286). Indeed, to judge Hastings's crimes in India without regard to local law would seem to re-perpetrate the oppressive degradation of their way of life practiced by the East India Company, rather than remedy it.

Burke's appeals to British and Indian law in his speeches and writings suggest that he continues to value—as he does in his other writings—local/national laws, customs, and standards as crucial to resisting arbitrariness and preserving freedom. Indeed, as Uday Mehta suggests in his reading of Burke's writings on India, Burke's condemnation of the East India Company's criminal uprooting of Indian forms of governance and his appeals to Indian laws and standards can be read as affirming what Mehta calls a "cosmopolitanism of sentiments"—that is, a mode of interacting with the other that is based in a respect for territorial and communal difference. As Mehta puts it, "[f]or Burke, territory or *place*, is a fundamental condition of collective and individual political identity."[20]

Burke's writings on the impeachment thus contain (at least) two, conflictual strands of argument: that Hastings must be judged by natural law because national/local law is insufficient to grasp his crimes *and* that Hastings must be judged by national/local laws because such territorially rooted, traditional laws are essential in resisting the rootless (and uprooting) oppressions of bodies like the East India Company (or, as he writes famously elsewhere, the French revolutionaries). Both sets of standards appear to be necessary for the Lords to adequately judge Hastings's crimes. Indeed, to call on the Lords to judge by natural law without regard to local precedents and practices would seem to undermine the very thing that Burke hopes to save through impeachment proceedings: British culture and autonomy, as well as Indian traditional culture and forms of government. Yet if Burke had turned to natural law without mention of local laws, he would appear to be turning to natural law like the French revolutionaries did (on his reading in the *Reflections*): as a way of breaking with local laws that they believed were so corrupt as to be beyond repair. Consequently, Burke would be vulnerable to the same critique that he levels against the revolutionaries: namely, that his appeal to natural law is not grounded in a set of experientially based checks on power that could restrain future uses of it, but instead is arbitrary and thus vulnerable to misuse by someone (perhaps even by Burke, himself) who is motivated by political considerations rather than by justice.

This is, in fact, the very criticism that was leveled against Burke by Hastings and his defenders. For example, Fanny Burney, a friend and admirer of Burke (even though she was a Hastings supporter), bemoaned what she viewed as Burke's persecution of Hastings in her journal entry about his opening speech: "Were talents such as these exercised in the service of Truth, unbiased by party and prejudice, how could we sufficiently applaud their exalted Possessor? But though frequently he made me tremble by his strong and horrible representations, his violence recovered me, by *stigmatizing his assertions with personal ill-will, and designing illiberality*."[21] John Scott, one of Hastings's agents, argues more forcefully than Burney that "the proceedings in Westminster Hall" are "a farce" as part of some private crusade to ruin Hastings and other "illustrious families."[22]

For Burney, Scott, and Burke's other critics, Burke's call for judgment unconstrained by British law revealed the prosecution as a lawless pursuit of private revenge, rather than a true pursuit of the public good. For Burney, in other words, it is Burke—not Hastings—who confuses public and private interest in ways that are damaging to the public good more generally. While there is little support in Burke's private letters or elsewhere for the claim that Burke's pursuit of Hastings was primarily personal, Burney's criticism nonetheless draws attention to a problem with Burke's claim to represent the true public good: namely, that Burke's appeals to mutually subverting sets of laws leave him unable to fully justify his claim that he is acting on behalf of the public good, because each set of laws' claim to validity stands in conflict with that of the other sets of laws.

Jennifer Pitts has argued that Burke's simultaneous turn to national and natural laws does not actually indicate a tension at all, but rather sketches a harmonious relation between the two spheres of law: a universalism that is based in local culture and practice. Pitts argues that "Burke believed that national sentiment, appropriately chastened, could underpin international justice."[23] For Pitts, Burke's appeals to natural law alongside local precedents and culture should be read primarily as markers of the limits of local thinking—that is, of how thinking in national terms can lead citizens to see members of other nations as inferior. Indeed, on Pitts's account, Burke ultimately saw the British failure to do justice to Hastings as due to "British disdain for Indians as inferior and barbarous."[24] Thus, for Pitts, Burke propounds a "universalism" in his speeches and writings on Hastings, but it is a "peculiar universalism"[25] because it is essentially a nationalistic outlook that is prevented, through acknowledgement of its limits, from turning into a "noxious nationalism."[26] Or, in Pitts's words, Burke is proposing "universalism as an enlarged mentality, resting on particular affections but attentive to the ways that such affections can slip into exclusion."[27] Pitts does not specify how Britons (on Burke's account) would prevent their nationalism from becoming noxious, but she seems to suggest that one important way this could happen is through "internal or immanent critique" like that practiced by Burke himself—that is, critique in which he presents "his audience with a portrait of their own self-understanding and then demonstrat[es] that they had failed to live up to it."[28]

Pitts's reading offers a compelling response to critics like Burney: that Burke's turn to natural law is meant to curb exclusionary nationalist sentiment by stressing the harmony between national and natural law, not to disregard national law and precedent in favor of private interest. Pitts's reading also has support in some parts of the text, especially in Burke's closing "Speech in Reply." In that speech, Burke appeals to a harmonious assemblage of national/local laws, all reflective of natural law: "[t]here is but one Law in the world, namely, that Law which governs all Law: the Law of our Creator, the law of humanity, Justice, Equity, the Law of Nature and of Nations and so far as any Laws fortify these, give them more precision, more energy, more effect by their declarations, these Laws enter into the sacredness of primeval Laws" (*WS* 7:280). Yet in other moments, Burke stresses the deep tension

and even incompatibility between natural law and local law. In particular, whenever he stresses the boundlessness of the Lords' authority,
he insists that their judgment, to do justice, must *exceed* and go *beyond*
local precedent. For example, Burke says in his opening speech that he
"hope[s] and trust[s] that there will be no rule, formed upon municipal
maxims, which will prevent the Imperial justice which you owe to
the people that call to you from all parts of a great disjointed empire"
(*WS* 6:277). For Burke, then, it is important, for the sake of justice,
to see national law and precedent not only as harmonious, but also as
standing in tension, with judgment according to the "eternal laws of
nature." Indeed, if we assumed that natural law and local law stood
completely in harmony, it would be impossible to do justice in a case
like Hastings's—where the very features that constitute the criminality
of his acts demand that we unmoor ourselves from most of our local
points of reference.

   We might, then, better read Burke's appeals to multiple sets of laws
as a *dissonant* (not harmonious) approach to transnational justice: one
that reveals that any attempt to adhere to one set of laws (national
or natural) is insufficient to do justice and, in turn, refers the judger
to other sets of laws indefinitely, with each in turn being revealed
as insufficient. Such an approach moves the judger—oscillates her—
between various sets of laws on behalf of justice, while insisting on
the insufficiency of these laws to judge crimes that exceed all of them.
This need to judge beyond these sets of laws, even while informed by
them, may be why Burke provocatively stresses in his closing speech
that the Lords must *give* or create law through their judgment, and not
just judge according to already existing law. He says, "And therefore
the issue before your Lordships is: *what law your Lordships shall give upon
this occasion?*" (my emphasis, *WS* 7:284). For Burke, doing justice to
Hastings's crimes demands the reflective exercise of judging Hastings's
deeds without being bound by existing sets of laws that do not fully
capture them. Not *only* law, but *also* reflective judgment that is not
bound by law, is the key to justice.

   Reading Burke's appeals to natural and local/national law as exemplary of a practice of reflective judgment does not, of course, fully
resolve or answer the criticism made by Burney and others—namely,
that his appeals may also be reflective of strategic opportunism and
a self-interested pursuit of revenge (a point I will return to later).

Indeed, the practice of reflective judgment is inherently vulnerable to this critique, since there is no existing rule that can fully validate its non-rule-governed judgments—a problem that will haunt Zola's and Arendt's judgments of Dreyfus's and Eichmann's trials, as well.[29] Put differently, judging without deference to rules leaves one singularly open to claims that one's judgment is a result of personal "bias" or self-interest. Yet as we will see, such a criticism misunderstands the register on which Burke's claims are pitched. He is not aiming to justify his claims according to an existing standard and thus to put them beyond contest—indeed, the only way he could do that would be to appeal to standards that mask Hastings's crimes. Rather, as I will suggest in the next two sections, Burke seeks to launch his claims about Hastings's guilt and his exemplary practice of dynamic reflective judgment into the contestatory public sphere in hopes of changing Britons' self-understanding and jolting them into recognition of the criminality of Hastings's acts. To put it in the helpful terms recently offered by Bonnie Honig, Burke seeks not justification, but political *vindication* of his claims from the Lords, and from a public that has been awakened (through his claims-making) to the paucity of its moral and political self-understandings and, in turn, to the need to practice a novel, non-rule-governed form of judgment to do justice to Hastings.[30]

THE PROMISE AND PROBLEM OF THE PUBLIC

Burke's call for the Lords to engage in dynamic reflective judgment of Hastings's crimes may seem to portray the judgment of the Lords as the cornerstone of justice in the trial—a reading that may also appear to confirm dominant judgments of Burke as an arch-conservative, relying on an aristocracy naturally endowed with broader and more perceptive powers of judgment than ordinary Britons. Yet if Burke appeals to elites to fulfill their role of safeguarding the public good from private interest, he is equally concerned in his public and private writings that these elites will not be up to the task—that they, perhaps even more so than ordinary members of the public, have been supporters and victims of the profit-driven mindset of the East India Company. For example, Burke writes in a private letter in December 1785 that "[w]e know

that we bring before a bribed tribunal a prejudged cause" (*C* 5:241; cf.
C 5:243). Similarly, he says in the speech opening the impeachment
that "[i]t is well known that great wealth has poured into this country
from India; and it is no derogation to us to suppose the possibility of
being corrupted by that which great Empires have been corrupted,
and by which assemblies almost as respectable and as venerable as your
Lordships' have been known to be indirectly shaken" (*WS* 6:277). For
Burke, the wealth of elites—and their staking of this wealth in part
on the East India Company—has made them vulnerable to the profit
mindset of the East India Company and complicit in its crimes.

Consequently, even as Burke appeals to the Lords with great passion in the trial, he does not, practically speaking, place much faith in
the Lords' ability to pursue the kind of judgment that Burke believes
would assure justice. Instead, Burke reveals in his private letters
that his hopes for the impeachment proceedings to do justice were
placed in an agent that most of his late twentieth-century and early
twenty-first-century readers—focused as they are on his writings on
the French Revolution—see him as distrustful of: "the publick." In a
letter to Dundas in November 1787, for example, Burke asks for the
trial to begin as soon as possible after the impeachment charges were
accepted by the Commons, "not only for the better arrangement of
every thing, but that the Business may proceed with a continuity cal-
culated to keep the whole series of Evidence in the minds of the Lords,
and under the attention of the publick" (*C* 5:356). Burke also tells Dundas
that he wants the trial held in Westminster Hall so that the public
can observe: "if we proceed under the publick Eye, I have no more
doubt than I entertain of my existence, that all the ability, influence
and power that can accompany a decided partiality in that Tribunal
can[not] save our criminal from a condemnation followed by some
ostensible measure of Justice" (*C* 5:357). Similarly, Burke writes in a
contemporaneous letter to General John Burgoyne that "[o]ur success
will in a great measure depend upon the publicity of the proceedings. Shut us up in a little chamber, and our cause is doomed from
the beginning. Nobody can bear witness to the procedure whilst it is
going on, and its voluminous nature will prevent all sort of interest in
it afterwards. It could neither be heard nor read" (*C* 5:358).[31]

Burke's turn to the public in Hastings's trial, however, does not portray the public in a uniform way. Even as Burke claims that only the

public can pressure the Lords to do justice in Hasting's trial, Burke also claims that this same public has turned into an uncertain agent of the public good and justice—primarily because of Britons' lack of connection with the Indians on behalf of whom Burke seeks justice. For example, in a letter to William Eden in May 1784, Burke says that "the havock and destruction of the species made in the East Indies does by no means touch the humanity of our countrymen, who, if the whole Gentoo race had but one neck, would see it cut with *the most perfect indifference*. To their own interest they have sensibility enough, but then it is only in the moment of suffering" (my emphasis, *C* 5:151). Burke argues that "all the Tyranny, robbery, and destruction of mankind practised by the Company and their servants in the East, is popular and pleasing in this Country" and "the Court and Ministry who evidently abet that iniquitous System, are somewhat the better liked on that account" (*C* 5:155). Consequently, as Burke writes in a 1788 letter to Burgoyne, "[w]e must be conscious that" in the impeachment "we have to deal with partial judges, unwilling and prevaricating witnesses, mangled records, a reluctant House of Commons, and *an indifferent publick*" (my emphasis, *C* 5:395).

Burke's turn to the public in the Hastings trial thus reveals an ambivalent picture of that public: as both the most capable agent of justice in a world characterized by elite failure *and* as too narrow-minded to actually embrace this role. Many scholars writing on Burke tend to focus on this latter aspect of his relationship to the public and thus to portray him as a proponent of the necessity of elite judgment, as well as elite guidance of public opinion.[32] Burke conforms to this reading most obviously in his writings on the French Revolution, where he famously dismisses the revolutionaries and their ilk as a "swinish multitude" that trample the customs, learning, and traditions of Europe under their feet (*RRF*, 176).[33] Here, the ambivalence of Burke's descriptions of the people in the Hastings impeachment collapses into a dichotomy between the true (elite/tradition-deferent) people and the false, swinish (arbitrary, irrational, leveling) multitude.

Yet Burke's concerns about popular power and his sometimes outright fear of it are matched in his work by his persistent claims that for Parliamentary representation to assure the public good, "the represented" and not just their representatives have a role to play in Parliamentary politics—that is, in eighteenth-century parlance, that representation must be actual, not just virtual. For example, in the "Thoughts on the Present Discontents," a text written about a different "crisis" in British life, a lack of public confidence in Lord North's administration in 1770, Burke also calls on the public to defend the public good in a moment when elites have abandoned it. He says, for instance, that "[t]he House of Commons can never be a controul on other parts of Government unless they are controuled themselves by their constituents" (*WS* 2:300).[34] Similarly, and in even stronger terms, Burke says later that "I see no other way for the preservation of a decent attention to public interest in the Representatives, but *the interposition of the body of the people itself*" to combat the movement by members of Parliament toward arbitrary power (*WS* 2:311).[35] Burke is not *only* a thinker of the public as the recipient of elite guidance; he is *also* a thinker of the public as an agent that guides elites.[36]

In the remainder of this section, I will take a "detour" through some of Burke's other writings—particularly the "Thoughts on the Present Discontents"—in order to examine this broader tension in Burke's understanding of the public. I will suggest, in contrast to other readings of Burke, that he *does* see the public as capable of discerning the public good—primarily because of their enmeshment in sentimental networks of care. However, I will also suggest that, for Burke, those sentimental networks of care are themselves vulnerable to corruption—in particular, when the influx of wealth from abroad leads citizens to identify the limits of those networks of care narrowly, as confined to Great Britain and not extending to India. My contention is that the contrast that Burke and other conservatives identify between elites (of broad vision and knowledge) and parochial members of the public is often decentered in Burke's thought by his encounter with moments of elite failure. In these moments, Burke focuses less on the elite/public contrast and more on the problem of soliciting the public on behalf of the public good. In such moments, the problem he faces is less the public's parochialism and more that their naturally reliable sentiments may be corrupted.

Hanna Pitkin has also attended to the tension in Burke's thought between his claim that Parliamentary elites are superior to ordinary citizens in their ability to pursue the public good—Burke says in one moment that these "experts" form a "natural aristocracy," without whom "there is no nation"[37]—*and* that virtual representation by elites (for example, in the case of Ireland) is inevitably insufficient to assure the public good; the represented have a role to play, too.[38] Pitkin ultimately concludes that Burke sees actual representation as important because it assures that citizens are able to speak up if representatives do *not* address their particular interest.[39] In other words, she sees citizens, in Burke's view, as capable of only seeking their particular interest—an interest that the representative then must harmonize with other particular interests into a broader public good.

Pitkin's reading finds support in some parts of the "Thoughts"—for example, when Burke suggests that "the people" will call for a return to the public good because they "have no interest in disorder" (*WS* 2:255). This suggests, as Pitkin argues, that the people's capacity to check their representatives' private interest is limited to voicing discontent about disorder—a voicing that reflects their concern with their particular interest, not the public good—and calling on those same representatives to remedy the situation by returning to the public good. One could thus read Burke as saying that it is only through guidance by a "natural aristocracy" that the people can be guided to discern, out of their particular interests, the common good—that is, to *be* a people as such.[40]

While this reading has the advantage of assuring a unified picture of Burke as a thinker who sees the public as always unable to discern the public interest better than the elite in Parliament, it also obscures the fact that Burke turns to the public in the "Thoughts" precisely because many elites have failed to discern the public good. This is why Burke asks the public in the "Thoughts" not only to call for Parliament to attend to the public good, but also to judge concretely *which* elites are concerned with the common good when both sides claim to be so concerned[41]—a judgment that demands some comprehension of a public, not just private, interest. Indeed, Burke suggests that the people will have the capacity to make precisely this kind of judgment when he argues that "[t]he people will see the necessity of restoring public men to an attention to the public opinion, and of restoring the constitution to its original principles" (*WS* 2:321). Burke similarly calls on the public in the Hastings trial to correct mass elite failure and to judge *which* elites are on the side of justice and the public good—a call which presumes that the public may be capable of discerning, at least in moments of crisis, the difference between private interest and the public good better than elites.

Burke's claims that the public may be more capable than elites of discerning the public good in both the "Thoughts" and his writings on Hastings is puzzling, given his claims throughout his work that elite guidance is necessary for the public to properly pursue the public good. However, it becomes less puzzling when put into the context of his broader sentimental depiction of the body politic, where he portrays popular concern with the common good as growing organically out of citizens' everyday experiences of caring and looking out for others. In the *Reflections on the Revolution in France*, Burke famously describes society as a system of relationships that ascend from care of the family to care of the symbols of the public good of the realm—the king, the aristocracy, the constitution. Burke says that "[t]o be attached to the subdivision, to love the little platoon we belong to in society, is the first principle (the germ as it were) of public affections. It is the first link in the series by which we proceed towards a love to our country and to mankind."[42] Similarly, Burke argues toward the end of the *Reflections*:

> We begin our public affections in our families. No cold relation is a zealous citizen. We pass on to our neighbourhoods, and our habitual provincial connections. These are inns and resting-places. Such divisions of our country as have been formed by habit, and not by a sudden jerk of authority, *were so many little images of the great country* in which the heart found something which it could fill. The love of the whole is not extinguished by this subordinate partiality. *Perhaps it is a sort of elemental training to those higher and more large regards, by which alone men come to be affected, as with their own concern, in the prosperity of a kingdom so extensive as that of France.*[43]

In other words, Burke suggests that the connections citizens form with their family and localities constitute, in lived reality, an image of the country as a whole—one which does not amount to private interest or "partiality," but rather to "elemental training" in discerning the public good—"those higher and more large regards." Familial and local relationships allow citizens to experience and understand the meaning of caring for the whole, in other words, because they train citizens in a system of manners—of showing respect and care for others—that, in taking on an aesthetically pleasing form, engage the affections of those participating in that system, *on behalf of that system of relationships, itself.* Put differently, Burke portrays ordinary people as enmeshed in networks of care that orient their relationship to the state—as an object to be cared for *and* as an entity that is responsible for protecting and enabling these networks of care throughout the state, in official and unofficial form. This lived experience of the importance of linkages of care in sustaining their private interests and concerns may make ordinary citizens more attentive than elites (whose wealth and power may make their interests feel independent of social supports) to the importance of representatives caring for the interests of all people within the state—that is, because such care for all sustains and promotes the interests of each.[44]

At the same time, however, Burke's portrayal of the popular ability to discern the public good as sentimental in origin explains why he sees the public, during Hastings's trial, as the best and yet also unreliable agent of justice. Specifically, and in contrast to Burke's portrayal of ordinary citizens in the *Reflections* as enmeshed in networks of affection, care, and sentiment that culminate in a love of the public good and of country, in his writings on the East India Company, Burke portrays those networks of affection and care as having been penetrated and turned upside down by the "birds of prey" whose work the public also enables and of which the public, to a certain degree, reaps the profit. Burke argues that when these birds of prey return to Britain—where their prey is lodged—the public good is not simply rendered subservient to private wealth, but rather that the British public and a public language of justice are corrupted by the enmeshment of these "birds of prey" within the sentimental life of the body politics: "In India all the vices operate by which sudden fortune is acquired; in England are often displayed, by the same persons, the virtues which dispense hereditary wealth.. . . They marry into your families; they enter into your senate" (*WS* 5:403). Whereas care for others in your "little platoon" used to culminate in a care for the public good—which is care for all—now caring for others appears to culminate in a public good that depends on pillaging and abusing the people of another country. Through the interplay between the public's active desire for Indian wealth and the oppressive actions undertaken by the birds of prey to attain it, vice is turned into virtue, and public votes are made on behalf of private interest.[45] Consequently, the proper public—the public that would recognize the importance of the public good over and against the boundless pursuit of profit, and would support legislation to reform the Company—is absent here. There is, on Burke's account, "no people to control, to watch, to balance against the power of office" in the East India Company (*WS* 6:286).

Burke's account of the sentimental public is thus ultimately ambivalent. While Burke suggests that the sentimental public is able, at least in moments of crisis, to act on behalf of the public good that elites have forsaken or lost sight of, he also suggests that this same (corrupted) sentimentalism blocks the public from imagining the public good outside imperial gain and oppression. Of course, one could argue that the ideal role that Burke imagines for the public is conservative in any case—aimed at simply restoring in both India and Britain traditional and hierarchical social relationships that were disrupted by the "rootless" effects of empire.[46] Yet the role that Burke imagines for the public is also a *sentimental* role, mobilized through and on behalf of affections—a role that in the eighteenth century contained the potential to transgress the social forms that it is also called on to sustain. Indeed, in late eighteenth-century Britain, sentimental novels and prose that appealed to sentiments of the heart were not uniformly or even primarily conservative, but often revelatory of social ills and, as in the case of anti-slavery sentimentalism, productive of social struggle on behalf of equality.[47] Burke's picture of a sentimental state—one that portrays our allegiance to the state as ultimately rooted in sentiment and affect rather than rational consent—thus is not inherently conservative. Rather, appeals to affect and sentiment may mobilize citizens to contest, as well as look away from, inequalities and oppression produced by social hierarchy, as Burke hopes they will in the Hastings trial.

SOLICITING A PUBLIC OF SYMPATHY

In Burke's speeches during Hastings's trial, he consistently appeals to the public to assure justice. How should we read those appeals? Burke's simultaneous depiction of the public as having lost the ability to discern the public good *and* as the only possible agent of justice in the trial suggests that we should not read his appeals to the public simply as attempts to persuade the existing public of the importance of finding Hastings guilty—indeed, the existing public is on Burke's account complicit in injustice and indifferent to the sufferings of Indians.

Rather, we would do better to read those speeches as attempts to use the very theatricality and publicity of the trial—and, in particular, its staging of the true public good—to *solicit* a public (that does not yet exist) on behalf of the public good and justice.

Indeed, Burke's appeals to the public in Hastings's trial occur in a historical context where claims to represent "the public" such as the one staged by Burke in the trial of Hastings were not claims of fact, but claims aimed at legitimating and producing a particular kind of state, governed by particular hierarchies and constellations of power. As Kathleen Wilson notes, "the claim to represent the 'sense of the people' became an important and legitimizing rhetorical strategy in the Hanoverian decades, a crucial part of the wider political contestation under way that had been produced by the emergence of a vibrant, national and predominantly urban extra-parliamentary political culture."[48] At stake in such claims, Wilson argues, was less the "fact" of a particular legitimating group than a social imaginary of the nation that would serve to enable and constrain certain forms of speech and public action: "'the people' as much as 'the nation' constituted an 'invented community' in eighteenth-century political argument, one conceived, significantly, as lying outside formal political structures and as having interests dichotomous or potentially dichotomous to those in power."[49] In other words, appeals to "the public" were a way of construing an imaginary of who makes up the public that in turn legitimates and circumscribes the proper political world.

Consequently, appeals to the public were not appeals to a concrete empirical group that everyone is trying to woo, but rather were expressions of broad political contest over the proper nature and composition of the public and the public good—contest which in this period was wide-ranging and fierce.[50] When Burke hopes to solicit a public on behalf of justice—that would replace the "indifferent publick" with which he was faced—he likely hopes to rouse a group of propertied, white, male Britons to his cause.[51] Yet he also certainly hopes to call them into action as part of a particular social imaginary of a public: specifically, as one that does not see the public good as synonymous with the relentless pursuit of private interest, but rather understands the public good as a care for the rule of law, the fair apportionment of goods, and for all individuals within the purview of the realm.

Such a public, on Burke's account, would consist in a public of *sympathy*—that is, one that would feel care and sympathy for Indians in the same way as, or at least analogously to, the way that Britons feel care and sympathy for those in their "little platoon." Burke discusses the importance of sympathy in the most depth in his closing speech in the trial. There, Burke discusses the problem of Britons' confusion of the public good with private interest, which he sees as preventing justice in the trial. Speaking almost harshly to the British public, Burke argues that by giving "soft, emollient names to vices and to crimes" (*WS* 7:241) the public not only fails to call "those people to an account" in Court "for that horrible crime which destroys the basis of human Society" (*WS* 7:244), but also "protect[s] its [own] corruption and its degeneracy." (*WS* 7:241).[52] In response to this confusion, Burke argues that it is the duty of the House of Commons "to give a more proper tone and a juster way of thinking to the public upon such an occasion" (*WS* 7:241)—specifically, a "juster way of thinking" guided by sympathy. Burke argues that doing justice to Hastings depends on what he calls a feeling of "sympathetic revenge": the desire to avenge a crime or injustice done to another. Through chastening "that wild stock of revenge" by "transferr[ing] [it] from the suffering party to the communion and sympathy of mankind" (*WS* 7:245), Burke says that it "yields all the charming fruits of justice." In contrast to those who see expressions of feeling as corruptive to justice, Burke argues that the danger when revenge is transferred to the public "Trustee and Delegate of justice" is that "he will not feel enough upon such an occasion, that he will be cold and languid in it" (*WS* 7:245).

Why is sympathy necessary to justice here? Wouldn't distancing oneself from partial feelings actually enable a fuller justice? On the one hand, Burke's argument on behalf of the importance of sympathy to justice reiterates the more general argument he makes about the social importance of sympathy in his earlier *Philosophical Enquiry into the Origin of our Ideas of the Sublime and the Beautiful*. There, Burke is interested in how sympathy bridges particularities and creates identification among disparate groups. Burke defines sympathy as the passion whereby "we enter into the concerns of others; that we are moved as they are moved, and are never suffered to be indifferent spectators of almost any thing which men can do or suffer" (*WS* 1:220). We should think of it, Burke says, "as a sort of substitution, by which we are put into the place of another man, and affected in many respects as he is affected" (*WS* 1:220–221). This is a common theme in sentimentalist writings of the period—for example, in those of Hume and Smith. Hume suggests, like Burke, that sympathy is what allows us to be social beings because, without it, the sentiments of others would have no claim upon us.[53] Similarly, Smith suggests that sympathy ensures that there will be "concords" in society, if not total harmony.[54] Yet Burke's formulation of sympathy's fundamental role in society stresses more than Smith and Hume its importance in ensuring that we come to the aid of those in distress. Indeed, Burke, in the *Enquiry*, is most interested in how sympathy can generate feelings of "delight"—that is, the experience of "danger or pain" felt "at certain distances" that is characteristic of the sublime (*WS* 1:217). Sympathy with others' feelings of pain so as to generate delight has, on Burke's account, salubrious social effects. Specifically, in pressing us to approach rather than "shun" "scenes of misery," our sympathy with those in danger and pain "prompts us to relieve ourselves in relieving those who suffer" (*WS* 1:222). For Burke, sympathy thus assures that people of all ranks and situations in society care for each other—and as a consequence, we might say, for the public good.

In his writings on the impeachment and trial, however, Burke suggests another crucial role for sympathy. Rather than simply assuring that we care for those in distress, sympathy also, on Burke's account, expresses natural feelings that re-orient us to the proper line between right and wrong, between the public good and private interest. For example, in a section of his "Speech on Fox's East India Bill" where Burke is describing the difficulty of "fixing our sympathy upon these objects" in India because of their cultural and physical distance from us, he defends the importance of displaying feeling and sympathy. While Burke there notes that a completely unrestrained display of feeling is detrimental to justice, he also says that "a cold style of describing actions which appear to me in a very affecting light is equally contrary to the justice due to the people, and to all genuine human feelings about them" (5:404). Burke illustrates the problem with a "cold style of describing actions" by reference to Tacitus and Machiavelli, whom he sees as sometimes exemplars of such a style: "It has been said (and, with regard to one of them, with truth) that Tacitus and Machiavel, by their cold way of relating enormous crimes, have in some sort appeared not to disapprove them; that they seem a sort of professors of the art of tyranny, and that *they corrupt the minds of their readers by not expressing the detestation and horror that naturally belong to horrible and detestable proceedings*" (my emphasis, *WS* 5:404). For Burke, to excise the "natural" feeling that accompanies observation of "horrible and detestable proceedings" is contrary to justice and morality because it suggests that actions like Hastings's *can* and perhaps should be assessed without regard to morality and natural feeling. It suggests, in other words, that what appears as a "crime" from a moral perspective can be, with equal validity, conceived merely as an act of state "necessity." The positive role of sympathy here is thus as an expression of natural feeling that insists that even acts supposedly justified according to "necessity" must be judged as morally right or wrong, as just or unjust, as serving the public good or private interest.

Other sentimentalists of the period similarly suggest that sympathy stands at the basis of our standards of justice and the public good. Hume argues, for example, that while "*self-interest* is the original motive to the *establishment* of justice," "a *sympathy* with *public* interest is the source of the *moral* approbation, which attends that virtue."[55] The importance of sympathy in securing justice is, for Hume as for Burke, its influence on public taste and (dis)approbation of the actions of those in power: "This latter principle of sympathy is too weak to controul our passions, but has sufficient force to influence our taste, and give us the sentiments of approbation and blame."[56] Yet in contrast to Burke, Hume does not suggest that sympathy sustains justice because it expresses *natural* feeling. Rather, for Hume, sympathy sustains justice because of its salubrious effects on social utility (noted by both Hume and Burke). Sympathy, on Hume's account, ties us to the (already acculturated) concerns and pains of others and gives us an interest in seeing them adjudicated fairly: "we have no such extensive concern for society but from sympathy; and consequently 'tis that principle, which takes us so far out of ourselves, as to give us the same pleasure or uneasiness in characters which are *useful or pernicious to society*, as if they had a tendency to our own advantage of loss."[57] The standard here that is instantiated by sympathy, on Hume's account, is not that of a natural morality, but of social utility. In contrast, Burke's argument for the importance of sympathy in sustaining justice rests on an understanding of feeling and sympathizing with pain as constitutive of a natural morality capable of crossing cultural boundaries.

In his closing speech, Burke suggests that it is precisely this natural feeling, rooted in common humanity, that can reorient the Lords and public to the proper line between right and wrong: "I hope that as you will sympathize with the great on account of their condition, that you will sympathize with all mankind on the ground of the common con- dition of humanity which belongs to us all" (*WS* 7:529). Indeed, Burke even seems to suggest, in the context of a particular set of injuries done to Indian women, that sympathy will *inevitably* lead to justice: "My Lords, if there is a spark of manhood, if there is in your breasts the least feeling for our common humanity, if the least feeling in your Lordships' breasts for the sufferings and distresses of that part of human nature which is made by its peculiar constitution to feel, if there is a trace of this in your breasts, *if you are alive to those feelings, it is impossible you can bear or tolerate that wicked Tyrant who is the cause of the whole of it*" (my emphasis, *WS* 7:537). Natural sympathy—an almost involuntary feeling for the pain of Indians—has on Burke's account an inevitable logic: the Lords and public will be redirected to the proper notion of the public good versus private interest, to the clear line between right and wrong.

Of course, Burke's very attempt to solicit a public that feels this natural sympathy alerts us to the fact that "natural" sympathy needs social and cultural supports. Siraj Ahmed argues that the dependence of sympathy on Burke's theatrical solicitations reveals that sympathy is actually not natural, but the product of "social mimicry" that obscures the natural savagery released in the East India Company.[58] Ahmed may be right that Burke's solicitation of sympathy obscures some aspects of the savagery of the oppressions of the East India Company—although Burke does in fact describe this "savagery" in great detail. However, Ahmed's reading neglects Burke's complication of the division between nature and culture in his conceptualization of social and political ties— a complication effected more broadly by sentimentalist thinkers in the mid- and late eighteenth century. For Burke, our "nature" is shaped and modified through historical tradition, customs, affective ties, and everyday practices; it becomes, in other words, a "second nature."[59] Thus, for Burke, to attempt to access a first nature *beyond* our second nature inevitably does violence to society and renders it vulnerable to arbitrary power—as, he argued, the French revolutionaries' appeals to pre-social natural rights rendered them unable to check arbitrary rule. Contra Ahmed, then, Burke's attempt to solicit a public of natural sympathy does not unmask nature as mimicry, but rather forms a part of Burke's broader view that our nature is only meaningfully fulfilled through its constitution and enmeshment in a particular society. However, Burke's solicitation of a public of natural sympathy *does* reveal that this sympathy is not as irresistible as he portrays it in the above passages—that is, that constituting our nature into an appropriate second nature is itself a contingent and uncertain project, dependent in this case on the response to his solicitation of an unreliable public.

STAGING SYMPATHY

Burke attempts to bring this unreliable public to identify as a public of sympathy through theatrically staging his own sympathy for Indians, as well as his own anger toward and disgust for Hastings. As Ahmed argues, Burke "intentionally made his speeches dramatic, rather than legalistic, because he wanted in effect to bypass the representatives and appeal to the represented."[60] Burke does this through speaking movingly and sometimes salaciously of the suffering of victims and by painting Hastings as almost a caricature of evil and wickedness. Brycchan Carey, in his study of British abolitionist rhetoric, calls this form of rhetoric "sentimental rhetoric" and argues that it is characterized by "the sentimental orator or author. . . seek[ing] out exceptional instances of suffering and emphasis[ing] them to gain the reader's or hearer's sympathy."[61] Such rhetoric is found in political speeches, sentimental novels and poetry, political writings, and letters of the period.[62] Anti-slavery rhetoric is the chief political exemplar of this form of rhetoric, but it was prominently used on behalf of all kinds of (often philanthropic) attempts to alleviate suffering—for example, on behalf of attempts to address poverty and cruelty to animals.[63]

Burke certainly makes use of this form of rhetoric in his speeches during the impeachment. Throughout his speeches, Burke rhetorically constructs Hastings not just as a criminal, but as the most villainous, wicked criminal Britain has ever seen. Hastings is the "Captain-General in iniquity," the "one in whom all the frauds, all the peculations, all the violence, all the tyranny in India are embodied, disciplined and arrayed" (*WS* 6:275). In the closing speech, Hastings is a "Weasel and a Rat" (*WS* 7:277) and a "plain cheat" (*WS* 7:663). Hastings's crimes in India "arose from his pride which arose from his malice and insatiable avarice, which arose from his abandoned tyranny and from that lust of arbitrary power. . ." (*WS* 7:299). Wherever Hastings went in India, Burke says, he was "pursued by the cries of an oppressed and ruined people, where they dared to appear before him" (*WS* 7:370). In Hastings's rule, we see "an industrious people, subjected to such a cursed anarchy under pretence of revenue, such a cursed tyranny under pretence of Government" (*WS* 7:371). Burke asks the Lords at the end of his opening speech, "Do we want a cause, my Lords? You have the cause of oppressed Princes, of undone women of the first rank, of desolated Provinces and of wasted Kingdoms. Do you want a criminal, my Lords? *When was there so much iniquity ever laid to the charge of any one?*" (my emphasis, *WS* 6:457).

Burke's most rhetorically inspired moments in his speeches, however, involve not only Hastings's wickedness, but also the injuries that he and his agents inflicted on Indians and Britons. Speaking of a local ruler supported and set up by Hastings, Burke says: "The tyrant Mr. Hastings set up cut and hacked the limbs of British subjects in the most cruel and perfidious manner; threw them into wells; and polluted the Waters of the Country with British blood" (*WS* 6:336). Perhaps most famously, Burke dwells in his opening speech on salacious injuries supposedly done by one of Hastings's deputies—Devi Singh—to Indians in his attempt to collect revenues.[64] Burke describes, for example, the torture inflicted on Indian men:

> The first mode of torture was this. They began by winding cords about their fingers until they had become incorporated together, and then they hammered wedges of wood and iron between those fingers until they crushed and maimed those poor, honest, laborious hands which never had been lifted to their own mounts but with the scanty supply of the product of their own labour. (*WS* 6:419)

Burke goes on to describe further torture in great detail:

> The Heads of villages, the parochial Magistrates, the leading Yeomen of the country, respectable for their situation, and their age, were taken and tied together by the feet, two and two, thrown

over a bar, and there beaten with bamboo canes upon the soles of
their feet until their nails started from their toes. And then, falling
upon them, while their heads hung down as their feet were above,
with sticks and cudgels, their tormentors attacked them with such
blind fury that the blood ran out of their mouths, eyes and noses.
(*WS* 6:419)

The torturers also "scourged these poor people with. . . thorns" while
"innocent children were brought out and scourged before the faces
of their parents" (*WS* 6:420) and "virgins were cruelly violated by
the bases and wickedest of mankind" in public (*WS* 6:421). Burke's
description culminates in his depiction of a horror supposedly inflicted
on women by Devi Singh's lieutenants:

> In order that nature might be violated in all those circumstances
> where the sympathies of nature are awakened, where the remem-
> brances of our infancy and all our tender remembrances are com-
> bined, they put the nipples of the women into the sharp edges
> of split bamboos and tore them from their bodies. Grown from
> ferocity to ferocity, from cruelty to cruelty, they applied burning
> torches and cruel slow fires.. . . These, my Lords, were the horrors
> that arose from bribery, the cruelties that arose from giving power
> into the hands of such persons as Debi Sing. (*WS* 6:421)

Through his detailed descriptions of Indian suffering and his own
performed feelings of sympathy for them, as well as his disgust with
Hastings, Burke hoped to stage the kind of sympathy that a proper
public would exhibit, and that it would use to guide its judgment of
Hastings. As Ahmed puts it, "[i]n providing an exaggerated performance of how the sentimental character responds to imperial atrocities,
Burke gave the British public a model of how it should act."[65] Similarly,
Uday Mehta has argued that Burke's "writings on India are the most
sophisticated and moving elaboration on the idea of sympathy—the
means through which one develops in oneself a feeling for another
person or collectivity of persons."[66] For Mehta, Burkean sympathy is
the cornerstone of a Burkean "cosmopolitanism of sentiments" that
seeks open-ended conversation and mutual understanding between
rooted cultures, rather than the liberal (Lockean) model of imposing
one mode of comprehension onto the other culture. In sum, Burke

stages his sympathy so as to offer a model of connection with Indian suffering with which the public could identify and emulate.

Yet does Burke's salacious and graphic account of the infliction of suffering, in hopes of kindling British sympathy with Indians, exemplify the kind of sympathy that Mehta is talking about? Mehta is certainly right that there are many parts of Burke's speeches that exemplify the possibility of a conversation between equals across cultural boundaries.[67] Yet there are other moments—as in the passages that I just quoted—where Burke's depiction of unfamiliar Indian suffering on behalf of sparking sympathy does not appear primarily as an attempt at mutual understanding. Instead, its obvious ploy to provoke sentimental response (which succeeded—many women in the audience burst into tears) seems to *use* an exoticized depiction of Indian suffering on behalf of achieving Burke's end of finding Hastings guilty. Burke's theatrical staging of his own sympathy for Indian suffering in this instance does not achieve mutual understanding, but subordinates such a project to his own end of provoking public response and assuring a guilty verdict. Not surprisingly, Hastings's supporters made precisely this critique of Burke: that is, that Burke's expression of sympathy with Indian suffering is a theatrical attempt to sidestep the public good and justice on behalf of private interest. One such critic, David Stewart Erskine, Earl of Buchan, writing anonymously as Albanicus, argues that Burke "has affected to espouse the cause of virtue and of the oppressed; he has collected the cries of the Indians, which, he says, were given to the seas and the winds, *and for the sake of private vengeance*, he has helped them on an evil head, under the name of punishing the guilty"—and "he has made use of every mode which his eloquence, his fancy, and his argument can furnish, to make you believe that his cause is that of thirty millions of your fellow Creatures."[68]

Burke's attempt to stage his own sympathy for Indians in a particularly provocative and graphic way thus reveals a tension within the pursuit of sympathy: that feelings of sympathy for others may not straightforwardly assure justice and protection of the public good, but can serve as cover and legitimation for—perhaps unintentionally— one's own pursuit of private interest, one's own political and moral agenda. While Mehta's portrayal of sympathy as the expression of true mutual understanding between cultures may reflect Burke's ideal of sympathy in the trial, Mehta insufficiently attends to the dangers inherent in the turn to sympathy: that this sympathy may be one way of staging the interest or agenda of one of the parties involved. This problem can be seen in contemporary politics, as well—for example, when white Western feminists claim to have "sympathy" with women of color and/or non-Western women. While this claim to sympathy may be well intentioned, it also may end up serving primarily to satisfy the desire of these women to be true representatives of feminism and to legitimate their sense of the right priorities for feminism, rather than to actually address the concerns of women of color and non-Western women.[69] Sympathy as a fantasy of connection—or what Lauren Berlant calls "national sentimentality, a rhetoric of promise that a nation can be built across fields of social difference through channels of affective identification and empathy"[70]—may serve the interests of the sympathizer to legitimate their political claims and agenda and perhaps even to sidestep the real causes of suffering (for example, imperialism, itself), rather than to truly address or seek to relieve the suffering of the other. The appeal to sympathy, then, may not resolve the confusion between the public good and private interest, but may instead heighten and re-stage that problem in a new register.

In his recent book, *The Rule of Sympathy*, Amit Rai makes a similar critical appraisal of eighteenth-century sympathy. There, he argues through readings of Hume and Smith on sympathy that the fantasy and practice of sympathy does not simply *obscure* hierarchies and injury, but rather *depends* on the existence of hierarchical relationships: "sympathy needs this abjected other, as the constitutive exclusion that would cohere its own fantasy of identity."[71] Without the existence of differences in power, Rai suggests that the fantasy of identity achieved through sympathy would not be so seductive—it would seem unnecessary. For Rai, this reveals that sympathy in the late eighteenth and nineteenth centuries ultimately "tied together subjects, families, communities, classes, nations, races, and colonies" through "normalization"[72]—not through some natural identification of feeling.

Rai's reading of sympathy has the virtue of pointing up the negative consequences of projecting a fantasy of identification from the point of view of the powerful as a condition of relieving the distress of the less powerful. Yet Rai also largely neglects the promising aspects of the turn to sympathy, as revealed in Burke's writings on the Hastings trial— aspects that are intertwined with the problematic aspects outlined by

Rai and that should not be simply excised. Specifically, Rai insufficiently attends to the promise inherent in the turn to sympathetic
feeling when it offers us a way to apprehend and respond to wrongs
that are not captured by formal legal categories *nor* by dominant cultural understandings.[73] Certainly, sympathy also promises a fantasy of
identification that it can never deliver—a fantasy that may obscure
and perpetuate the very hierarchical relationships that make sympathy
necessary in the first place (the problem with sympathy that Mehta has
missed). However, we could read this tension not as showing sympathy
to be an instrument of normalization and oppression almost *tout court*,
but as an ambivalent resource for justice: one that seems to offer a way
of pursuing justice beyond existing legal forms while also reaching
limits in achieving true understanding of the suffering of the other.[74]
Or to push the point further, we might read the ambivalence inherent
in Burke's appeal to sympathy as gesturing toward the importance of
(if not authorizing) a chastened appeal to a sympathetic public in times
of legal and popular insufficiency—an appeal to sympathy that allows
us to identify the shortcomings of existing law and cultural norms,
while remaining cautious about the ability of sympathy to provide full
redress for those shortcomings and do full justice.

In the next section, I will suggest that we might glean such a chastened approach not primarily from the impeachment writings themselves, but from Burke's later attempt to grapple with his ultimate
failure to secure a guilty verdict in the trial. Burke's response to that
failure is not to turn away from the ambivalent and unreliable public
altogether, but to appeal to it in a different register—as a public that
mourns.

MOURNING SYMPATHY

In a letter written late in his life to French Laurence, after his retire-
ment from the House of Commons, Burke asks Laurence to remember
his promise to publish a history of the impeachment.[75] Burke wanted
such a history published so that Hastings's acquittal would not be the
last word on the trial. Rather, Burke hoped that the history would
restage that acquittal as itself an injustice. "Above all," Burke says,
"make out the cruelty of this pretended acquittal, but in reality this

barbarous and inhuman condemnation of whole Tribes and nations, and of all the abuses they contain" (*SL*, 398). In other words, the history that Burke envisions would be a "lost cause narrative"—that is, a narrative of Hastings's trial that, in publishing Burke's speeches alongside those of Hastings's defenders, would reveal the cause of justice as one that could have been won (had the public intervened), but was not. In this Burkean counter-narrative of the trial, the Indian suffering on behalf of which Burke had waged the impeachment—and on behalf of which he had solicited a sympathetic public—had not in the end been alleviated by the trial, but rather deepened and obscured by a verdict that cemented it in place as "justice."

For Burke, the point of publishing a history of the impeachment is not simply that Britons will remember the trial differently, but that it might serve as a spark for a response by a belated public: "[i]f ever Europe recovers its civilization that work will be useful. Remember! Remember! Remember!"; "there will be a Season for the appearance of such a Record; and it ought to be in Store for that Season" (*SL*, 398). Burke does not say in what way this record might be "useful." Yet he seems to imagine that by preserving a record of Hastings's acquittal as injustice, this acquittal might not only mark the end of the story of his pursuit of justice, but also the beginning of other pursuits of justice—pursuits sparked by Burke's dedication to his "lost cause" (even after the acquittal) and, in turn, dedicated in some way to alleviating the suffering of those under the yoke of British imperialism or, perhaps, under the yoke of any imperialism. Burke acknowledges that there may never be such a public when he asks Laurence to ensure that this "cruel, daring, unexampled act of publick corruption, guilt, and meanness go down—*to a posterity perhaps as careless as the present race*" (my emphasis, *SL*, 397). However, Burke nonetheless wants the record—*his* record—of the trial to be preserved for a possible future, receptive, belated public.

One might read Burke's desire for a history of the impeachment as an attempt to project the call he made in the impeachment to a sympathetic public across temporal divides—to solicit this same public in the future. Yet Burke's call to a future public, based as it is in the experience of failure, reflects a shift in register. Specifically, Burke's hoped-for history of the impeachment would solicit a public that would have to grapple with Hastings's trial precisely as a "lost cause"—as a trial where justice could have been done if the public had heeded Burke's call for justice, but was not. Put differently, Burke's hope that the history of the impeachment would solicit a future public is implicitly a hope that the history will call out a public ready to address the failure of sympathy in Hastings's trial—that is, a public that would acknowledge that sympathetic feeling is not automatically shared by all and that it may fail to assure justice.

The contention of this section is that Burke envisions a public that would negotiate this failure of the sympathetic public to appear through the practice of mourning. I find the primary support for this reading in Burke's request to Laurence that a history of the impeachment should not only be published, but also stand as his (Burke's) monument: "Let my endeavours to save the Nation from that Shame and guilt, be my monument; The only one I ever will have. Let every thing I have done, said, or written be forgotten but this" (SL, 397). Writers on Burke have commented on or noted this gesture of his, and some have noted that this indicates the importance of the impeachment to him, in the context of his broader oeuvre.[76] Yet none to my knowledge has asked what he means by a monument, and what it means to understand the impeachment as a monument to him. By "monument," Burke does not seem to be referring to the kinds of monuments intended to commemorate great rulers or great war commanders, such as the statue commissioned by Anne of herself as an imperial monarch. Rather, given his various references to his impending death in the surrounding passages, he seems to be referring to his own funeral monument. Indeed, Burke begins his letter with a rumination on his impending death[77] and, right before asking Laurence to remember his promise to publish a history of the impeachment, Burke notes that "it is possible that my stay on this side of the Grave, may be yet shorter, than I compute it" (SL, 397). Similarly, after asking Laurence to let these writings stand as his monument, Burke goes on to say that "I wish after my death, to have my Defiance of the Judgments of those, who consider the dominion of the glorious Empire given by an incomprehensible dispensation of the Divine providence into our hands as nothing more than an opportunity of gratifying for the lowest of their purposes" (SL, 398). Burke's writings and speeches on Hastings—and not some great physical monument—will memorialize him in and after death.[78]

In asking that the history of the impeachment stand as his monument, Burke is certainly attempting to control in advance how he will
be remembered—not as his detractors paint him (as a vengeful, fanciful
pursuer of private interest), but instead as the pursuer of justice and the
public good. Yet in casting the impeachment history as a future memorial of a dead individual (himself), Burke's request also suggestively
calls for a public relationship to the impeachment's failure in the register of mourning. Burke does not elaborate on how such a mourning
public would respond to the history of the impeachment. However,
by considering late eighteenth-century understandings and practices
of mourning, especially in relation to funeral monuments, we might
cobble together a sense of Burke's "mourning imaginary." When put
in conversation with Burke's hope for a history of the impeachment to
serve as his monument, I will argue that this "mourning imaginary"
reveals an understanding of mourning as a productive public practice
of negotiating and responding to failures and insufficiencies in public
life—in particular, here, the failure of sympathy.

Burke's Mourning Imaginary

Unlike our contemporary era, where monuments and tombstones are
for the most part cordoned off from everyday life, funeral monuments
in the late eighteenth century were deeply entwined in the ordinary
lives of British subjects. Monuments to those of elite status (or, as of
the seventeenth and eighteenth centuries, to those who could buy their
way into the company of such elites) were mostly placed in churches,
which Britons were required to attend, and those of lesser status in
churchyards—thus placing British subjects in weekly communion with
these commemorations of the dead. Funeral monuments underwent
huge growth in the seventeenth and eighteenth centuries, with many
more people of the bourgeois and even lower classes commissioning
monuments of varying grandeur to the dead.[79] Thus, not only did
British subjects interact with monuments weekly in and around church
(and sometimes, literally interact, as when monuments in the shape of
the deceased person kneeling were put next to the altar of the church),
many of them also actively participated in imagining what an appropriate monument to the dead would be.[80]

In so doing, British citizens in late eighteenth-century Britain
would have largely thought about the purpose of monuments in two

ways: as having commemorative and didactic purposes. As commemorative objects, monuments were meant to represent the dead person in their absence—to offer continuity to living friends and relatives (or in the case of royalty or nobility, to subjects) who experience disruption through the loss.[81] In this sense, monuments were meant to represent the dead—to make them present to the living and to offer a site on which grief may focus and be expressed. Monuments were also meant, however, to offer lessons of virtue to a broader public. Epitaphs to the dead were meant to instruct the living on how to live a virtuous life, and sculpted images of the dead offered in more elaborate monuments were meant to demonstrate the virtue of the dead as well as to instruct. As the eighteenth century progressed, these images changed from being stills of the dead—for example, lying recumbent or semi-recumbent, or kneeling in prayer—to more narrative sculptures of the dead in a particular (metaphorical or real) vignette or event, meant to be exemplary of their life. David Bindman quotes an eighteenth-century guide's description of Roubiliac's monument to Joseph Gascoigne and Lady Elizabeth Nightingale, which, Bindman notes, "could easily be describing a theatrical performance":

> Above is represented a Lady expiring in the Arms of her Husband; beneath, slily creeping from a Tomb, the King of Terrors presents his grim Visage, pointing his unerring Dart to the dying Figure, at which Sight the Husband, suddenly struck with Astonishment, Horror, Despair, &c. would fain ward off the fatal Stroke form the distressed Object of his Care.[82]

Such monuments offered a picture of a virtuous death, but they also instructed the spectator on the appropriate mode of response to death. For example, Roubiliac often incorporated an observer within the sculpture itself—often a grieving widow who "acts both as *exempla virtutis* and paragons of tender feeling which they arouse empathetically in others.. . . They represent ideal female conduct in response to grievous loss, but their physical separation from the monument also invites the visitor, especially a female one, to enter fully into their sorrow."[83] Such monuments blurred and combined the commemorative and didactic functions of the funeral monument—teaching citizens, through the example of one grievous loss, about a more general virtuous relationship to death and loss.

As the eighteenth century progressed, the didactic purpose of monuments was increasingly associated with feeling—with evoking feelings
of the loss of virtue and, in turn, desires for imitations. While Addison
is writing at the beginning of the eighteenth century, a passage from
his essay on this subject is nonetheless instructive. He writes:

> When I look upon the tombs of the great, every emotion of envy
> dies in me; when I read the epitaphs of the beautiful, every inor-
> dinate desire goes out; when I meet with the grief of parents upon
> a tomb-stone, my heart melts with compassion; when I see the
> tomb of the parents themselves, I consider the vanity of grieving
> for those whom we must quickly follow; when I see kings lying by
> those who deposed them; when I consider rival wits placed side by
> side, or the holy men that divided the world with their contests and
> disputes, I reflect with sorrow and astonishment on the little com-
> petitions, factions, and debates of mankind. When I read the sev-
> eral dates of the tombs, of some that died yesterday, and some six
> hundred years ago, I consider that great day when we shall all of us
> be contemporaries, and make our appearance together.[84]

In this passage, Addison's response to the monuments offers an ideal
eighteenth-century model for apprehending them. His spectatorship
of funeral monuments sparks feelings of grief and a sense of insignifi-
cance that in turn lead him to reflect on how death should affect the
life of the living—what kind of virtuous behavior it should cultivate
in us.

When Burke imagines the history of the impeachment serving as
his funeral monument, he thus likely imagines it as having two purposes: first, as commemorating his public virtue and the virtue of his
pursuit of justice in Hastings's trial as solace for the loss of both; and,
second, as a didactic lesson in just action for a broad public. Yet as we
can see in Addison's example, the lesson of just action that emerges
from the experience of mourning is one that is chastened by the spectator's mourning of loss. For Addison, the experience of mourning
teaches about the importance of justice and virtue, but it also reveals
the inevitable limits of human activity in the figure of death. The
practice of mourning Burke (the person) via the monument of the
impeachment history thus may generate an attunement to his call for
sympathetic justice as important *and* limited, virtuous *and* incomplete.

Indeed, we can find this model of mourning in sentimental novels of the period that Burke likely read, such as Henry Mackenzie's wildly successful *The Man of Feeling*, published in 1771. *The Man of Feeling* contains two exemplary graveyard vignettes. In the first moment, the sentimental hero (the man of feeling), Harley, accompanies his old friend Edwards, along with Edwards's grandchildren, to the grave-stone of Edwards's son (after having journeying for weeks to find him, Edwards had just learned of his son's death). Mackenzie describes the moment thus:

> There was an old stone, with the corner broken off, and some letters, half covered with moss, to denote the names of the dead: there was a cyphered R.E. plainer than the rest: it was the tomb they sought. 'Here it is, grandfather,' said the boy. Edwards gazed upon it without uttering a word: the girl, who had only sighed before, now wept outright; her brother sobbed, but he stifled his sobbing. "I have told sister," said he, "that she should not take it so to heart; *she can knit already, and I shall soon be able to dig: we shall not starve, sister, indeed we shall not, nor shall grandfather neither.*"—The girl cried afresh; Harley kissed off her tears as they flowed, and wept between every kiss.[85]

In this moment, the simplicity of the gravestone offers commemoration of Edwards's son's simple virtue, and works both didactically and as a site of grief. It allows the children and Edwards to grieve the loss of the particular individual they knew, and it allows Harley to grieve the loss of virtue more generally. The feeling of the loss of virtue in turn sparks a more intense desire to be virtuous oneself—to replace or supplement what was lost. Here, the grief of virtue leads Edwards's grandson to seek to emulate his father's virtue in taking care of his family.

The second and more striking moment in *The Man of Feeling* consists in the narrator's description of his own response to Harley's grave—a description that concludes the book. Harley dies in the novel, essentially as a result of feeling too deeply the loss of Miss Walton (his virtuous beloved) to another. The narrator notes that Harley was buried in the old churchyard near his mother, in a spot where the narrator and Harley had spent time and "counted the tombs."[86] The narrator says, "I sometimes visit his grave; I sit in the hollow of the tree. It is worth a thousand homilies! every nobler feeling rises within me! every beat of my heart awakens a virtue!—but it will make you hate the world—No: there is such an air of gentleness around, that I can hate nothing; but, as to the world—I pity the men of it. FINIS."[87] Here we see again, but in more pronounced fashion, the didactic function of the funeral monument entwined with, and sparked by, feelings of grief and loss. Simply by contemplating the tombstone of the virtuous individual, and grieving his loss, the narrator is spurred himself to virtue and nobility. Yet the narrator also suggests that contemplating Harley's grave makes him pity the men of the world, and to almost hate the world, because Harley's virtue, it is intimated, could not survive on this earth. The narrator's response to Harley's tomb, in other words, is to both contemplate the impossibility of true virtue like Harley's on earth *and* the importance of pursuing such virtue oneself, to try to supplement its absence with an imperfect substitute. Thus, in both of these vignettes (and especially the last one), feeling grief at the loss of a virtuous person spurs an acknowledgement of the impossibility of perfect virtue on earth and the desire to nonetheless enact that virtue, in chastened form, as best one can in one's own person.

Chastened Sympathy

In the context of this "mourning imaginary," Burke's call for the impeachment history to serve as his monument appears to solicit a mourning public that would (like the spectators of funeral monuments in Mackenzie's novel) acknowledge the impossibility of the virtues represented by Burke's trial of Hastings and yet feel called to pursue those virtues (*im*perfectly) anyway. Specifically, a public that meditates on and grieves the loss of Burke's pursuit of Hastings, and of Burke himself, would be called on to see the virtues of sympathy for justice, but would also be more attuned than Burke himself to the inevitable limits of sympathy. These limits would be marked not only by mortality—that Burke's pursuit of sympathy could not survive his death—but also by the failure of the trial that Burke, in calling for a history of it to serve as his monument, portrayed as an analogue to, or symbol of, his own mortality. The sympathy into which a mourning public would be interpolated would be, in other words, a *chastened* sympathy: a sympathy that calls us to address sufferings and wrongs not captured by existing standards and laws, but which is attentive to its own limits and insufficiencies.

Such a chastened sympathy, reconceived through the practice of mourning, would be politically distinct from the sympathy that Burke called for during Hastings's trial. Whereas during the trial Burke asked Britons to identify with and seek to relieve the sufferings of Indians, the practice of mourning sympathy directs us to attend to the ways in which sympathy may hinder, as well as aid, comprehension of those injuries—for example, by sentimentally focusing attention on particular damages rather than the system of hierarchy that produces them. Further, if Burke believed that sympathy could re-orient the public to the natural line between right and wrong during the trial, a chastened sympathy generates questions about how sympathetic identification of wrongs may not only help to redress suffering, but also traffic in and reiterate the victimization of others. Finally, where Burke calls in his trial writings for the public to sympathetically pursue connection across cultural boundaries, a sympathetic public attuned to its own limits would seek such connection while also asking whether it is a ruse that sustains hierarchy.

In sum, the practice of mourning sympathy would encourage a belated public to be attentive to how the desire to right a wrong may obscure aspects of the injury they hope to redress; to question whether their moral sense of wrong may be felt in a cross-cultural context as a form of imposition; and, finally, to be attuned to the possibility that their feeling of connection across cultural boundaries may mask points of *dis*connection created, for example, through economic and cultural hierarchies. Through the practice of mourning sympathy, sympathy thus appears differently: not as the final answer to problems of transnational injustice, but as one important way of pursuing justice beyond traditional legal and cultural categories that is also potentially problematic in its normalizing and hierarchical effects.

A form of sympathy that admits its inevitable failure would certainly offer less certain legitimacy to law, and less certain guidance about the line between the public good and private interest, than the form of sympathy *qua* natural morality advocated by Burke in his impeachment writings. Yet an imaginary of a public constituted through a comportment of mourning or grief toward the ideal of sympathy might better prepare citizens and publics to acknowledge and address moments of the failure of sympathy to achieve perfect community and identity— moments when, as Berlant has argued in the contemporary context, appeals to feeling work to instantiate a fantasy of identification across class, race, and gender boundaries that masks rather than remedies the structural causes of inequality. The acknowledgement and mourning of failure, Burke's example suggests, might itself offer novel possibilities—occluded by a turn to standards of legitimacy—for imagining ourselves as a public and, in turn, for imagining the actions we might take on behalf of relieving suffering, combating injustice, and pursuing the public good.

A PUBLIC TASTE FOR TRUTH

Zola's Literary Appeals to the People in the
Dreyfus Affair

*The impossibility of our saying the truth, even when we feel it, makes us
speak as poets. . .*
—Jacques Rancière, *The Ignorant Schoolmaster*[1]

In many ways, the Dreyfus Affair is an affair of and about writing, about writing's capacity to reveal truth and dissimulate, to enlighten and mystify. At the heart of the Affair lies the *bordereau*—the scrap of paper outlining French military secrets that a maid found in the wastebasket of the German attaché, Schwartzkoppen, and delivered to French army intelligence. While the French military claimed that handwriting experts had identified Dreyfus's handwriting as that on the *bordereau*, Zola and others would proclaim that it was so obviously the handwriting of the actual traitor, Esterhazy, that "any child" could recognize it. All around the *bordereau* other forms of false and true writing proliferated, mixing together in a grand conflagration: the forged documents of Colonel Henry that were designed to assure a guilty verdict for Dreyfus, the anti-Semitic newspapers devoted to whipping up public hatred of Jews and shoring up the honor of the army, the newspaper writings of Zola and other Dreyfusard "intellectuals" on behalf of justice. The Affair, in other words, is not just an affair of and about writing, but of and about *democratic* writing—writing available to all, with no restrictions on style and content, except those imposed by late nineteenth-century newspaper publishers and journal editors (which is to say, almost none at all). In this late nineteenth-century atmosphere of democratic writing, there is no presumed elite or even bourgeois readership, as in the late eighteenth century. The public is the mass public.

While Burke never stopped to consider that the very medium through which he communicated with the public—writing—was itself potentially deceptive and misleading, Zola's writings on the Dreyfus Affair stand, in the context of late nineteenth-century worries about the decline or "degeneration" of the public into the mass public,[2] as a protracted attempt to distinguish true forms of writing from false ones, forms of writing that appeal to a true public versus forms that appeal to the mob. Indeed, for Zola, the worst crime of the Dreyfus Affair is not the injustice done to Dreyfus—which could have been remedied if the army had been willing to acknowledge its errors—but rather the government and the army's "crime against society": their willful deception of the French public about Dreyfus's guilt, mainly through writing (the forged documents, the rabid anti-Semitic newspaper coverage sanctioned by the army). Zola's attempt to distinguish a true form of communicating with the public from the false one practiced by the army is intimately linked to concerns with justice and autonomy. For Zola, only a truthful public can assure justice and only an autonomous public—seeking truth for itself, rather than deferring to the judgment of others—can be truthful.

This attempt to discern truth from image and true communication from dissimulative rhetoric is, of course, nothing new. Both Plato and Rousseau count among those who have pursued, as a condition of autonomy and justice, truth and transparency untainted by image and social dissimulation. Contemporary theorists such as Jürgen Habermas and Joshua Cohen have also attempted to isolate the criteria by which we may assess the truth of statements in politics.[3] The contention of all these thinkers (with Plato excepted, who did not think in these terms) is that true democratic autonomy is interlinked with the ability to distinguish truth from falsity. If the demos is not able to distinguish truth from falsity, it will always be vulnerable to manipulation by others and thus will never achieve true self-rule. As Hannah Arendt puts the point in her discussion of the government's willful deception of the American public about the true situation in Vietnam: without "the right to unmanipulated factual information," "all freedom of opinion becomes a cruel joke."[4]

Yet if Zola's concern with identifying the form of writing proper to truth restages the concern of past thinkers, his concrete experience of the failure of this attempt in the context of the Dreyfus Affair raises important questions about the efficacy and democratic fruitfulness of approaching the problem of truth in politics through what Foucault calls an "analytics of truth"[5]—that is, by attempting to identify criteria for assessing the truth of statements. Specifically, Zola's writings during the Affair, as well as his novels and literary criticism, show that the attempt to resolve the problem of truth in politics—by offering criteria for pursuing or assessing it—is itself connected to the relations of rule that Zola, as well as the thinkers mentioned earlier, see as detrimental to democracy. Experts' attempts to teach the public to discern truth inevitably capture the public in a relationship of subordinate to superior, with the public deferent to the expert who offers them truth, rather than pursuing truth autonomously. While Habermas, for example, suggests that the force of the better argument is (or should be) self-evident—thus releasing citizens from relations of deference and subordination in truth-telling—Zola's writings suggest that in the realm of democratic politics, the persuasiveness of justificatory, true speech depends on its enmeshment in aesthetic registers of speech (mythical and rhetorical) that place democratic speakers in unequal relations to each other.[6] Zola's writings, in other words, portray the people's pursuit of truth as necessarily in tension with itself: dependent on persuasive enlighteners (like the Rousseauian lawgiver) whose practice of enlightening may betray the democratic autonomy and ability to discern truth that they seek to inculcate.[7] Zola's writings on the Affair resonate in this sense with Arendt's claim in "Truth and Politics" that the two realms (truth and politics) will always be to a certain degree hostile, insofar as claims to truth demand assent rather than the exchange of opinions and affirmation of plurality characteristic of the political realm.[8] Similarly, Zola's writings suggest that the attempts to resolve the problem of truth in democracy will necessarily be a failure insofar as they compromise the autonomy that they also endeavor to cultivate.

While we could read this inevitability of democratic failure in Zola's writings as cause for despair, I argue in this chapter for reading it as revealing an important truth: namely, that the demos' pursuit of truth is inevitably shot through with forms of speech,

relations of hierarchy, and practices of contestation that hinder as
well as enable the people's attempt to identify truth and, hence, to do
justice. Rather, then, than attempting to finally resolve the problem
of the democratic pursuit of truth (as do Cohen, Habermas, and, in
some moments, Zola), I argue that we might better re-conceive the
democratic pursuit of truth as necessarily enmeshed in a set of risks
that demand democratic awareness and response. I find the beginnings of such a reconception in Zola's re-narration of the democratic
failure to acknowledge truth and do justice in the Dreyfus Affair as
an occasion for democratic response: namely, via a dissident practice
of truth-telling that reveals perspectives on events occluded by official narratives. If legal institutions pursue (and often fail to achieve)
formal justice, Zola argues that a dissident practice of truth-telling
may pursue "poetic justice"—that is, justice in the realm of public
memory and storytelling. Yet Zola's own practice of poetic justice—
found in his rewriting of the Dreyfus Affair in his posthumously
published novel, *Vérité*—leads him to seek to do away with writing
altogether in favor of transparency. In other words, Zola remains
captured by what Jean Starobinski has called the Rousseauian opposition between transparency and obstruction,[9] even as he acknowledges the inevitable failure of transparency in his other writings,
and seeks to inaugurate a democratic form of response to it in the
form of "poetic justice." I argue in the conclusion for reconceiving
democratic truth-telling as a practice of "poetic justice" that would
proceed through attunement to its own risks—the risks of being
captured by false perspectives, on the one hand, and, on the other
hand, the risk of taking flight from the democratic practice of negotiating truth into the dream of the transparent and absolute.

Before turning to the tensions between truth and myth, between
the true public and the mob, in Zola's writings on the Affair (especially in "J'Accuse!"), as well as in his novels and literary criticism,
I first briefly discuss the Dreyfus Affair as a whole.

THE AFFAIR

On December 19, 1894, Alfred Dreyfus was found guilty of treason by
a French military tribunal. The main pieces of evidence were the *bordereau* and Colonel Henry's (false) statement in court that a decent person

(who supposedly had to remain anonymous) had accused Dreyfus. He was sentenced to a ceremony of public shaming and to imprisonment for life on Devil's Island. At the time of his conviction, almost no one doubted his guilt and only the anti-Semitic, rightist papers devoted a high degree of attention to the trial and public shaming. About two years later, Mathieu Dreyfus (Alfred's brother) started to make progress toward proving his brother's innocence when he discovered the identity of the actual traitor (Esterhazy) and enlisted Bernard Lazare in the Dreyfusard cause. Lazare wrote an important pamphlet laying out the facts of the case and arguing that Dreyfus's conviction was a judicial error.[10] He also worked tirelessly to recruit writers, scholars, and political figures in the cause. Lazare was successful in enlisting many important figures, but at this point, his appeals to one writer, Emile Zola, went unheralded. Zola expressed sympathy with the cause, but declined to take an active role. It wasn't until a year later, in November 1897, when an influential Alsatian senator (August Scheurer-Kestner) adopted the cause and solicited Zola's help, that Zola agreed to write on behalf of Dreyfus.[11]

Zola's involvement in L'Affaire began with an essay he published in late 1897 defending Scheurer-Kestner in Le Figaro, spiked in importance with the publication of "J'Accuse!" and ended only with his death in 1902. Unlike other early prominent Dreyfusards—Scheurer-Kestner (a member of the Senate) and Lazare (who, at least initially, was allied with the Dreyfus family)—Zola had no official role or personal interest in the case. Instead, Zola's writings on the Affair articulate his role as an important, but unofficial, democratic one: the role of the truth-teller. The truth-teller is an important democratic figure because she stands up to the people when she believes they are misguided and attempts to reveal the truth and recall the people to their true nature, desirous of the common good. Without truth-tellers—those individuals whom Arendt describes as witnesses, reporters, judges, and historians—political judgments and opinions become meaningless, or perhaps even harmful, disconnected from the factual reality that they are supposed to address.[12] And indeed, Zola proclaims the importance of truth—and its denigration in the injustice done to Dreyfus—in almost every essay he writes on the Affair, as well as throughout his literary criticism. For Zola, without truth, there cannot possibly be justice.

Yet even as Zola declared the truth of Dreyfus's innocence in newspapers, pamphlets, and books, and achieved some success, along with other Dreyfusards, in converting public opinion and spurring official action on a retrial, the outcome of the Dreyfusard struggle was by no means unambiguously positive. While Dreyfus ultimately received a retrial, he was once again convicted by a military tribunal and then pardoned by the president—a pardon which Zola and most other Dreyfusards saw as a defeat, since Dreyfus was required to admit guilt as a condition of the pardon. Even more unjustly, in Zola's view, a year later, the Legislative Assembly passed an amnesty bill—giving amnesty to everyone involved in the Dreyfus Affair, including those military officers and governmental officials who framed Dreyfus. While Dreyfus was ultimately rehabilitated in 1906 (an event Zola did not live to see), the outcome of the Dreyfus Affair remained a matter of contestation within France, where many continued to regard him as guilty and to see his rehabilitation as an injustice. For example, after Charles Maurras, a Vichy collaborator, leader of *Action Francaise*, and anti-Dreyfusard, was convicted in 1945 of "complicity with the enemy," he responded by claiming "C'est la revanche de Dreyfus!" ("This is the revenge of Dreyfus!"). Zola's writings thus stand not only as an example of the importance of truth-telling in politics, but also as an example of a writer confronting the problems and blockages surrounding truth-telling in democracy.

The intensity of the debates and protests over the Dreyfus Affair can be explained in part by the fact that the Affair had inherently contentious issues at its heart—anti–Semitism, government corruption, and treason (among others). Yet this intensity was also fueled by the uncertainty and sense of insecurity that marked *fin-de-siècle* France. France was still smarting from its loss to Germany in the Franco-Prussian War and its consequent loss of Alsace, as well as from the political upheavals surrounding the Commune and the intrigues of the Third Republic. As a result of this turmoil, national identity was in flux and military figures, as well as citizens, were increasingly fearful of a united Germany moving against the fraught French republic.[13] As Louis Begley argues, the "trauma" of "the humiliating defeat suffered by the French army in the Franco-Prussian War of 1870" and the "efforts that followed to rebuild the army, in large measure explain the vehement, indeed hysterical, response of nationalist politicians and journalists, as well as wide segments of the French public, to the danger of disclosures that would impugn the honor of the army chiefs and potentially expose them to prosecution."[14] Further, in the wake of the Jules Ferry education laws,

old aristocratic structures were being ruptured by republican structures of education, which allowed Protestants, Jews, and to a certain
degree women into the hierarchies of state and martial power. Even
the authority of an old intellectual elite was being challenged by new
university professors (such as Durkheim and Bergson). In this context, the French army often served as a site of citizens' devotion—a
symbol of French honor and national identity that persisted through
political intrigue and corruption. Indeed, after a scandal involving the
president's son-in-law selling Legion of Honor medals, a large part
of the French public briefly united around the charismatic General
Boulanger, whom they perceived as a heroic figure who could unite
and restore honor to France.

Considered in light of the role played by the French army in citizens'
understandings of French national identity, and the fear that citizens
had of another German defeat, the deep controversy caused by the
Dreyfus Affair becomes more explicable. Citizens were not only debating the guilt or innocence of one man, they were debating French
national identity and honor, as well as whether the honor of France
was best preserved through acknowledging the army's judicial error
and the anti-Semitic and deceitful tactics later employed by the government, army, and press, or by remaining loyal to the army at all cost.

A CRIME AGAINST SOCIETY

Zola's writings on the Affair obviously take the former position, arguing that the honor of France is best preserved through acknowledging and remedying the injustice done to Dreyfus. Throughout these
writings, Zola defends Dreyfus's innocence and claims that it has been
proved beyond any kind of reasonable doubt.[15] Yet most of Zola's writings on the Affair also focus on how and why the public, the army, and
the government continue to ignore this proof and to virulently fight
against any attempt for a revision of the trial. For Zola, this vocifer-
ous denial of the truth, and hence justice, is an "extraordinary crime"
(DA, 20)—that is, a crime of "refusing to acknowledge, even when
confronted with indubitable proof, that a mistake has been made" (DA,
13). In two of his most important writings on the Affair—his "Letter
to France" and "J'Accuse!"—Zola calls this crime a "crime against

society." For him, a crime against society consists in a willful misleading of the public on behalf of assuring public continued support of the existing government and the army and, hence, of injustice.

In his most famous essay on the Affair, "J'Accuse!" Zola places the primary blame for the "crime against society" on the General Staff of the Army, with the complicity of the press and government: "It is the General Staff who wanted this trial [that acquitted Esterhazy]; it is they who judged Dreyfus; and they have just judged him for the second time" (DA, 46). Zola argues that the army and the government lied to the public out of the misguided belief "that falsehood is indispensable to the salvation of France"—in particular, to saving the honor of the army (DA, 69). For example, Zola zeroes in on the (false) claims made in Dreyfus's and Esterhazy's trials by Henry and Sandherr that:

> . . . there was a damning but secret document; they cannot reveal it but it makes everything legitimate and we must bow before it, as before an invisible and unknowable God!. . . No! No! It's a lie! And what makes the whole business all the more odious and cynical is that they are lying with impunity and there is no way to convict them. They turn France inside out, they shelter behind the legitimate uproar they have caused, they seal mouths, by making hearts quake and perverting minds. *I know of no greater crime against society.* (my emphasis, DA, 46)

In this passage, Zola alludes to Henry and Sandherr's perjury: they lied about the existence of a document that proved Dreyfus's guilt and that supposedly "concerns the national defence" (DA, 46).[16] Yet Zola's diagnosis of a "crime against society" also makes a broader claim: that the detrimental social ramifications of their deception—their turning of France "inside out"—is itself criminal and constitutes an injustice.

In his "Letter to France," Zola says that the "crime against society" is "perpetrated by anti-Semitism." The problem with anti-Semitism—besides its obvious bigotry—is that it distorts truth in favor of a form of thinking structured by stereotypes. For example, Zola argues that the public is ready to believe lies about Dreyfus because they were already prepared with the stereotype of the "Jewish traitor": "A Jewish traitor, betraying his country: that goes without saying. But what if no human motive can be found for the crime? What if he is rich, of good conduct, hard-working, unswayed by any passion, leading an irreproachable life? Well, he's Jewish—isn't that enough?" (*DA*, 24). Anti-Semitism, especially when reinforced and spread by the press, distorts ordinary moral categories by allowing the public to believe that guilt can be assessed by reference to (Jewish) identity, rather than by examining the facts. This results in a broader reversal of values: in the Dreyfus Affair, "the foul press is saturating the public too heavily with lies and calumny" and "[t]he press is over determined to *turn decent people into knaves, and knaves into decent people*" (my emphasis, *DA*, 41). Through anti-Semitic stereotypes and scapegoating, injustice becomes justice and falsity becomes truth.

For Zola, the army and the government's willful deception of the people is a crime because it undermines the people's capacity for self-rule and justice by rendering them (unknowingly) subservient to the will of some government and army officials. Since "public opinion is arrived at on the basis of those lies, those idiotic and extraordinary tales the press prints every morning" (*DA*, 38), the people pursue falsity (masquerading as truth) and injustice (masquerading as justice): "[h]ow could you [France] possibly demand truth and justice when they are doing so much to denature your legendary virtues, the clarity of your intelligence and the sturdiness of your reasoning?" (*DA*, 38)[17] Invoking a common late nineteenth-century contrast between the true people and the irrational mob, Zola says that the French public has turned into a "mob gone mad," incapable of self-rule (*DA*, 22): "Lies spread wider and wider, the serious newspapers gravely print the silliest stories, *the entire nation seems to have gone mad*" (*DA*, 13). In short, for Zola, the government and the army's mass deception of the people is a crime because it endangers their ability to *be* a true people—that is, to rule itself freely, justly, and equitably. As he puts it in "J'Accuse!" "It is a crime to lead public opinion astray, to manipulate it for a death-dealing purpose and pervert it to the point of delirium. It is a crime to poison the minds of the humble, ordinary people, to whip reactionary and intolerant passions into a frenzy while sheltering behind the odious bastion of anti-Semitism" (*DA*, 51).

Sometimes, Zola suggests that the people are simple victims of this crime against society—naively misled into embracing injustice and turning into a mob. For example, in "J'Accuse!" Zola depicts the army as crushing a popular desire for truth in favor of lies: "They [the General Staff] have crushed the nation under their boots, stuffing its

calls for truth and justice down its throat on the fallacious and sacrile-
gious pretext that they are acting for the good of the country!" (*DA*,
50) However, if the "crime against society" is a problem *for* democracy
that exceeds the scope of formal legal institutions and rules, Zola also
portrays it as a problem *of* democracy: Zola suggests that the people
are themselves complicit in, and even actively desire, the deception
practiced upon them by the army and the government. He says, "You
[France] look healthy enough—but suddenly little blotches appear on
the skin: death is there, inside you" (*DA*, 39). For Zola, the people are
susceptible to these anti-Semitic deceptions—"idiotic stories" that go
"too much against the grain of sheer common sense and integrity"
(*DA*, 41)—because they have a latent desire to be ruled, rather than to
rule themselves. Zola says that there is a "growing hatred of freedom"
among the people that make them vulnerable to the lies fed to them
by the press (*DA*, 40). This "hatred of freedom" is growing, on Zola's
account, because of a popular loss of trust in their republican system of
government, especially in the wake of the Panama Scandal, in which
many members of Parliament were implicated in corruption.[18]

In the context of this broad mistrust of government, Zola argues
that French citizens long for leaders that seem to stand above and outside ordinary corruption: army leaders, like General Boulanger, and
the church. He says:

> Ask yourself frankly: was it really your army you were rushing to
> defend when no one was attacking it? What you suddenly needed
> to cheer on was the sabre itself—isn't that the truth?. . . [W]hat
> I hear, in the noisy ovation they are given, is the reawakening
> (unconscious, no doubt) of the latent Boulangism you are still
> infected with. The blood that flows in your veins is not yet repub-
> lican blood. Whenever any plumes and ribbons go parading by,
> your heart beats faster! Whenever a king comes along, you fall in
> love with him! You're not thinking of your army at all—you just
> want to go to bed with its general!. . . France, if you're not careful,
> you're heading straight for dictatorship. (*DA*, 39)

This "hatred of freedom" also leads the public to turn to other hierarchical institutions and reactionaries: "The Republic is overrun by
reactionaries of every stripe; they adore it with a harsh and terrifying
love, they stifle it with kisses. *All you hear, on all sides, is that the idea of*

freedom is bankrupt. And when the Dreyfus Affair broke out, it supplied *the growing hatred of freedom* with an astonishing opportunity; passion began to blaze, even in the most oblivious people" (my emphasis, *DA*, 40). The people's complicity in the "crime against society" is thus not only due to their misguided belief in Dreyfus's guilt, but to their desire to defer judgment to someone else—to not rule themselves freely, but to *be ruled by* someone else. The traits of the mob that Zola had identified as the outgrowth of the army's deception of the public—its irrationality, its susceptibility to be ruled by others, its love of injustice rather than justice—here appear in contrast as emanating from the people themselves.

Zola thus offers an ambivalent account of the "crime against society": an account that places blame on the army and the press for misleading the public, while also placing blame on the public for enabling and being complicit in this deception. Inherent in this account of the "crime against society" is a similarly ambivalent account of the people: as both public and mob. On the one hand, Zola depicts the people as a true public that is rational, seeks truth, loves freedom, and has merely been hoodwinked by the army, the military, and the press. Yet on the other hand, Zola portrays the people as an irrational mob that loves falsity, desires to be ruled, and due to its irrationality also *needs* to be ruled. This mobbish image of the people was common in the late nineteenth century. For example, Gustav Le Bon—who published *The Crowd* in 1895, contemporaneously with the Dreyfus Affair—argues that the late nineteenth century was the age of "the crowd."[19] By this, he means that democracy was no longer (if it ever was) an affair of debate and deliberation; instead, it consists in crowd acclamation or declamation of leaders—that is, essentially a form of dictatorship that is crowd-driven. For Le Bon, crowds lose their rationality because their members lose their individuality and become a "collective mind" that "thinks in images" rather than using logic, and thus is vulnerable to the suggestion of leaders.[20] This transformation from individuals to crowd occurs, first, because of *contagion*: "[i]n a crowd every sentiment and act is contagious, and contagion to such a degree than an individual readily sacrifices his personal interest to the collective interest";[21] and second, because of *anonymity*: "a crowd being anonymous, and in consequence irresponsible, the sentiment of responsibility which always controls individuality disappears entirely."[22] As Susanna Barrows notes, this depiction of the people as crowd or mob was not unique to Le Bon. Rather, many writers, such as Hippolyte Taine and Gabriel Tarde, depicted the crowd as "a horrifying beast. They stressed its irrationality, its primitive and savage mentality, its insatiable thirst for alcohol, its 'hypnotic' leadership, and its female character."[23]

Yet while Zola's image of the mobbish public bears similarities to Le Bon's crowd, his view of the people ultimately differs from Le Bon's because Zola portrays the people as composed of conflicting elements: the desire for freedom *and* the desire to be ruled, the desire for equality *and* the desire for hierarchy, the desire for justice *and* the desire for scapegoating. In short, Zola does not see the people as a mob, but rather as a site of ongoing conflict between characteristics of the true public and those of the mob.[24]

"ENLIGHTENING THE LITTLE PEOPLE": THE PROBLEM OF DEFERENCE

While Zola's writings on the Affair reflect an uncertainty about whether he should address the French public as a mob or public, he most often responds to this problem by framing the people as a public whose mobbish moments are inauthentic—produced by demagogic and ill-intentioned manipulative elites. For example, after Zola's conviction in his libel trial, *L'Aurore* published an interview with him, conducted at his home. The interviewer notes that in the course of their discussion, "[t]he detestable demonstrations which had occurred the day before yesterday in front of the Palais de Justice came up in the course of the conversation" (*DA*, 62). Zola said, "I do not hold Paris responsible for what happened. It is not Paris—the Paris I love so much!—that was shouting and yelling death threats in the hope of drowning out our voices. I would never confuse the great and generous people of Paris with a gang of fanatics and braying bullies, hired for the occasion" (*DA*, 62). Zola thus frames the "mob" as an irrational, temporary manifestation of the true people that will ultimately fade away in favor of rationality and justice. While Zola insists that "France cannot possibly be France any longer if it can be duped to this extent, whipped to a frenzy against a poor unfortunate man" (*DA*, 18), he also claims that "France"—the true France—"is always ardent in support of just and righteous causes" (my emphasis, *DA*, 18). Speaking to France, Zola says, "You will always reawaken, you will always triumph amid truth and justice!" (*DA*, 43).

For Zola, this reawakening of France to its "true" self—its abandonment of its temporary mobbish manifestation—is a condition of justice being done to the "crime against society" perpetrated by the army, the government, and the press (and by itself). Indeed, Zola suggests in his "Letter to France" that this "extraordinary crime" can (and will) be tried and judged in an extraordinary way, through "an outpouring of sovereign generosity":

> One of these days the public will suddenly gag on all the filth it has been fed. It is bound to happen. And just as in the Panama Canal scandal, you'll see that in this Dreyfus Affair as well, the public will bring its weight to bear. In *an outpouring of sovereign generosity, the public will decide there are to be no more traitors; it will call for truth and justice*. Thus, anti-Semitism will be tried and sentenced for its evil deeds, for the two mortally dangerous follies it has led this country into and for the loss of dignity and health this country has suffered as a result. (*DA*, 41)

In this passage, Zola connects the reassertion of true popular sovereignty with the public's ability to discern truth and seek justice. For anti-Semitism to be judged and "sentenced" (to die), the people must reassert their sovereignty against the officials who have misled and manipulated them. However, they must also do it in a way that is "generous," that challenges the insider/outsider categories that define anti-Semitic nationalism. Sovereignty, in other words, must be reborn as a true expression of the popular will for equality, truth, and freedom, rather than appearing falsely dependent on excluding Jews and other "outsiders."

Yet even as Zola suggests that autonomy and a reassertion of sovereignty—a return to being a true people rather than a mob—are the conditions of the people's pursuit of truth and justice, his arguments for how the French public could become such a sovereign, truthful public seem to rely on the public remaining, to a certain degree, deferent to authorities. Specifically, Zola suggests that the public can reassert its sovereignty and come to know truth through being enlightened by truth-tellers like him. In his "Letter to France" and many other essays,

Zola argues that his duty is to enlighten public opinion. Zola says, "Oh, I'll speak to them, all right—with all my might. I'll speak to the ordinary people, the humble people, the humble people who are being poisoned and forced into delirium. That and that alone is the mission I assign myself" (DA, 36). His goal is to "enlighten the little people, the humble people who are being poisoned and forced into delirium" (DA, 42).[25] For Zola, the public must be enlightened by truth-tellers such as he because other, false truth-tellers are working so diligently to *mis*lead public opinion.

However, if the problem with the "crime against society" is that it undermines, through deception, the people's ability to rule themselves, then the solution proposed by Zola may not only be a solution, but also a problem. Specifically, Zola's attempt to enlighten the people may continue, in different form, the relationship of rule between leader and people (as in the Le Bon mobbish image of democracy), and may enable a continued desire to be ruled on the part of the public, insofar as the enlightener (who knows) purports to be able to teach the truth to the public (who does not know). Thus, while Zola takes on the role of truth-teller in the Dreyfus Affair, his writings also articulate that role as a problem for the autonomous, truthful people he hopes to call into being. There is some indication that Zola worries about this problem, too. For example, in "Justice," he protests against his critics that "[i]t would be unworthy of me if anyone, even for an instant, was able to confuse me with the vile exploiters of mass movements" (DA, 130). While Zola's protestation claims the need to distinguish between exploiters and enlighteners, it also suggests that they *can* be confused— both, after all, encourage and rely on public dependence on experts rather than independence—and that there is no easy way to discriminate between them.

"J'ACCUSE!": THE TENSION BETWEEN TRUTH AND MYTH, PUBLIC AND MOB

I suggest in this section that Zola's most famous attempt to enlighten the public during the Dreyfus Affair—the publication of "J'Accuse!"— is itself inhabited by this tension between the cultivation of deference and autonomy. I make this claim in three parts. First, I argue for reading "J'Accuse!" as a mythical narration of the facts of the case that, like the anti-Dreyfusard writings that Zola criticizes, obscures truth and encourages public deference. In particular, I will suggest that Zola's desire to solicit the public on behalf of justice leads him to obscure the public's complicity in the crime against society—and hence, the need to call them to account for it—in favor of a simplified (and somewhat deceptive) myth of heroes and villains. From this perspective, "J'Accuse!" appears to pursue justice by cultivating deference and sanctioning deception, rather than through soliciting an autonomous, truthful public. However, I then question Zola's (and my) association of myth with mobbishness, deference, and deception through examining Zola's pursuit of truth in his naturalist fiction. While Zola criticizes myth as Romantic deception in his literary criticism, his novels enact mythical narration as necessary to truth-telling—in particular, as necessary to jolting the public free from false myths and freeing them to see the world without myth. On the basis of this reading, I then revisit "J'Accuse!" and argue that it is more ambivalent than I first supposed—that it can be read as a myth that aims to allow the true public to announce its freedom from myth *and* as pandering to the mob. Finally, I argue for acknowledging the inevitable entanglement of truth and myth, the public and the mob, in democratic politics.

"J'Accuse!" as Myth

In "J'Accuse!" Zola spends a good deal of time describing the details of Dreyfus's situation and the injustice done to him. Yet Zola's narrative in "J'Accuse!" also exaggerates and obscures facts to create a mythical picture of the central struggle of the narrative—here, between the agents of justice and injustice. In particular, Zola's narrative rhetorically heightens the import of one "villain" of the Affair (Paty de Clam) and obscures another (the public). Zola focuses on and exaggerates the role of Paty de Clam (the army official who originally arrested Dreyfus) in the original injustice done to Dreyfus. Just as Burke rhetorically embellished Hastings's role to create a symbol of a broader systemic injustice, so, too, does Zola's account overstate the role of Paty de Clam. Zola says, "One wicked man has led it all, done it all: Lt-Col du Paty de Clam. . . He *is* the entire Dreyfus Affair" (*DA*, 44). Zola accuses Paty de Clam of purposefully framing Dreyfus—specifically, of "dictat[ing] the *bordereau* to Dreyfus" and examining it "in a room

entirely lined with mirrors" (*DA*, 44)—and holds him up as a figure
of fun, a misguided man who is slightly deranged, as if made drunk by
the idealistic fiction that Zola criticizes in his writings on the novel.[26]
Zola ridicules, for example, Paty de Clam's idea of "intending to slip
into the cell where the accused man was sleeping and flash the light on
his face all of a sudden so that he would be taken by surprise and blurt
out a confession" (*DA*, 44). Yet Zola also suggests that Paty de Clam's
feverish imagination is responsible for literally hypnotizing others to
follow his lead: Paty de Clam "led those men by the nose. He hyp-
notized them. Yes indeed, he also dabbles in spiritism and occultism;
he converses with spirits" (*DA*, 45). Paty de Clam is the stereotypical
villain—a kind of evil genius—who masterminded the entire plot.

At the same time, Zola noticeably does *not* mention the complicity
of the public in the "crime against society" in "J'Accuse!"—a point
I will return to later. Instead, he portrays the General Staff of the Army
and government officials as Paty de Clam's fellow "villains." If Paty de
Clam did the work of framing Dreyfus, the General Staff and government officials sanctioned "the dreadful denial of justice which has laid
France low" (*DA*, 45). In particular, Zola notes the complicity of gen-
erals (Billot, de Boisdeffre, Gonse, [*DA*, 48]) and the war minister (*DA*,
47) in Paty de Clam's plot, as well as complicity of the handwriting
experts, the War Office, and the judges of the court martial (*DA*, 52).

If Zola exaggerates the role of Paty de Clam and obscures the role
of the public as "villains," he diminishes the role of several Dreyfusard
"heroes" in "J'Accuse!" Specifically, Zola downplays the significance
of the efforts of Scheurer-Kestner, the Alsatian member of Parliament
who was the first official to publicly demand justice for Dreyfus, and
Picquart, the military whistleblower who insisted on Esterhazy's
guilt. While Zola portrays Scheurer-Kestner as a "hero" in an earlier piece on the Affair (*DA*, 11) and in "J'Accuse!" calls Picquart a
"decent man" who sought to do his duty in revealing the truth (*DA*,
48), he depicts both of them in "J'Accuse!" as unable to address the
"crime against society" committed by the government and the army
because they assumed that facts and rule-following would be enough
to rebut falsity and injustice. Scheurer-Kestner could not address it
because he "assumed that truth alone would be enough—could not
help but be enough, since it was plain as day to him," and Picquart
followed the "discipline" of the army while "his superior officers were

busy slinging mud at him" (*DA*, 51). Scheurer-Kestner and Picquart thus appear in "J'Accuse!" no longer as heroes, but as "two victims, two decent, stout-hearted men, who stood back to let God have His way—and all the while the devil was doing his work" (*DA*, 51). While Scheurer-Kestner and Picquart revealed truth, the Government, Army, and complicit press continue to lie "with impunity and *there is no way to convict them*" (my emphasis, *DA*, 46).

Zola's portrayal of Scheurer-Kestner and Picquart as victims (and his failure to even mention other important Dreyfusards, such as Bernard Lazare) sets the stage in "J'Accuse!" for a new hero to emerge: Zola himself. Indeed, at the end of the essay, Zola does not turn to officials to do justice, but demands a libel trial for himself: "In making these accusations, I am fully aware that my action comes under" the article that "makes libel a punishable offence. I deliberately expose myself to that law. . . Let them dare to summon me before a court of law! Let the inquiry be held in broad daylight!" (*DA*, 53). Where Scheurer-Kestner and Picquart have failed to achieve justice through formal legal means, Zola can achieve justice as a heroic public intellectual, brandishing his pen against the swords of the army.

While Zola does not mention the public directly in "J'Accuse!", his mytheical account of the Affair seems aimed at soliciting a truthful public that would affirm the truth he offers. Indeed, Zola's demand, at the end of the letter, to be tried for libel is a demand that the case be judged by the people (via the jury) rather than elites: "dare to summon me before a court of law" and "[l]et the inquiry be held in broad daylight." As Henri Mitterand puts it, while the official addressee of "J'Accuse!" is the president, "lequel n'est là qu'en trompe-l'oeil et pour accroître le car-actère spectaculaire de la declaration, établir un dialogue direct, tendu, sans échappatoire, avec le people entier des lecteurs, et avec chaque lecteur en particulier" ["this is nothing but a 'trompe-l'oeil' to enhance the dramatic character of his declaration, established in a direct, tense dialogue with no way out, with the entire people of readers, and with each reader in particular"].[27] Zola's demand to be put on trial for libel is, implicitly, a demand for Dreyfus's case to be judged not by the army or the government, but instead by the public. This demand, alongside his whitewashing of the public's complicity in the "crime against society," seems to offer a chance for the public to emerge as a mythical hero who, through vindicating Zola in the libel trial, regenerates and saves France.

However, in his hopes of rousing the public to identify with the myth of a just public that will do justice to those who have misled it, Zola's narrative of the Affair in "J'Accuse!" also hinders doing justice to the "crime against society" insofar as it obscures the public's complicity in it. To put the problem in terms of Roland Barthe's famous discussion of myth, Zola's narrative obscures the complex reality on which it is also parasitic for its power.[28] In a telling example in *Mythologies*, Barthes discusses the "young Negro in a French uniform" on the cover of *Paris-Match*, who is "saluting, with his eyes uplifted, probably fixed on a fold of the tricolour."[29] While this young man certainly has a unique and complex history, "one must put the biography of the Negro in parentheses if one wants to free the picture, and prepare it to receive its [mythic] signified"[30]—namely, the myth that "France is a great Empire, that all her sons, without any colour discrimination, faithfully serve under her flag, and that there is no better answer to the detractors of an alleged colonialism than the zeal shown by this Negro in serving his so-called oppressors."[31] Yet at the same time, for the myth to appear *real*, this biography must serve as a distant "nutrient" for the myth, an assurance of its reality.[32] The complex historical reality of the Negro soldier's life becomes the guarantee of the reality of the myth that, at the same time, displaces and obscures this complex truth.[33]

Read in Barthes's terms, Zola uses the complex reality of the Affair as a "nutrient" that will sustain, but also will be hidden by, the simple myth of a fight between good and evil that he offers to the public in "J'Accuse!" While this myth could have rallied the public to free Dreyfus, it would likely not, when seen through the lens offered by Barthes, have cultivated a public desire to know the factual reality of life and to do justice in the way that Zola hopes. Instead, Zola's mythical solicitation of the public may spark an unquestioning deferral to the authority of the myth itself—a deferral that is at odds with the practice of acknowledging truth, desired by Zola. Read in this way, Zola's myth-making does not solicit a truthful public, but instead shores up the authority of myth at the expense of democratic autonomy. To put the point another way, Zola's turn to myth to solicit a truthful public reintroduces the problem of the people's mobbish deference to authority that prevents them from being fully truthful.

On this reading, Zola's appeal to the public in "J'Accuse!" appears to be a fatalistic narrative of democratic failure. Zola assumes that the public is not capable of understanding the truth on their own—that to "save" democracy, they must have the truth packaged for them in a simple myth by someone better capable of seeing truth (Zola, the expert). Zola's narrative of the democratic failure of the Affair encourages habits of deference to authority, which allowed the injustice to persist and fester in the first place.

However, as I show in the next section by examining Zola's approach to the problem of truth in his literary criticism and novels, the entwinement of myth and truth, and the relationship of deference that it implies, need not be understood as *opposed* to a popular practice of truth-seeking and truth-telling. Rather, it may be a condition of such a practice.

Zola's Naturalism and the Problem of Myth

While Zola's journalistic essays on the Dreyfus Affair were his first real foray into the realm of public affairs, his critique of the crime against society perpetrated by the press and the army, and desired by the public, has an analogue with his earlier published critique of Romanticism in literature. In his major text in literary criticism and theory—"The Experimental Novel"—Zola criticizes representatives of Romanticism, such as Victor Hugo and Renan, and defends the "experimental," or naturalistic, novel as practiced by himself (he writes Balzac, Stendahl, and Baudelaire into this "tradition" as well). Zola's critique of the Romantic novel opposes its supposed mythical, emotional qualities with the scientific, rational qualities of the naturalist novel. Where idealists, according to Zola, "base their works on the supernatural and the irrational" and "admit. . . the power of mysterious forces outside the determinism of phenomena," naturalists ground their novels in "observation" (description) of real world conditions and then introduce an "experiment" aimed at revealing the truth of human behavior, instinct, and motivation.[34]

For Zola, the problem with the idealist or Romantic novel (or drama, or academic lecture) is, as he says in "A Letter to the Young People of France," that it pushes youth to turn away from "reality." He says that in "recent events," "[t]here has been a flight into the ideal, an escape from the earth and a soaring in mid-air, in sort of counter charge on the part of poetry against the scientific spirit" (*EN*, 57). Such a "flight into the ideal" leaves French youth ill-equipped to meet the

challenges of an increasingly scientific, complex, and diverse world.
Zola says that "if we wish tomorrow to belong to us we must be new
men, marching toward the future by method, by logic, by study, and *a
full appreciation of reality*" (my emphasis, *EN*, 60). Yet might it be important for French youth to embrace ideals that offer them guideposts in
dealing precisely with the new challenges of the approaching twentieth century? Perhaps. But Zola insists that the Romantic literary style
warps and obfuscates the reality that youth are attempting to address.
Indeed, Zola says that young people today "are made drunk with lyri-
cism; their heads are filled with words; their nervous systems are dis-
tracted with this music to such an extent that they come to believe that
morality and patriotism only consist of the well-turned phrases of the
word-mongers" (*EN*, 97). Romanticism masks reality and intoxicates
youth by depicting ideal—rather than realistic—characters aimed at
sparking emotion among readers and spectators. For example, Zola says
that Victor Hugo's play, *Ruy Blas*, is a "piece of beautiful music" that
is also "a lie" (*EN*, 61–62): "It is a construction of language aimlessly
beating the air" (*EN*, 65). Why does Zola call *Ruy Blas* a "lie"? He
does not say, but given the play's depiction of ideal-type characters and
improbable plot twists—a nobleman disguising a slave as a nobleman in
order to fool the queen (and make a fool of her), the later murder of the
nobleman by the slave, and the suicide of the slave—Zola likely calls it
a "lie" because, like anti-Semitism, it offers misleading characterizations of humanity: abstractions aimed at cultivating emotion in spectators, rather than depictions of real people and problems that demand
rational investigation and response.

   Yet while Zola criticizes Romanticism for obscuring truth with
myth and abstractions, he does not suggest that truth can be found by
attempting to strip off all interpretation and perspective so as to access
unmediated facts. Rather, Zola's naturalist fiction attempts to reveal
truth by exploring the multidimensionality of mediated reality: that
is, by revealing, and inviting his readers to inhabit, diverse perspectives on reality. As Zola says in his discussion of a potential naturalistic
theater: "[N]o more abstract characters in books, no more lying inven-
tions, no more of the absolute; but *real characters, the true history of each
one, the story of daily life!*" (my emphasis, *EN*, 114–115). Thus, in contrast
to Hugo and other writers in the Romantic tradition, who believed
that the poetic genius of the individual writer accesses the absolute

(which can then be displayed, prophetically, for the public), Zola suggests that it is only through moving between the perspectives of different individuals that we can approach truth.

Zola's oscillation between perspectives in his novels reveals truth as contested and immanent, rather than unified and transcendent. For example, in *Germinal*, Zola's narrative repeatedly switches between the perspectives of Étienne Lantier (the central character, and instigator of the strike), various miners and their wives (especially Maheu and La Maheude), and the bourgeois mine owners and supervisors. These diverse perspectives allow us to understand the reality of the miners' desperate situation in the context of the Second Empire, but these perspectives do not weave together into a harmonious whole. This is particularly clear in an important scene in the novel that takes place at the outset of the miners' strike.

In the scene (which we see from several viewpoints, and to which Sandy Petrey has also importantly drawn attention), a group of miners go to the home of their supervisor, Monsieur Hennebeau, to state their demands. The first viewpoint the reader is offered is that of the Hennebeaus and Gregoires (members of the bourgeoisie with ruling interests in the mine), who are sitting in the dining room while they hear the miners being shown into the drawing room:

> The guests, who were still sitting round the table, felt momentarily unnerved, and exchanged worried glances. But then they started joking again: they pretended to put the remains of the sugar in their pockets, and spoke of hiding the silver. But the manager refused to laugh, and the laughter died away, to be replaced by whispering, as the heavy footsteps of the delegates being shown into the drawing-room and trampling over the carpet reverberated close at hand.[35]

For these uneasy members of the bourgeoisie, the miners' delegates appear to be an almost animalistic mob—trampling on the carpet that represents the wealth and comfort of the bourgeoisie. Yet as Petrey has shown, from the perspective of the miners in the same scene (described by Zola in the following chapter), this same carpet and the objects of the bourgeoisie appear differently. Here is Zola's description:

> [T]he miners, left on their own, did not dare sit down, feeling embarrassed, although they were all perfectly clean, and had shaved

that morning.. . . . They fingered their caps uneasily, and looked out
of the corners of their eyes at the furniture, which was an amalgam
of every style imaginable that the current taste for antiquity had
made fashionable: Henri II armchairs, Louis XV chairs, an Italian
cabinet from the seventeenth century and a Spanish *contador* from
the fifteenth, an altar-front used as a mantelpiece, and gold braid
taken from antique chasubles and sewn onto the *portieres*. All this
old gold and tawny-hued silk, with its air of ecclesiastical luxury,
filled them with respectful discomfort. *The Oriental carpets seemed to
entangle their feet in their deep woolen pile.*"[36]

Whereas for the bourgeoisie, the miners are trampling on their wealth,
the miners experience that wealth and opulence as holding them in
place. In Petrey's words, "[t]o the intimidated miners, the carpet is
tying their feet. To the intimidated bourgeois, the same carpet is being
crushed to death."[37] For these two groups, the same world and the
same situation appear in irreconcilable terms. By seeing the world from
these two vantage points, we thus see that truth—the nature of reality—is itself contested, seen differently by different classes and groups.

In this moment and others in his fiction, Zola's portrayal of diverse
perspectives solicits a public of truthful novel-readers that would be
constituted through a willingness to inhabit multiple, perhaps incom-
mensurable perspectives on reality. On the one hand, this model of
truth-telling offers an apparent resolution to the problem of the elite
truth-teller's imposition of authority onto a public which, to be truthful, needs to be autonomous—namely, because in this model, every
truth-teller is also necessarily a truth-receiver who must (to apprehend
truth) inhabit the perspectives of others, not just of themselves. A public's autonomy would here be constituted by reciprocal truth-telling and
truth-receiving—a practice that calls to mind an Arendtian "enlarged
mentality." Yet on the other hand, Zola's perspectival portrayal of truth
suggests that "truth" may not be as easily identifiable, nor as objective a
notion, as he often implies in his writings on the Dreyfus Affair. That
is, in portraying truth as constituted in and through multiple perspectives, Zola's fiction does not appear to offer a rule by which to judge
which perspectives are *really* true and which are false.

This does not mean, however, that Zola's novels fail to make judgments about truth. Indeed, Zola's novels often do make judgments

about truth—specifically, by presenting diverse perspectives in the register of myth, where some perspectives are represented as more just and generative than others. In particular, as Philip Walker has shown, Zola's novels present diverse perspectives in the terms of the myth of degeneration and regeneration, Death and Life.[38] Perhaps one of the most dramatic mythical portrayals of degeneration and the hope of regeneration in Zola's fiction comes in *Germinal*, where the apocalyptic destruction of the coal mine (created by the enigmatic Souvarine) seems to issue at the end of the story (when the survivor of the apocalypse, Étienne, is walking toward Paris) in a potential for rebirth:

> [F]ar below, beneath his feet, the stubborn tapping of the picks continued. His comrades were all down there, and he could hear them following his every step.. . . High in the sky the April sun now shone down in its full glory, warming the bountiful earth and breathing life into her fertile bosom, as the buds burst into verdant leaf, and the fields quivered under the pressure of the rising grass. All around him seeds were swelling and shoots were growing, cracking the surface of the plain, driven upwards by their need for warmth and light. The sap flowed upwards and spilled over in soft whispers; the sound of germinating seeds rose and swelled to form a kiss. Again and again, and ever more clearly, as if they too were rising towards the sunlight, his comrades kept tapping away. Beneath the blazing rays of the sun, in that morning of new growth, the countryside rang with song, as its belly swelled with a black and avenging army of men, germinating slowly in its furrows, growing upwards in readiness for harvests to come, until one day soon their ripening would burst open the earth itself.[39]

Zola's portrayal of the failure of the coal miners' strike as part of regenerating French society—germinating through their example and labor a future of freedom, equality, and justice—envelopes the diverse perspectives of *Germinal* within a narrative that depicts some perspectives (those of the miners) as more attuned to reality, and more in tune with the future, than those of others (the bourgeoisie). Zola's fiction, then, does not entirely leave judgment of truth to his readers. Rather, his fiction presents those perspectives within a mythical narrative that anticipates and solicits a particular kind of judgment from his readers. His novels may attempt to reveal and participate in a model of truth-telling where everyone is a truth-teller and truth-receiver, but Zola also occupies the role of the truth-teller who enlightens the public, insofar as his narratives tutor his readers in the nature of the proper judgment he asks them to make.

Read in this way, Zola's novels appear closer to his depiction of Hugo and the Romantics than he would admit—that is, insofar as he seems to make sense of various social and political problems (the capitalist system, workers' misery, etc.) through a myth of natural death and rebirth that may distract us from the importance of concrete political and social struggles.[40] In a famous letter to Henry Ceard, Zola discusses this tension in his novels and claims that myth is not in fact a corruption of truth-telling, but a necessary part of it. Specifically, he says: "je crois encore que je mens pour mon compte dans le sens de la Vérité. J'ai l'hypertrophie du detail vrai, le saut dans les étoiles sur le tremplin de l'observation exacte. La Vérité monte d'un coup d'aile jusqu'au symbole."[41] ["I still believe that I myself lie in service of truth. I enlarge true details, jumping to the stars on the springboard of exact observation. Truth rises in the blink of an eye to the realm of the symbolic."[42]] For Zola, in other words, truth-telling proceeds not simply through revealing perspectives and "details," but also through creating a broader myth or symbol out of those facts: in *Germinal*, the possibility of regeneration out of degeneration.

Why would the practice of revealing truth depend not only on true details, but also on generating a symbolic or mythical narrative out of those details? One possibility, perceptively suggested by Philip Walker, is that Zola's mythical truth-telling aims to announce the truth prophetically—in the register of what is to come. For Walker, the kind of "truth" that Zola aims at telling on this reading is not only or primarily factual truth, but a higher truth about human nature: "the modern myth of a material cosmos endowed with a single life,. . . of a godlike nature engaged in a single, perpetually self-renewing vital process in which all the elements are so inextricably involved that human life and death in the traditional sense have lost their meaning."[43] Truth-telling would depend on myth on this reading because only myth can reveal the higher meaning implicit in factual reality.

Walker's reading suggests that Zola's fiction essentially pursues the same strategy as the Romantics—mythologization on behalf of a higher truth—that Zola explicitly critiques, and claims to be departing from, in his literary criticism. While this reading of Zola as contradictory (failing to practice in his fiction what he preaches in his criticism) is not without basis, it neglects another possibility that is more in tune with Zola's attempt to release the public from mystification: that Zola turns to myth not to announce a higher truth that exceeds or stands behind our existing reality, but instead to prophetically announce the coming-into-being of a truthful public that would be *freed* from myth, free to examine and address concrete reality. Such a public would not need a myth of truthfulness in order to see a *higher* truth that escapes their current vision, but rather to spur them to look more closely and accurately *at what they already see*, to acknowledge and seek to address facts that they might already know, but that have been obscured via Romantic lenses of ideology and mystification. We could think of this distinction in Linda Zerilli's recent formulation of the difference between knowing and acknowledging truth[44]—that is, that Zola's prophetic myth-making aims not to reveal a higher truth that the public does not know, but rather to spur the public to acknowledge and more actively attend to the reality that they already see around them.

Zola himself suggests this in his essay, "Naturalism and the Stage." There, Zola suggests that the point of novel reading is not only or primarily to *reveal* truth, but also and perhaps more primarily to give individuals a *taste* for truth: "[T]he public," he says, "will certainly acquire a taste for reality in reading novels" (*EN*, 147). What is this "taste for reality"? As Zola describes his own "taste for truth," it consists in a yearning for reality that is itself a pleasure: "I yearn for life with its shiver, its breath, and its strength; I long for life as it is" (*EN*, 156). Similarly, he describes it is an aural or sensory capacity: "Truth has a sound about it which I think you can never mistake" (*EN*, 214). Zola prophecies that a public that reads more and more naturalist novels will continue to have a greater and greater taste for truth: "the public itself, that cannot very well boast of great delicacy of sense, clearly hears the works which ring with truth; it turns more and more toward them. . ." (*EN*, 214). On this reading, Zola's mythologization of the diverse perspectives he reveals aims not to release the public from Romantic myth in order to capture the public in the web of a new myth. Rather, Zola's mythologization is done on behalf of soliciting a public with a taste for truth that would have no more need of myth, that could "long for life

as it is" and seek truth simply through exchanging perspectives, con-
ducting experiments, and displaying facts for each other.

Revisiting "J'Accuse!": The Ambivalence of the People

My analysis of Zola's fiction suggests that the dependence of truth-telling
on myth need not only encourage mobbish deference. Rather, Zola's
use of myth also seeks to jar readers free from stereotypes and obfusca-
tory myths on behalf of calling them to attend to the reality that stands
in front of them. If we revisit "J'Accuse!" in the context of this reading, it may not appear as fatalistic as I earlier suggested. Rather than
seeing the use of myth in "J'Accuse!" as *only* cultivating deference, we
could—building on my analysis of Zola's fiction—read "J'Accuse!" as
also a prophetic solicitation of a public that aims to release the public
from myth. It may be, in other words, that Zola is writing for the
public in "J'Accuse!" *as if* the public already had a taste for truth. By
addressing it as a public that already seeks and values truth, Zola calls
on the public not to defer to, but rather, through their actions and
judgment, to vindicate his claim to truth.

Indeed, this is how Zola argues that naturalist writers should write
theater for mass audiences that have not yet developed a taste for truth
through novel-reading. For Zola, theater audiences, like all mass audiences (such as the one he addresses in "J'Accuse!"), are less hospitable
to the multi-perspectival, detailed picture of reality that Zola offers in
his naturalist novels: spectators, "taken *en masse*, are seized with prudishness, with frights, with sensibilities of which the author must take
notice" (*EN*, 145).[45] Yet at the same time, Zola holds out hope that, if
correctly appealed to, the crowd could be a powerful force on behalf of
truth: "[t]he wonderful power of the stage must not be forgotten, and
its immediate effect on the spectators. There is no better instrument
for propagating anything" (*EN*, 150). Specifically, Zola suggests that
playwrights should write for a public with a taste for truth *even before
that public actually exists*. Zola writes that such naturalistic drama should
proclaim that it has no connection to the isolated reader, "but with a
crowd who cry out for clearness and conciseness" (*EN*, 150). While
theater cannot cultivate individual desires, habits, and reflections the
way that novels can, naturalistic theater may nonetheless postulate a
public that desires to have such habits—a public with a taste for truth.
Such an approach, in other words, would solicit the mass public that

could or might have been cultivated by the naturalistic novel, but that may in fact not have been so cultivated. Zola's comment seems to gesture toward the importance of understanding the people as a "claim," in Jason Frank's words—that is, as a political claim that demands response and affirmation by the public in whose name, or on behalf of whom, the claimer claims to speak.[46] By writing for a public with a taste for truth—before that public actually exists—we can understand Zola as making a political claim on behalf of that public, a claim that has its "validity" not in a preexisting reality that it reflects, but in the response that it hopes to elicit.

Read in this way, Zola's myth of the Affair in "J'Accuse!" aims to solicit a sovereign public that would do justice to the "crime against society" in two ways: first, by judging Zola to be innocent of libel and, hence, judging the army and the government as guilty of deception (of course, this did not come to pass); and second, as enacting, through such a judgment, the freedom and generous sovereignty that had been denied to the people by the army's and the government's deception. On this reading, Zola's myth of the Affair highlights the failure of Scheurer-Kestner and Picquart to teach the truth to the public and assure justice so as to frame that failure as an occasion for democratic transformation and rebirth.

I do not mean, however, to argue that we should read "J'Accuse!" as resolving the tension between the public and mob. Rather, I am suggesting that we see its mythical solicitation to the people as ambivalent—as soliciting a true public *and* mob, speaking in the registers of myth *and* truth, rhetoric *and* rationality. One way to respond to this tension between truth and myth, between the people and the mob, is to attempt to resolve it by isolating the form of communication proper to truth. In her analysis of the Dreyfus Affair in *The Origins of Totalitarianism*, Hannah Arendt—perhaps surprisingly—pursues such an approach. There, she (like me) identifies the mobbish dimensions of Zola's mythically inflected appeals to the French public. Arendt writes that while "[t]he first to wean the workers, at least partially, from their mood of indifference was that great lover of the people, Emile Zola," he was also, "[i]n his famous indictment of the republic. . . [,] the first to deflect from the presentation of precise political facts and *to yield to the passion of the mob* by raising the bogy of secret Rome."[47] For Arendt, the problem with attempting to persuade the public of Dreyfus's innocence through recourse to the claim that the pope is pulling the strings in the Affair (a claim that Zola does occasionally make[48]) is that even if the mob is convinced of Dreyfus's innocence, Zola has done nothing to interrupt the mob's general desire to scapegoat others for social ills. Zola's form of address to the mob thus validates rather than interrupts its politics of scapegoating—a politics that, as Arendt notes, works in the form of anti-Semitism as "an almost magic formula. . . for reconciling the masses to the existent state of government and society."[49]

Arendt argues that the better approach to the injustice of the Affair can be found in Clemenceau's acts and writings. Arendt dubs Clemenceau the true "hero" of the Affair[50] because he appealed not to a *myth* of "'secret Rome" or "secret Judah"[51] to invoke the resentment and outrage of the mob, but instead to *abstractions* of equality, justice, and freedom that sparked a desire for justice in "the people." For Arendt, "[t]he greatness of Clemenceau's approach lies in the fact that it was not directed against a particular miscarriage of justice, but was based upon such 'abstract' ideas as justice, liberty, and civic virtue."[52] Arendt argues that, ultimately, Clemenceau's abstractions were revealed in the Affair as *"actually nearer to political realities* than the limited intelligence of ruined businessmen or the barren traditionalism of fatalistic intellectuals."[53] For Arendt, these abstract principles—freedom, justice, equality—enabled clearer vision than myth because they enabled individuals to look beyond their "interests" (in particular, class interests that led many socialists to stay away from the Dreyfus Affair because they saw him simply as part of the bourgeoisie) to the political importance of preventing oppression for everyone. As Arendt says of Clemenceau, he was one of the "true friends modern Jewry has known just because he recognized and proclaimed before the world that Jews were one of the oppressed peoples of Europe."[54] Indeed, "Clemenceau, in his consuming passion for justice, still saw the Rothschilds as members of a downtrodden people."[55] Clemenceau's abstractions revealed oppression where it was otherwise invisible, or nearly so.

Arendt's critique of Zola thus is not an argument against myth on behalf of unmediated reality as the only key to justice. Rather, she is criticizing the *way* in which he mediates reality—via myth—on behalf of a different way of mediating or revealing truth, namely, through abstractions. However, as Arendt herself notes later in *Origins* in her discussion of how the abstractions of "human rights" obscured rather than addressed the problem of statelessness in the pre- and post–World War II world,[56] abstractions can function as myths, too. Abstractions, like Zola's narratives, may hide the complexity of political problems and the messiness of political responsibility. This suggests that the attempt to identify the correct way to mediate truth to the public—an attempt made by both Zola and Arendt in different moments—may simply restage rather than resolve problems of hierarchy and mystification. Such attempts also hide the ambivalence of myth and relations of hierarchy in democratic politics: that is, that myth and hierarchy (relations of teacher/student) can enable truthfulness *and* hinder it, that myths that appeal to "mobs" may not be cleanly separable from the exercise of political persuasion and claims-making that appeals to "the people."

Rather than attempting to draw a clean line between mob and people and the forms of discourse appropriate to each—as both Zola and Arendt do in different moments—perhaps we would do better to acknowledge the attempt to isolate a form of communication proper to truth in democratic politics as a (likely inevitable) moment of democratic failure. It will likely issue in democratic failure for two reasons: (1) because every attempt to teach the people truth, or to identify the proper means of identifying truth, ends up involving the truth-teller and the people in relations of superior/subordinate that undermine the aspiration to autonomy that underlies the pursuit of truth in democracy; (2) because attempts to solicit a public on behalf of truth involve forms of communication (myth, abstractions, symbols) that appeal to traits we usually understand as "mobbish" (deference, passions), as well as to traits that we see as characteristic of a "true" people (rationality, autonomy). Attempts to teach or reveal truth to the people, in other words, will likely be democratic failures because it will never be fully or only the "true people" that responds—even if the people affirms the truth that one is trying to teach. The people will always also be the mob, and the teacher/revealer will always be both equal citizen and superior.

This inevitability of failure may appear as cause for despair—and indeed, this is how Arendt narrates Clemenceau's reaction to the Dreyfus Affair. She argues that he, like Zola, could "scarcely distinguish the mob from the people" and that this led him to ultimately despair of democracy altogether—that is, it led to "his despair of the people, his contempt for men, finally his belief that he and he alone could save the republic."[57] As a way of warding off this turn to anti-democratic elitism, Arendt says that Clemenceau should have recognized and claimed this "heterogenous minority"—"only those who heeded him"—as the "true people of France."[58] Arendt, in other words, argues for avoiding rather than addressing and negotiating the experience of democratic failure that I am diagnosing here (that the people *cannot* be fully separable from the mob) on behalf of saving Clemenceau's, and perhaps our, faith in democracy.

Yet the experience of democratic failure need not result in despair of democracy. Indeed, I will suggest in the next section that when that failure is re-narrated as a lost cause—a cause that could have been won if the people had acted differently—it may appear as a promising occasion for re-imagining how the public might respond to the failures and risks of mythologization discussed by Arendt. I will make this claim by turning to Zola's late writings on the Affair, where Zola grapples with the failure to appear of the truthful public he solicited. In these writings, Zola no longer calls for the people to enact a mythical sovereignty that obscures their "mobbish" complicity in injustice, but rather to embrace a non-sovereign responsiveness to democratic failure in the form of what Zola calls "poetic justice": that is, the practice of writing alternative narratives of the Dreyfus Affair that are missed by official, legal narratives.

POETIC JUSTICE: THE TRIAL BEFORE MANKIND'S "UNIVERSAL CONSCIENCE"

Zola's late writings on the Affair address and seek to come to terms with what he views as France's ultimate failure to do justice to the "crime against society" perpetrated by the government and the army. Specifically, Zola criticizes—even as he applauds—the pardon for Dreyfus following his re-conviction at Rennes, as well as the later blanket amnesty for everyone involved in the Affair. In his open letter to Alfred Dreyfus's wife, Lucie, following the pardon, Zola stresses that he sees it as an injustice, even if it is a victory for Dreyfus and his family: "No matter how much I as a citizen may be in mourning, no matter how much painful indignation, how much rebellion and anxiety just souls may continue to feel, I share with you the exquisite tearful moment when you hold the resurrected man in your arms" (*DA,*

141). For Zola, the pardon is an injustice because it grants Dreyfus freedom only on the condition that he admit guilt. Dreyfus "has only been granted as an act of pity what was due him as an act of justice" (*DA*, 145). While Dreyfus has rightly been freed, the pardon sustains the reversal of values produced by the Affair: injustice continues to masquerade as justice, falsity as truth.

Zola critiques the blanket amnesty passed by the Senate in even stronger terms. "[T]his amnesty," Zola says, "comes and closes one of the last doors opening onto the truth" (*DA*, 163). The blanket pardon makes no judgment about truth and suggests that people on both sides were lawbreakers or law-upholders: "the amnesty would be applied against us, the upholders of the law, in order to save the real criminals, by shutting our mouths through an act of hypocritical and injurious clemency and placing decent people in the same category as scoundrels" (*DA*, 155–156). In enacting a blanket pardon, the government "bur[ies]" rather than "expiate[s]" crimes (*DA*, 157) and invokes "political necessity" as a reason to do injustice (*DA*, 155). The blanket pardon, in other words, presses France to move beyond the Dreyfus Affair without holding individuals accountable for their crimes—a lack of accountability that enshrines a precedent of sanctioning injustice.

In these late writings, Zola sometimes seems to despair of the French people who failed him during the Affair and fantasizes about an unequivocal legal ruling that would assure the truth and transparency that he and other Dreyfusards failed to achieve. He says in his letter to Lucie Dreyfus: "some legal punishment is necessary. The decisive argument is this: if no awe-inspiring example is set, if justice does not strike those in high places who are guilty, the ordinary people will never know how great the crimes have been. The pillory must be erected so that the people will know, at last" (*DA*, 131). Similarly, he argues in his essay critiquing the blanket amnesty that unequivocal legal punishment of the wrongdoers is needed to secure public judgment of the truth: "the Dreyfus Affair must finish in the only way that can restore calm and strength to this country. The guilty parties must be punished, not so that we can rejoice in their punishment but so that the people will know the truth at last and justice can provide the only true and lasting balm" (*DA*, 161). In these moments in his writings, Zola seems—like Arendt's Clemenceau—to have despaired of democracy altogether in favor of a regime where elites display truth for a people who are incapable of achieving it on their own.

Yet Zola's fantasy of regenerative legal judgment is matched in these writings by his sense of the failure of law to assure justice. Specifically, Zola suggests that the failures of the public and law to assure formal, legal justice reveal the importance of the pursuit of another kind of justice: *poetic* justice. Zola argues that even if the formal court system does not acquit Dreyfus and convict the guilty, the "other trial" that is happening through public opinion will do so: "it is the poets. . . who nail the guilty parties to the pillory" (*DA*, 147). Zola frames this alternative form of justice as a perennial response to the inevitability of formal *in*justice: "Immanent justice has reserved this punishment as its own; it has instructed the poets to single out, as objects of loathing down through the ages, those whose social malfeasance and merciless crimes exceed the scope of ordinary tribunals" (*DA*, 147). Failure of law and people may lead to a certain form of despair—and to the fantasy of full legal punishment and instantiation of truth—but it may also be re-narrated as an occasion for democratic responsiveness through writing. Indeed, Zola makes sense of his own writings in this context— that is, as documents that aim not only to reveal the truth, but also to enact justice through writing. For example, in an earlier piece (on his own libel trial), Zola says, "[w]hether I am convicted or acquitted is of no importance to the only real trial, the one taking place before mankind's universal conscience" (*DA*, 54). In the wake of the failure of law and public to do justice, Zola foregrounds the importance of citizens performing that justice otherwise: in the form of literature. A public that would perform and respond to such literature would not be the sovereign public that Zola envisioned in his early writings on the Affair. Yet the non-sovereignty of this belated public—their sense that they are entering into and responding to events that they cannot fully control and which they are too late to provide full remediation for anyway—may allow its members to respond, through writing and narration, to the likely failure of all forms of communication to elicit a "true" public.

Zola situates "poetic justice" as the outgrowth and continuation of collective action and solidarity, in contrast to the heroic individualism he enacted in "J'Accuse!" In his letter to Lucie Dreyfus, Zola argues that even with the injustice done to Dreyfus in the pardon, the Affair has had a positive effect in creating a new universal solidarity on behalf of truth and justice: "For the first time ever, all of mankind uttered a single cry for liberation. . ., as if all mankind were but one sole people, the single and fraternal people of whom the poets dream" (*DA*, 147). Dreyfus, Zola says, is the symbol of this new "religion" (*DA*, 47). While the Dreyfusards failed to achieve the complete justice they sought, their writings and action on behalf of justice in Dreyfus's case nonetheless created new international solidarities that remain valuable resources for and symbols of justice. Indeed, we could see the "cry of liberation" of these movements as itself a practice of poetic justice: a claim of democratic failure and a demand for a broader, fuller justice than was done—or could have been done—in courts of law.

Zola's conception of "poetic justice" thus suggests that the capacity of writing that he sees as dangerous in the Army's perpetration of falsity—writings' capacity to *re*-narrate events, to display them otherwise—is also why it is important to democracy. While citizens' ability to narrate events differently may lead to the proliferation of false perspectives (as during the Dreyfus Affair), Zola suggests that this same ability allows democratic citizens to address entrenched, false claims to truth—such as the government and the army's official story of Dreyfus's guilt. Zola's appeal to poetic justice in his late writings on the Affair thus reflects a shift in emphasis from his earlier writings. Whereas in those early writings he worried primarily about defending the truth of Dreyfus's innocence and indicting the government's falsity, in these later writings, Zola seems more concerned about the dangers of dominant narratives of truth going unchallenged.

Zola's appeal to poetic justice also suggests that writing may have its most important role in democracy not as the handmaiden of great deeds—that is, in its capacity to express or monumentalize them—but in its capacity to rhetorically transform moments of democratic failure into occasions for democratic response. Arendt's description of the Declaration of Independence in *On Revolution* offers the opposite formulation, emphasizing the ability of writing, in contrast to speech, to monumentalize action: "since we deal here with the written, and not with the spoken word, we are confronted with one of the rare moments in history when the power of action is great enough to erect its own monument."[59] This written monument reminds us of the freedom and public happiness inherent in the Revolution—not of its later failures, as diagnosed by Arendt in the same book—and thus orients us to contemporary democratic failures as problems to be overcome through the kind of democratic action exemplified in the Declaration of Independence. The Declaration, in other words, works in the register of inspiration: encouraging democratic actors to imitate the political action of the Founders to overcome or address political problems. Yet what if democratic actors are faced with the ongoing failure of political action to address political problems, and to assure justice? This is where Zola's practice of "poetic justice" may offer more resources than Arendt's monumentalizing practice of writing— namely, insofar as Zola's call for "poetic justice" suggests that democratic writing has an important role to play precisely in moments when no exemplary democratic action exists, in responding to moments of democratic failure through offering alternative perspectives on events that are occluded by official narratives. Zola's image of "poetic justice," in other words, suggests that even when democracy appears at its bleakest, collectively acting and writing one's judgment or one's narrative of events has the potential to generate responsiveness on behalf of justice, kernels of democratic solidarity that may enable the pursuit of justice today, or tomorrow.

VÉRITÉ: A UTOPIA WITHOUT WRITING

If one impulse of Zola when faced with failure is to value writing as a practice of re-narrating democratic failure on behalf of democratic response, we can find a different impulse in his final, and posthumously published (in 1903), novel, *Vérité*, where he portrays writing as danger-ous to democracy except in moments, as in founding, when it monu-mentalizes and expresses a perfect moment of democratic unity and action. In this novel, Zola himself pursues poetic justice by essentially rewriting the Dreyfus Affair in novelistic form and offering an alterna-tive, more just ending to the saga (an ending toward which Zola also gestures in his final writings on the Affair).[60] However, in his pursuit of poetic justice, Zola also undermines its core premise: the need to pluralize narratives of events, given the inevitable failure of law and official institutions to do full justice. He does so by charting an alterna-tive ending to the Dreyfus Affair: an ending in which the people have so achieved truthfulness that writing, as the practice of inhabiting and narrating alternative perspectives, is no longer needed.

Vérité, like the Dreyfus Affair, tells the story of a wrongly accused Jew (here named "Simon"), who is unjustly found guilty of a crime and is removed from his family for many years while his champions seek justice. Yet unlike Dreyfus, Simon is not a wealthy member of the army, but a poor schoolteacher. Also, Simon is accused not of treason, but rather of the murder of his young nephew, Zephirin, who had been in his charge after the death of the boy's parents—a scenario that bears more resemblance to the Calas than the Dreyfus Affair (and suggests that Zola's attempt to do "poetic justice" in *Vérité* may also be a response to Voltaire's earlier call for justice in the Calas Affair).[61] However, despite these differences, the broad narrative of *Vérité* mimics the Dreyfus Affair: Simon is wrongly convicted, sent away to an isolated prison camp for many years, finally recalled for a new trial after the hard work of his defenders produces new facts disproving the original verdict (and after being granted a revision by the Court of Cassation), then found guilty *again* in a new trial in a rural conservative town, and finally pardoned. The main difference in plot is that no broad amnesty law follows the pardon of Simon. Rather, the pursuit of truth and justice goes on and justice (both legal and social) is finally done, as I will describe later.

Vérité, like "J'Accuse!" is mythical in structure, but unlike "J'Accuse!"—whose ending Zola could not control—*Vérité*, which ends with justice and truth, turns into utopia. Just as in "J'Accuse!" Zola portrays the story in *Vérité* as a struggle between larger forces of justice and injustice. Here, the main hero is a young schoolteacher (who ages as the novel goes on)—Marc Froment—who is animated by the desire for truth that Zola sought to spark in the public during the Dreyfus Affair. As Zola puts it in the novel, "Marc's mind was one that sought logic and light. His clear and firm judgment demanded in all things a basis of certainty. Thence came his absolute passion for truth. In his eyes no rest of mind, no real happiness, was possible without complete, decisive certainty. He was not very learned, but such things as he knew he wished to know completely in order that he might have no doubt of the possession of the truth, experimental truth, established for ever."[62] Opposed to Marc and his small band of other truth-seekers (mainly other teachers in secular schools) in *Vérité* are the representatives of the

Catholic Church, who lie behind the continuing miscarriage of justice in the novel. Zola portrays priests and monks as literally responsible for hiding evidence of the true criminal's guilt from the authorities (the true criminal, it turns out in the end, is a monk).[63] However, Zola also blames the church (as he blames the army, the church, and the press during the Dreyfus Affair) for educating citizens incorrectly—namely, teaching them to see mystery and faith as the source of truth and justice, and to see reason as the source of error and vice.[64] Just as in his depiction of the Dreyfus Affair, Zola (via Marc) calls the misleading of the public by the church and the (Catholic) press a "crime against society": the crime of willfully deceiving a people in ways that prevent them from seeing truth and making just judgments. Zola writes, "To penetrate among the simple by affecting bluff good nature, and then to mingle arsenic with every dish, to drive the masses to delirium and to the most monstrous actions in order to increase one's sales, *I know of no greater crime!*"[65] In sum, Zola narrates the "Simon Affair" in *Vérité* as representing a clash between reason and mystification, secularism and religion.[66]

Yet at the heart of *Vérité* is the notion that not only the church or other agents of injustice are responsible for this crime against society—and the deception and domination it entails—but also the very practice of writing that Zola claims is typical of poetic justice: writing as re-narration, as the practice of re-presenting diverse perspectives. Specifically, the novel suggests that the further writing moves from the attempt to simply reflect reality, the more it becomes an instrument of deception and domination, rather than of truth and justice. For example, the novel contrasts Marc's estranged wife's reading of the court transcript from the retrial of Simon with her reading of Church-run newspapers: the former (an attempt to merely represent reality in writing) led her to see Simon's innocence, while the latter (guided by church-run anti-Semitic ideology) led her to see him as guilty. And in contrast to the struggle against injustice during the Dreyfus Affair, which took place mainly in the medium of writing, Marc's pursuit of justice through teaching underscores the dangers of turning to writing as a means of becoming truthful. Marc sees teaching as the only way to "*create a people of truth who, then alone, would become a people of justice.*"[67] Yet Marc's "love of truth and his desire to educate his students in truth" was:

why Marc kept such a careful watch over the books which the curriculum compelled him to place in the hands of his pupils; for he well knew that the best of them, written with the most excellent intentions, were still full of ancient falsehoods, the great iniquities consecrated by history. *If he distrusted phrases and words*, the sense of which seemed likely to escape his little peasants, and endeavoured to interpret them in clear and simple language, he feared yet more the dangerous legends, the errors of articles of faith, the abominable notions set forth in the name of a mendacious religion and a false patriotism. There was often no difference between the books written by clerics for the Brothers' schools and those which university men prepared for the secular ones.[68]

One could read this passage as suggesting simply that books written in a culture that embraces falsehood invariably repeat narratives that hide truth. Yet the passage also suggests a deeper distrust of language—Marc distrusts not only books, but also "phrases and words, the sense of which seemed likely to escape his little peasants." The problem with "phrases and words" is that they seem to mask, rather than reveal, reality. This is why Marc does not try to inculcate his students' love of truth through lectures or books, but rather through oral question and answer (he explains things they are puzzled about) and through experimentation and discovery in the natural world. This education, in other words, teaches students to be naturalists and empiricists, to identify truth through observation and experiment rather than through reading the accounts of others or through inhabiting their perspectives.

The culminating moment of full justice in *Vérité* celebrates a form of writing appropriate to this new, truthful public: namely, a completely transparent form of writing. This culminating moment takes place after a long process of education (of several generations) that finally results in a people who love truth and justice[69] (Indeed, we might say that if Burke saw mourning the failure of a sympathetic public as necessary to an always incomplete pursuit of justice, Zola here portrays the sacrifice, via their literal death, of ignorant generations as necessary to justice). At this point, Simon is rehabilitated[70] and brought back to Maillebois for a "festival of reparation.[71] The "public reparation"[72] offered to Simon is a house built on the site of an old Jewish ghetto that had been razed (representing the end of the Jews' second-class status).[73] Yet importantly, in a book that portrays writing and language as deceptive, this house would bear an inscription on a "marble slab" above the entrance: " 'Presented by the Town of Maillebois to Schoolmaster Simon, in the name of Truth and Justice, and in reparation for the torture inflicted on him.' And the whole will be signed: 'The Grandchildren of his Persecutors.' "[74] When this inscription is revealed at the festival of reparation, "there arose a last mighty acclamation, which rolled on like thunder—an acclamation in which all at last united, none henceforth daring to deny that truth and justice had triumphed."[75] The inscription, in other words, exemplifies and monumentalizes the kind of truthful language that would be ushered in by a truthful, sovereign people—a transparent language that means the same thing to everyone (it provoked "an acclamation in which all at last united"). Yet such a truthful society also seems, after having inscribed this one, truthful phrase—and thus fully united in truth—to no longer need writing at all, or at least, to no longer need writing as poetic justice, as a practice of re-narrating events from the vantage point of alternative perspectives. Indeed, even in situations where there is disagreement over truth—Zola depicts two of these at the end of *Vérité*—the situation is easily resolved through investigation and frank speaking. The public of transparency is Zola's people of "sovereign generosity," for whom there are no traitors.

Vérité thus offers a redemptive vision of the Dreyfus Affair, in a similar register as much of Zola's fiction. That is, the Simon Affair hastens the degeneration of a society, but in so doing, it also sparks a desire for truth and justice in a few that germinates throughout society and ushers in a new people of truth and justice. The new people of truth and justice, Zola shows in the novel, have no need of the combative newspapers of the late nineteenth century because they all see events clearly and, even if they disagree on the cause of an event, this disagreement can be cleared up through investigation. Such a vision of a future people must have been a comfort to Zola in his last days, offering him the possibility that the terrible anti-Semitism and crowd violence of late nineteenth-century France could usher in a new era. Zola's sacrifice and writings on behalf of truth, in other words, would not be in vain, but would serve as a seed for a new people to come.

Yet Zola's sacrifice of writing in *Vérité* may also entail a sacrifice of justice. In *Vérité*, the emergence of utopia is premised on the disappearance of religion and, in particular, on the decline and death of the Catholic Church. The Catholic Church, in other words, is—as Arendt argues in her critique of Zola—turned into the scapegoat, the willful lover of falsehood that, once sacrificed, enables the emergence of a truthful people. Thus, the utopia of truth without writing is actually premised on injustice, on *suppressing* one perspective on truth in order to achieve a sovereign, transparent public. Yet in Zola's utopia, there is no practice of writing available through which this injustice could be named as such and through which an alternative perspective on the Church—or on the utopia—could be made known. Rather, the practice of poetic justice that Zola affirms in his late writings on the Affair has, in *Vérité*, been written out of the picture.

WRITING AND JUSTICE

Zola's narrative of the Dreyfus Affair thus ends in a tension between Zola's *call* for poetic justice—the pluralization of narratives of events—and his *practice* of poetic justice that fantasizes about doing away with poetic justice altogether. On the one hand, we could read this tension as suggesting that Zola ultimately despairs of the people that he had hoped to rally to truth and justice—that he looked to again play the expert for a mob that he believed incapable of identifying truth on its own. On this reading, Zola's writing of *Vérité* is not only understandable as an act of seeking solace (as I suggested earlier), but also as an act of despair—that is, an attempt to reject a medium of writing that seemed to have thoroughly betrayed the purpose of revealing truth and enabling justice that Zola ascribed to it in his fiction and in his late writings on the Affair. Just as Arendt depicted Clemenceau as a man who began to see his own judgment as superior to that of the people after his despair at their mobbish character during the Dreyfus Affair, so, too, might we see Zola, in the wake of the democratic failure of his pursuit of ushering in a truthful public, as having despaired of democratic writing and turned to his own writing, his own utopia, as superior to the writing of the people. On this reading, in the end, Zola saw the people simply as a mob that must be led to truth by an expert who then does not allow them to have access to the writing that might allow them to turn away from truth, to see things from another perspective.

Yet we could also read the tension between Zola's call for "poetic justice" and his practice of it differently: as revealing that responsiveness to democratic failure through poetic justice does not *resolve* the risks of pursuing truth in democracy, but is also vulnerable to them. In *Vérité*, Zola's attempt to pluralize narratives of the Dreyfus Affair turns into the claim that his own narration of events is absolutely true, beyond contest or interpretation. Poetic justice may work as a rejoinder to dominant state narratives of justice that obscure injustice, but it may also attempt to silence other voices.

This vulnerability of poetic justice to anti-democratic relationships of rule suggests that the tensions and problems inherent in the democratic pursuit of truth are not fully resolvable. Indeed, in Zola's writings on the Affair, we see not only that laws, experts, and the people betray truth and justice; so, too, in the end does Zola's practice of dissident truth-telling. In other words, the attempt to assure truth, and to bring a people into being who would assure truth, appears as a persistent site of democratic failure. This persistence appears to drive Zola into moments of despair. Yet it also offers a productive democratic re-orientation to the problem of truth: namely, as a political problem that demands diffuse re-narration, rhetorical persuasion, political action, and solidarity. In other words, seeing the aspiration for full democratic agreement on truth as a failing aspiration better attunes democratic actors to the ongoing possibility of such failure (false claims used to undermine democratic freedom) *and* better positions them to see an engagement in poetic justice as part of the pursuit of truth and justice rather than only a dangerous form of dissimulation (as it is pictured in *Vérité*). Seeing the aspiration to resolve the problem of truth in democracy as a site of failure does not shut down the aspiration to truth, but rather positions democratic actors to pursue it democratically: through inhabiting and narrating diverse perspectives on behalf of challenging the relationships of deference in which they are always already caught up.

COMEDY AND/OF
JUSTICE?

LAW, POLITICS, AND PUBLIC OPINION IN ARENDT'S
WRITINGS ON THE EICHMANN TRIAL

*[I]f I was going to write, I had to say the way things are. I am not doing
that with anyone else, and I am, I think, halfway capable of maintaining
my façade. I give my lectures, have a lot of students, and, on the outside,
things appear to be going along normally. In the end, you believe, we
believe, the truth will out. But that is a belief. And the question of
whether one will live to see that day is not answered by it.*

—Hannah Arendt, letter to Karl Jaspers[1]

W hen Hannah Arendt decided to attend the Adolf Eichmann
trial in Israel in 1961, she opted to occupy the role of trial
reporter for *The New Yorker*.[2] In contrast to the role of the
prosecutor seeking a conviction (Burke) and the role of the intellectual seeking to convince the public of the truth (Zola), Arendt
described her role as simply discussing "the matters which were
treated in the course of the trial, or which in the interests of justice
should have been treated" (*EJ*, 285). Yet in describing the trial as it
appeared to her, Arendt placed herself in a critical position vis-à-vis
the state of Israel's prosecution. She claimed that the trial, focused on
the charge of "crimes against the Jewish people," obscured and failed

to do full justice to Eichmann's "crimes against humanity." She also famously took issue with the prosecution's (and the Court's) narrative and framing of events on many other issues—for example, its focus on Jewish suffering (in the form of testimony by Holocaust survivors) rather than Eichmann's deeds, and the prosecution's portrayal of Eichmann as exemplifying fanatical evil (for Arendt, Eichmann revealed "the banality of evil"). Arendt's narrative of the trial in *Eichmann in Jerusalem*, we could say, exemplifies Zola's practice of "poetic justice" in action—narrating events otherwise on behalf of revealing truth and seeking justice.

In recent years, Arendt's narrative of the trial in *Eichmann in Jerusalem* has increasingly been read as a juridical one—that is, as a text framed by what James Tully has described as a juridical "form of thought" occupied with "assessing our morals and politics predominantly in the juridical terms of 'right,' 'rights,' 'law' and 'universal.'"[3] For example, Shoshana Felman (a critic) argues that Arendt seeks a "purer justice" through austere adherence to rules—a justice that the politically infused trial in Jerusalem could not deliver and which, according to Felman (who is sympathetic to the Israeli prosecution), it should not have delivered.[4] Another juridical reader of the text, Seyla Benhabib, sees more promise in Arendt's text than Felman, but similarly argues that Arendt's priority is to call for standards of moral right that Eichmann's trial obscured in the morass of local politics. In particular, Benhabib argues that Arendt criticizes the Jerusalem trial because it failed to vindicate the new juridical category of "crimes against humanity."[5] For both Benhabib and Felman, Arendt mourns the failure of existing rules and institutions in Eichmann's trial on behalf of moral and legal standards that could reassert the priority of right over force and violence.[6]

I will argue, in contrast, in this chapter for reading *Eichmann in Jerusalem* as a narrative of democratic failure, where the juridical outlook that Benhabib and Felman see Arendt as lauding actually participates in and enables the failure of the trial to do full justice. I will suggest that, for Arendt, the Court's juridical approach led the judges to feel helpless to legally respond to Eichmann's novel crimes and, in turn, led them to judge those crimes according to existing laws that failed to capture them. Just as Burke criticizes the Lords for obscuring Hastings's crimes in their reliance on existing rules, so, too, does Arendt criticize the well-intentioned Jerusalem Court for hiding the unprecedented nature of Eichmann's crimes behind inadequate precedents.

I will also argue, however, that Arendt's portrayal of democratic failure in *Eichmann in Jerusalem* re-narrates that failure as a "lost cause" and, in turn, as an occasion for democratic response: namely, when she portrays political actors' contestation of legal constraints as empowering of legal responsiveness. She does so when she portrays the courtroom audience's challenge to procedural strictures on behalf of truth as enabling of (rather than detrimental to) justice and when she offers a "could have been" narrative of the trial that reveals how a world public could have demanded a new international court on behalf of justice and, in turn, solicits one that might do so in the future. In these moments, Arendt portrays the human capacities to resist legal compulsion and to found new institutions as the condition of rendering law responsive to new events and dangers. Building on these moments in Arendt's text, I argue that *Eichmann in Jerusalem* authorizes not a juridical, but an *agonistic* approach to law: that is, an approach that casts the political contestation of law as the condition of law's viability as a stabilizing force for political life. Consequently, I suggest that her analysis of Eichmann's trial directs us to attend to political action, contestation, and practices of resistance—what Tully has called "the free agonistic activities of participation themselves"[7]—as crucial to the stability of our legal world.

Yet if *Eichmann in Jerusalem* authorizes an agonistic approach to law and shows the problems of a juridical form of thought, Arendt's response to the risks of agonistic contestation in the controversy over *Eichmann in Jerusalem*—where the book solicited a public opposite of what Arendt hoped for—is to attempt to regulate those risks through drawing what I argue is a quasi-juridical distinction between proper contestation (motivated by "public spirit") and improper contestation (spurred by "public opinion"). Arendt's attempt to distinguish inauthentic from authentic contestation has the virtue of allowing her—as she argues retrospectively Clemenceau should have done—to avoid despairing of democracy altogether (since those who contest her book are framed as a "mob," rather than part of democracy). Yet it also leads her to obscure the problem Zola grappled with: that the problem of the mob—here in the work of "public opinion"—does not represent the failure of democracy, but rather an inevitable risk *of* democracy that stands in need of ongoing response.

I argue, in contrast, for responding to the riskiness of an agonistic approach to law—its vulnerability to failure—by cultivating broader and more diverse forms of democratic receptivity to failure. I find an argument for one such form in Arendt's review of Nathalie Sarraute's fiction, published in the *New York Review of Books* at the height of the Eichmann controversy. In this review, Arendt thematizes comedy and laughter as important practices of responsiveness to the victory of "the they." While laughter can serve a disciplinary function (disciplining dissident judgments into conformity), Arendt suggests that ironic laughter may create a community of laughers—a plural "we"—that acknowledges, but does not succumb to, the uniformity and rule-bound ethos of "the they." Arendt's review of Sarraute, I suggest, amounts to another lost cause narrative about the Eichmann controversy—displaying laughter as a way of responding to failure that might have enabled independent judgment and democratic solidarity on behalf of justice, and that might still enable such solidarity (and perhaps justice, too) in the future. Laughter and comedy might appear incongruous with the pursuit of justice (which seems to demand seriousness and solemnity). However, I suggest, through a discussion of Arendt's references to comedy and laughter in *Eichmann in Jerusalem*, that broadening our understanding of "proper" forms of democratic receptivity to failure—to include, for example, laughter as well as solemnity or despair—might allow democratic actors and theorists to see and pursue novel forms of democratic responsiveness on behalf of justice.

In the following, I first examine Arendt's diagnosis of the problem of addressing the unprecedentedness of Eichmann's crimes in a rule-bound court and suggest that this diagnosis illustrates the dangers of a juridical form of thought. In the next two sections, I turn to Arendt's discussion of the human capacities that addressed or could have addressed Eichmann's unprecedented deeds: first, the human capacity to resist legal compulsion and reveal truth that she affirms in the courtroom audience; and second, the human capacity to found new institutions that she calls for in her appeal for an international court. Next, I discuss her response to the public failure to respond to her call for justice and her thematization of comedy and laughter as productive practices of responsiveness to the failures of conformity and rule-following. I close by examining the relationship between laughter and justice.

THE PROBLEM OF THE UNPRECEDENTED

Arendt argues in *Eichmann in Jerusalem* that the "greatest moral and even legal challenge of the whole case" was the challenge of judging Eichmann's unprecedented crimes within a rule-bound court (*EJ*, 26). According to Arendt, Eichmann's crimes are "unprecedented" (*EJ*, 273) in two ways. First, they are unprecedented because of the huge gap between Eichmann's motives as a self-confessed "law-abiding citizen" (*EJ*, 24) and the horrific character of his deeds. While the prosecution's case "rested on the assumption that the defendant, like all 'normal persons,' must have been aware of the criminal nature of his acts" (*EJ*, 26), Arendt's observations of Eichmann suggest that this assumption is seriously flawed. For Arendt, what we learn by looking at Eichmann is that conscience is not an unchangeable moral faculty, but is susceptible to social, political, and legal influence. Indeed, Eichmann's motivations to participate in the "Final Solution" seem to have had less to do with fanaticism and more to do with his desire to please his betters and follow the law: Eichmann said that "he would have had a bad conscience only if he had not done what he had been ordered to do—to ship millions of men, women, and children to their death with great zeal and the most meticulous care" (*EJ*, 25)—a point that, as Arendt notes (in perhaps the greatest understatement of the book), "admittedly, was hard to take" (*EJ*, 25).[8] Yet it is not just Eichmann's conscience that is new and "unprecedented" (*EJ*, 263). It is also, and second, the character of his crimes—that is, that he committed genocide (and not just murder), a crime that violated the "order of mankind" and not just the order of a particular people (*EJ*, 272). While Israel and the international community had categories like "expulsion," "pogroms," "anti-Semitism," and "murder" at their disposal to talk about and judge crimes like Eichmann's, none of these described the precise character of his acts: that he attempted to wipe an entire people off the face of the earth—a crime that could be directed against any people, not just the Jews (*EJ*, 272–273). For Arendt, this twofold unprecedentedness of Eichmann's crimes—his lack of *mens rea* and the horrific novelty of his deeds—makes the task of judgment in a rule-bound court difficult: How can the Jerusalem Court accurately judge Eichmann's deeds when they defy the categories and precedents by which the Court judges?

This challenge for the Court was, on Arendt's account, made even more difficult by attempts of the Israeli prime minister (Ben-Gurion) and lead prosecutor (Hausner) to turn the trial into a "show trial" and use it for purposes of state-building (EJ, 4).[9] Arendt argues that the prosecution portrayed Eichmann's crimes not as "unprecedented," but rather as part of "the most horrible pogrom in Jewish history" (EJ, 267). For the Israeli prosecution, eternal anti-Semitism and "history. . . stood at the center of the trial" (EJ, 19).[10] Arendt understands why Jews would adopt this narrative of the trial (EJ, 263), but she also worries that this meta-narrative of anti-Semitism ultimately ascribes responsibility for Eichmann's acts to a historical force, rather than to Eichmann himself (EJ, 19). For Arendt, Hausner's and Ben-Gurion's focus on the suffering of the victims—and of Jews in general—betrays the purpose of a trial: "to weigh the charges brought against the accused, to render judgment, and to mete out due punishment" (EJ, 253).

While the prosecution sought "the limelight," Arendt says the judges shunned it and for the most part kept the trial focused on Eichmann's deeds (EJ, 5–6). Arendt describes the chief Justice, for example, as "someone who serves Justice as faithfully as Mr. Hausner serves the state of Israel" (EJ, 5). And in the "Epilogue," Arendt argues that, thanks to the judges, the "main purpose" of the trial—"to prosecute and to defend, to judge and to punish, Adolf Eichmann—was achieved" (EJ, 273). However, Arendt also argues that the Jerusalem Court failed to accurately judge the twofold unprecedentedness of Eichmann's crimes (EJ, 274). The judges were "helpless" when "confronted with the task they could least escape, the task of understanding the criminal whom they had come to judge" (EJ, 276). Further, they never considered the possibility that Eichmann's crimes "might be more than a crime against the Jewish or the Polish or the Gypsy people, that the international order, and mankind in its entirety, might have been grievously hurt and endangered" (EJ, 276). The judges kept the Israeli prosecution from turning the trial into a "show trial," but they never, Arendt says, "rose to the challenge of the unprecedented" (EJ, 263).

At stake for Arendt in the judges' failure to accurately judge the unprecedentedness of Eichmann's crimes is, at least in part, justice. In Eichmann in Jerusalem and elsewhere, Arendt argues that the main purpose of criminal trials is to do individual justice. As Arendt puts it in "Civil Disobedience," it is "the grandeur of court procedure that it is

concerned with meting out justice to an individual and remains uncon-
cerned with anything else."[11] Similarly, Arendt argues in *Eichmann in
Jerusalem* that "[j]ustice insists on the importance of Adolf Eichmann"
(*EJ*, 5)—on the "man of flesh and blood" (*EJ*, 285)—and not on ideologies, history, or moralities. The "ideologies of the time" (*EJ*, 286) and
the history of anti-Semitism are relevant to the trial only insofar as
they are "circumstances of the crime" (*EJ*, 289) or its "background"
(*EJ*, 287)—they are not themselves on trial.[12] If, as Arendt says, "[t]
he purpose of a trial is to render justice, and nothing else" (*EJ*, 253),
then the judges' failure to judge the unprecedentedness of Eichmann's
crimes matters because they failed to do full justice.

This would seem to support juridical readings of *Eichmann in Jerusalem*,
which portray Arendt as concerned with justice above all else. Yet
Arendt's criticism of the Court breaks with this juridical reading in at
least two ways. First, Arendt suggests that the Court's failure to judge
the unprecedentedness of Eichmann's crimes is most consequential not
because the judges failed to do justice—after all, the "main purpose" of
the trial, judging and punishing Eichmann, was achieved (*EJ*, 254)—
but rather because they failed to advance the *political* project of building
international laws and institutions.[13] For Arendt, the Court's failure to
judge the unprecedentedness of Eichmann's crimes meant that the trial
would "no more, and perhaps even less than its predecessors, serve as
a valid precedent for future trials of such crimes" (*EJ*, 272)—a point
important because of the very real "possibility that similar crimes may
be committed in the future" (*EJ*, 273). Given the political stakes of the
trial, Arendt says—seemingly in strange contrast to her argument that
trials must focus only on individual deeds—that "[s]uccess or failure in
dealing with the hitherto unprecedented can lie only in the extent to
which this dealing may serve as a valid precedent on the road to international penal law" (*EJ*, 273). Consequently, and second, Arendt suggests that judges must judge unprecedented crimes in a less rule-bound
way. She argues that due to the "unfinished character of international
law," it is reasonable to "demand" that "ordinary trial judges" judge
unprecedented crimes "without the help of, or beyond the limitation
set upon them through positive, posited laws" (*EJ*, 274).

Arendt's criticism of the Jerusalem Court's failure thus leads her not
to call for the rehabilitation of the Court's failed juridical outlook—
bound by rules, precedents, and existing institutions—but instead to

call for them to *break* with that outlook on behalf of a political project of building international law and institutions. This turn in her argument is puzzling. Especially given her appreciation for the Jerusalem Court's legalistic resistance to the Israeli prosecution's showmanship, why would Arendt suggest that going *beyond* rules and bringing political concerns to bear on the trial is the best response to the Court's failure to judge the unprecedentedness of Eichmann's crimes? Next, I address Seyla Benhabib's and Leora Bilsky's responses to that question and then offer my own, alternative response.

Benhabib's Response: The Tension Between the Universal and the Particular

Seyla Benhabib's reading of *Eichmann in Jerusalem* responds to this question by casting Arendt's demand that courts judge crimes against humanity beyond positive, posited law not as the expression of a *political* concern, but of a (universal) moral one. For Benhabib, Arendt's combined sympathy with the Court's adherence to Israeli law and her criticism of this adherence exemplify the "unresolved tension between the universal and the particular" in Arendt's work more generally, between Arendt's dual commitment to "the ideal of humanity" and "the fact of human particularity and diversity."[14] Arendt seems to support Benhabib's point when she says in the "Epilogue" that "[i]nsofar as the victims were Jews, it was right and proper that a Jewish court should sit in judgment; but insofar as the crime was a crime against humanity, it needed an international tribunal to do justice to it" (*EJ*, 269)—a statement that seems to suggest that *justice* (Benhabib's universal morality) was best served in an international court, even though there were *political* reasons to try Eichmann in a Jewish court.

For Benhabib, this apparent tension in Arendt's thought is what makes her work valuable. As Benhabib argues in her recent work on cosmopolitanism, *Eichmann in Jerusalem* pushes us to reflect on the "inevitable and necessary tension between those moral obligations and duties resulting from our membership in bounded communities and the moral perspective that we must adopt as human beings *simpliciter*."[15] Yet Benhabib finds Arendt's response to this tension to be lacking. In particular, Benhabib is "baffled" by Arendt's suggestion in the "Postscript" to *Eichmann in Jerusalem* that while "[i]t is quite conceivable that certain political responsibilities among nations might some day be adjudicated in an international court; what is inconceivable is that such a court would be a criminal tribunal which pronounces on the guilt or innocence of individuals" (Arendt *EJ*, 298).[16] Benhabib takes Arendt's apparent retreat from her argument for an international court as a "den[ial] that an International Criminal Court is conceivable"[17] and casts it as symptomatic of Arendt's broader skepticism about the import of moral values and especially moral universalism in politics.[18] For Benhabib, this skepticism is problematic because it leaves Arendt (and us) unable to respond critically to state- and majority-sanctioned inequalities and human rights violations: "If we do not differentiate between *the moral and the ethical*, we cannot criticize the exclusionary citizenship and membership practices of specific cultural, religious and ethnic communities. If we do not differentiate between *morality and legality*, we cannot criticize the legally enacted norms of democratic majorities."[19]

Arendt's apparent retreat from, rather than confrontation of, the tension between the universal and the particular leads Benhabib to develop her own approach to it—one based in Habermasian discourse ethics that she calls "democratic iterations." Democratic iterations mediate *"between the moral and the ethical, the moral and the political"*[20] by "making sense of an authoritative original in a new and different context"[21]—in particular, by making sense of universal moral norms in a local context: "By *democratic iterations*, I mean complex processes of public argument, deliberation, and exchange through which universalist rights claims are contested and contextualized, invoked and revoked, posited and positioned throughout legal and political institutions as well as in the associations of civil society."[22] "Democratic iterations" are important because they provide a way for citizens to "judge the legitimacy of a range of variation in the interpretation of a right claim"[23]—in other words, to evaluate whether local "interpretations" of universalist principles are democratically legitimate, or truly in accord with universal moral norms.

Benhabib aims to bring together moral universalism and critical democratic contestation in her "democratic iterations" and thus help Arendt (against Arendt) better justify her turn to an international court. Yet Benhabib's reading of Arendt's "demand" that the judges judge "beyond. . . positive, posited law" as a gesture toward moral universalism dismisses rather than addresses Arendt's concerns about seeing morality as the ground of law and politics. While Benhabib sees morality as a check on legality, Arendt's examination of the perversion of Eichmann's conscience—how "an average, 'normal' person, neither feeble-minded nor indoctrinated nor cynical could be perfectly incapable of telling right from wrong" (*EJ*, 26)—suggests that it may be dangerous to assume that we can rely on moral standards to offer guidance in novel situations. As Villa puts it, Arendt's examination of the malleability of Eichmann's conscience in a totalitarian regime suggests that "it is self-deluding to expect either the voice of conscience or traditional moral yardsticks to pick up the slack or present a genuine obstacle" to such regimes.[24] Benhabib's casting of Arendt as a would-be rehabilitator of universal moral categories seems to sidestep the concern identified here: that relying on moral categories can help us avoid rather than address new moral and political problems.

The problem with sidestepping this concern is not simply that Benhabib misrepresents Arendt; it is also that Benhabib's reading of Arendt as a seeker of universal moral standards keeps us from asking questions about why Arendt calls for the judges to *break* from a rule-bound approach to justice. Benhabib's reading of Arendt's comment at the end of the "Postscript" is a case in point. Recall that Arendt says at the end of the "Postscript" that while "[i]t is quite conceivable that certain political responsibilities among nations might some day be adjudicated in an international court; what is inconceivable is that such a court would be a criminal tribunal which pronounces on the guilt or innocence of individuals" (*EJ*, 298). Benhabib reads Arendt here as saying that an International Criminal Court is "inconceivable" in general. Yet when we put the passage into the context of Arendt's argument in the "Postscript" about the importance of keeping collective and individual responsibilities separate (*EJ*, 296–297), we can see that Arendt may be making a different point—not that *no* criminal court could exist at the international level, but that *whatever* court adjudicates political responsibilities among nations would not *also* be a criminal court that judges individual actions (it "is inconceivable that *such a court* would be a criminal tribunal" [*EJ*, my emphasis, 298]): individual and collective responsibility are different matters. Rather than indicating a retreat from Arendt's gesture toward universalism (Benhabib's reading), then, this passage may reiterate Arendt's concern with the importance of correctly judging individual deeds, especially in cases involving the unprecedented. When Benhabib translates this passage into a worry about the viability of an international court (and universalism) without addressing this alternative possible reading, she casts the problem of judging the unprecedented as a problem that must be resolved by finding the *right* (universal) rule, rather than as a problem that may call for us to judge *without* such moral guideposts.

Benhabib's failure to address this alternative possible reading reflects a broader failure to ask whether Arendt's criticism of the judges—and her demand that they judge in a less rule-bound way—may reflect a worry about juridical approaches to law and politics more generally, rather than a call to rehabilitate such approaches. Indeed, given Arendt's worries about seeing morality as the ground of politics, might it not be likely that Arendt's demand that judges judge "*beyond. . .* positive, posited law" reflects a concern about the viability of the Court's juridical approach as such, rather than a call to rehabilitate that approach on universal moral grounds?

Bilsky's Response: A Turn to Reflective Judgment

Leora Bilsky's reading of *Eichmann in Jerusalem* seems to respond to this problem in Benhabib's approach. Where Benhabib casts Arendt's "demand" to the judges as a gesture toward universalism, Bilsky—more sympathetic to Arendt's worries about morality in politics—reads Arendt's "demand" as a gesture toward the importance of incorporating reflective judgment into trials involving the unprecedented. Given the failures of "determinative judgment" in Eichmann's trial—"which attempts to explain unfamiliar crimes by analogizing them to more familiar ones"—Bilsky argues that Arendt's "demand" is meant to call on judges to practice "reflective" aesthetic judgment of the particular *qua* particular: judgment that proceeds through imagining ourselves inhabiting different perspectives on the object or issue at hand.[25] In her casting of Arendt as authorizing a less-rule-governed approach to legal problems, Bilsky takes up the challenge of Arendt's resistance to the judge's juridical approach more fully than Benhabib.

Yet even as Bilsky casts reflective judgment as the answer to the problems of Eichmann's trial, she suggests that reflective judgment, to be successful, must be tethered to a liberal conception of justice. She frames this argument as a response to a worry about reflective judgment—a worry that she believes is Arendt's. Specifically, Bilsky suggests that Arendt ultimately pulls back from affirming reflective judgment in trials because of the threat that judgment unstructured by rules poses in the courtroom (for example, in allowing in irrelevant witness testimony): "Guarding the line between the political and the legal, she [Arendt] criticizes the prosecution's efforts to give a stage to the victims' stories."[26] Rather than asking why Arendt may affirm *and* worry about non-rule-governed judicial judgment, Bilsky suggests that Arendt's worries about allowing reflective judgment into the trial—that it will politicize the pursuit of justice—are not warranted. These worries, Bilsky says, persist only if we fail to identify criteria that distinguish between "legitimate" and "illegitimate" reflective judgment—criteria that Bilsky finds within Arendt's own thought.[27] Specifically, Bilsky says that reflective judgment is legitimate when it fulfills three characteristics:[28] plurality (occupying a variety of viewpoints in coming to a judgment,[29] natality (judging the particular *qua* particular),[30] and narrativity (judgment through telling a story that "binds together actors and spectators in a human community").[31] These criteria, Bilsky says, also happen to be key values of a liberal-democratic society. Consequently, a public and a judiciary skilled in reflective judgment would not only have a better chance of judging crimes like Eichmann's accurately; they would also produce a pluralistic society[32] and a "legal system capable of fostering equality among our diverse embodied selves."[33] Like Benhabib, then, Bilsky sees Arendt's "demand" not as indicating a worry about juridical approaches in general, but instead as expressing hope for a *better* juridical approach. Unlike Benhabib, though, Bilsky sees this new juridical approach as necessarily flexible—guided by a liberal ethos, rather than by unshakeable moral norms.

In her liberal reformulation of Arendtian reflective judgment, Bilsky thus hopes to create a fuller solution to the problem of judging the unprecedented than Arendt herself offers. Yet Bilsky's turn to reflective judgment neglects Arendt's worries about whether such judgment is sufficient to achieve adequate judgment of the unprecedented. Specifically, Bilsky does not attend to Arendt's suggestion in the "Postscript" that the judges in Eichmann's trial actually *had* "judged freely" (*EJ*, 294) in their judgment—but without accurately judging Eichmann's crimes. The problem was, Arendt says, that the judges "more or less convincingly sought to justify their decisions" with "standards and legal precedents" that did not apply to Eichmann's crimes (Ibid.), including older international precedents and the Nuremberg precedent, itself.[34] Arendt thus does not portray reflective judgment as the solution to the problems of Eichmann's trial, but rather suggests that reflective judgment is caught within the parameters of another problem: the judges' inability (real or imagined) to articulate their free judgment freely in their public decision.

Bilsky is certainly right that *Eichmann in Jerusalem* reveals a crisis in judicial judgment. Yet Arendt's comments about the insufficiency of reflective judgment in the trial suggest that liberal reflective judgment may not offer a solution to that crisis. Rather, Arendt's comments suggest that the judges' ability to practice meaningful reflective judgment is contingent upon our response to another problem: the judges' apparent helplessness to do in public what Arendt says they were doing privately-namely, judging Eichmann's crimes freely, beyond positive, posited law. Might Arendt's worry about the judges' juridical approach—and her reasons for demanding that they break with it—be in part a worry about this sense of helplessness, and not just about the particular standards that guide them?

Switching the Problem: From Judges to the Audience

Indeed, throughout Arendt's depiction of the Jerusalem Court, she suggests that the judges' juridical approach to the trial not only failed to offer sufficient categories for judgment. Their approach also produced a sense of *disempowerment* vis-à-vis the law: the judges seemed to have a limited horizon for judgment and a dampened sense of their capacity for action. For example, foreshadowing later critiques of jurisdiction, such as Robert Cover's,[35] Arendt argues that the Court's failure to judge the unprecedentedness of Eichmann's crimes was due to the judges' "firm belief that *they had no right to become legislators*, that they had to conduct their business within the limits of Israeli law, on the one side, and of accepted legal opinion, on the other" (my emphasis, *EJ*, 274). Similarly, Arendt argues that the Court believed that the "weight" of its "authority. . . depends upon its limitation" (*EJ*, 254). The Court's sense that their authority depended on the connection of their judgment to existing rules led them to feel that the possible bounds of their judgment were circumscribed—and that this circumscription was out of their control. Indeed, Arendt notes that the judges felt "helpless" to act or judge otherwise (*EJ*, 267). For Arendt, the judges' sense that right judgment depends on its connection to appropriate standards engendered a lack of confidence in their ability to respond to new dangers and events.[36]

Yet if Arendt's worry about the judges' juridical approach is about their sense of helplessness, and not just about the particular standards that guided them, then her "demand" to them seems a curious response. After all, given that Arendt herself admits that the judges are trapped by a sense of helplessness to judge "beyond positive, posited law"—and that she even appreciates this sense when the Court resists the Israeli prosecution's attempts at politicization—why does she demand that they do otherwise (*EJ*, 273)? Is she merely being utopian or provocative—drawing our attention to this problem, but not seriously expecting any positive response? Perhaps—but there is another possibility: namely, that Arendt is modeling a non-formal demand for justice that may not have official bearing on the proceedings, but which nonetheless may have *political* and perhaps even legal importance. That is, Arendt's "demand" to the judges may be a way of modeling how demands that do not come from judges—and not even from prosecutors or witnesses—may still be important and exert influence on the proceedings, and perhaps even on the project of international world-building that Arendt supports. If this is right, then we can glean more than an important diagnosis of the dangers of the judges' juridical approach from Arendt's story of Eichmann's trial. Her "trial report" may also be exemplary of the role that spectators must play in trials like Eichmann's—not practicing liberal reflective judgment, but instead *resisting* the judges' juridical approach and initiating new ways of addressing the unprecedentedness of Eichmann's crimes.

Indeed, as I will show in the next section, Arendt picks out for special attention moments when the courtroom audience exerts pull in the courtroom, sways the proceedings, and creates or reveals narratives of Eichmann's crimes. Specifically, Arendt highlights moments when audience spectatorship and theatricality display truths about Eichmann's crimes that the Court's procedural strictness might otherwise have silenced. If, as I have argued above, Arendt's politically inflected criticism of the Jerusalem Court expresses a worry about how identification of judgment with legal rules engenders disempowerment, her appreciation of spectators' action in court may gesture toward a

rejoinder to this tendency—namely, spectators claiming law as constituted by political action, not just rule-following. Rather than drawing
attention to the problem of finding the right rule or flexible criteria
for judgment, Arendt may thus be drawing our attention to a different
problem altogether—namely, that law's ability to respond to new events
may, perhaps strangely, depend on the actions and demands of political
actors who challenge or exceed legal categories and procedures.

THE COURTROOM AUDIENCE: SPECTATORSHIP AND THEATRICALITY

Arendt's contemporary interpreters rarely discuss her descriptions of
the courtroom audience in *Eichmann in Jerusalem*. This may reflect their
sense that for her, the audience is not an actor in but only recipient of
the proceedings and, thus, that the important considerations about the
trial have to do with judges, laws, and official legal actors. Yet Arendt
actually devotes a fair amount of attention to the audience throughout the book and suggests that its members were uniquely resistant to
the Israeli prosecution's narrative of the trial. At the very outset, for
example, Arendt notes that the composition of the courtroom audience resisted the Israeli prosecution's attempts to use the trial to teach
a nationalist lesson—that "only in Israel could a Jew be safe and live
an honorable life" (*EJ*, 8). While the prosecution had hoped to see the
audience filled with "young people" who did not yet know the story of
the Holocaust, Arendt says that instead "[i]t was filled with 'survivors,'
with middle-aged and elderly people, immigrants from Europe, like
myself, who knew by heart all there was to know, and who were in no
mood to learn any lessons and certainly did not need this trial to draw
their own conclusions" (Ibid.). Rather than being the passive recipient
of the prosecution's lessons, Arendt suggests that this audience may be
taking away lessons that the prosecution does not intend—using the
trial rather than being used by it.

However, Arendt does not just urge us to see the audience as a source
of passive resistance to the prosecution's narrative. She also draws our
attention to several moments—especially in her chapter on "Evidence
and Witnesses"—when the audience or some of its members resist the

Court's procedural strictness and theatrically push the proceedings to attend to truths that would otherwise have been excluded. Shoshana Felman has also attended to the "Evidence and Witnesses" chapter, but takes issue with what she sees as Arendt's narrow juridical approach to the trial. Felman argues that Arendt wrongly seeks to keep drama and theater out of the proceedings in favor of a trial that is "a thoroughly ascetic, disciplined, conceptual experience."[37] In this section, I suggest, contra Felman, that Arendt is not categorically opposed to drama in court. Rather, Arendt approves of drama that is generated by the audience's response to the proceedings, while she resists attempts by official legal actors (witnesses, lawyers) to use the trial to impose theatrical lessons on the public.

Felman reads Arendt's "Evidence and Witnesses" chapter as exemplifying a juridical perspective because, in it, Arendt heavily criticizes one witness (K-Zetnik) for theatrically failing to follow the rules and lauds a more circumspect witness, Zyndal Grynzspan, whose testimony adheres to the rules. Arendt criticizes K-Zetnik's testimony because, on her account, his theatrical appearance fails to issue in meaningful testimony: K-Zetnik describes his internal struggle to deal with his time in Auschwitz, and ultimately faints (*EJ*, 224). Arendt disdainfully recounts K-Zetnik's failure to tell his story and approvingly notes the efforts of the Jerusalem Court and even the prosecutor to make him give testimony according to the Court's rules. By contrast, Arendt lauds Zyndal Grynzspan because he knows how to tell his story without digression or theatrics. Arendt notes that Grynszpan had not volunteered to testify, but that once there he needed no prompting to tell his story in line with courtroom rules: Grynszpan "carefully answer[ed] questions put to him by the prosecutor" and "spoke clearly and firmly, without embroidery, using a minimum of words" (*EJ*, 228). This exemplary testimony pushes Arendt to think "foolishly" that "[e]veryone, everyone should have his day in court" (*EJ*, 229).

For Felman, Arendt's affirmation of Grynszpan and criticism of K-Zetnik is indicative of her broader affirmation of a narrow juridical understanding of justice and devaluation of the Jewish narrative of suffering that the trial articulated for the first time—a narrative that on Felman's account (and contra Arendt) was crucial to understanding the unprecedentedness of Nazi crimes.[38] Arendt's criticism of K-Zetnik is particularly troubling for Felman, though, because Felman argues that

Arendt diminishes the kind of testimony that K–Zetnik in fact gave through fainting on the stand—namely, testimony to the inexpressibility of the trauma of the Holocaust.[39] While Arendt sees this as a "failure of narration," Felman argues that the inability to tell a story "is itself an integral part of the history and of the story of the Holocaust."[40] Indeed, for Felman, K–Zetnik's testimony ensures that the trial did not falsely suggest that it could bring final closure to the Holocaust. Rather, speaking the "truth" of the Holocaust calls on us to both tell the story (as Hausner and his witnesses did) *and* admit that the story can never fully be told (as K–Zetnik's testimony did).[41]

Felman's reading thus frames Arendt as favoring (false) legal closure over artistic openness, while Felman casts herself as embracing the tension between the two as productive of legal meaning. Yet it is not clear that Arendt occupies a single side of this antagonism. Indeed, Arendt's account of Grynzspan's testimony, which Felman reads as favoring legal closure over Hausner's "folktale of justice" *and* K–Zetnik's "failure" of testimony, actually challenges (rather than reinforces) the strictures of the court. Listening to Grynzspan leads Arendt to resist—even if "foolishly" and just for a moment—her own resistance to K–Zetnik and to *any* limitations on testimony: *everyone* should have their day in court. Arendt's response to a rule-governed witness thus leads her to embrace, at least momentarily, an excessively anti-legalistic, open-ended stance.[42] The difference between Arendt and Felman here, then, seems to be less a difference between an embrace of legal closure (Arendt) over a vision of law haunted by artistic openness (Felman) and more a difference between two ways of embracing a tension between (legal) closure and (artistic) openness. While Felman sees K–Zetnik's inability to tell his story as exemplary of the insufficiency of language and law to fully grasp the reality of the Holocaust, Arendt approves of Grynzspan's inspiring example because it gestures toward the importance of an open-ended capacity for storytelling not captured by legal procedure and precedent.

Felman's version of this tension may seem more appealing than Arendt's because Felman is more concerned than Arendt with ensuring that all victims' testimony is valued—and, indeed, her embrace of K–Zetnik's testimony in contrast to Arendt's harsh dismissal of him seems, on its own, to recommend her view. Yet Felman's reading of the trial, while usefully drawing our attention to one limit of law (its inability to speak the truth of trauma), also obscures the limit that Arendt identifies—that law, judges, and other official actors are limited in their ability to inaugurate a new legal framework that can meaningfully address the crimes of the Holocaust. Felman's embrace of the state's narrative of the trial instead leads her to take for granted the trial's ability to found what she (following Robert Cover) calls a "folktale of justice" that can ground future trials of criminals like Eichmann. Arendt's criticism of both Hausner and the Jerusalem Court leads us to ask, in contrast, whether it is a good idea to rely on state and legal actors to address and narrate crimes like Eichmann's. Indeed, for Arendt, the prosecutor's alignment with the state and the judges' alignment with legal precedent mean that they may be the actors least capable of judging new crimes and creating new institutions. Felman is right to take Arendt to task for her dismissal of K-Zetnik, but her embrace of the state's narrative of the trial leads her to be insufficiently attentive to the problem diagnosed by Arendt: that relying on state and legal actors to address new crimes may lead us to fail to inaugurate an adequate response to those crimes.

Felman's claim that law and its agents/official actors *can* provide new legal meaning—that only trauma escapes—also has another important effect. It leads her to be less attentive than Arendt to how the audience—and not just official legal actors—may play a formative role in creating legal meaning. In particular, Felman does not urge us to attend (as Arendt does) to the drama created by the audience's *response* to the proceedings: drama that does what the judges were unable to do on Arendt's account—resist juridical limits, reveal truths, and create worldly contexts where new judgments can occur. Arendt draws attention to just such a moment (later in the same chapter) when she describes how the entire courtroom was compelled to see an important truth about Eichmann's crimes and about the Nazis' crimes more generally—not because official courtroom actors brought it to light, but because the audience's spectatorship riveted attention on it. This "dramatic moment" (*EJ*, 230) occurred during the testimony of a witness, Abba Kovner, when he described his interactions with Anton Schmidt, a German soldier who aided the Jewish underground—"the first and the last time that any such story was told of a German" (*EJ*, 231). Arendt writes that during the minutes when Kovner was discussing Schmidt, which were like a sudden burst of light in the midst of impenetrable, unfathomable darkness, a single thought stood out clearly, irrefutably, beyond question—how utterly different everything would be today in this courtroom, in Israel, in Germany, in all of Europe, and perhaps in all countries of the world, if only more such stories could have been told. (Ibid.)

Arendt does not specify how things would be "utterly different. . . if only more such stories could have been told" (Ibid.), but at least in the Jerusalem courtroom, she suggests that this story revealed an important truth that would not have come to light otherwise—namely, that "under conditions of terror most people will comply but *some people will not*" (EJ, 233). Through revealing this truth, Kovner's testimony orients spectators to Eichmann's crimes as specific deeds for which he is *individually* accountable (if someone *didn't* follow orders, then "just following orders" is no excuse). This moment thus does not reveal "facts" about Eichmann's deeds—which, as Arendt notes, were "beyond dispute" (EJ, 265)—but rather reveals a truth about how they must be judged: Eichmann must be held individually responsible for his deeds, no more and no less.

Yet while Arendt's appreciative recounting of this moment is understandable, given the truth revealed in it, it is also puzzling, since (unlike Grynzspan's testimony) this moment occurred when legal procedures were not in control of the courtroom—during the judges' "almost desperate attempt to bring the proceedings back under the control of normal criminal court procedures" (EJ, 230). Given Arendt's worries about departing from procedures that are so evident in her descriptions of K-Zetnik and her criticism of the Israeli prosecution's grand narratives in the trial, it is striking that Arendt has nothing critical to say about this procedural lapse. Why doesn't Arendt criticize this departure from rule-following? Arendt does not give a reason for this, but her description of the moment suggests that her appreciation was compelled by the courtroom audience's response to Kovner's testimony. When Kovner began talking about Schmidt, Arendt tells us that the audience became quiet and listened in rapt attention: "it was as though the crowd had spontaneously decided to observe the usual two minutes of silence in honor of the man named Anton Schmidt" (EJ, 231). The spontaneous response of the audience interrupted the judges' attention to (failing) procedures and compelled them to pay attention to Kovner's story: "a hush settled over the *courtroom*" as a result of the audience's riveted attention, Arendt tells us, not just over the courtroom audience (my emphasis, Ibid.).

Why did the response of the courtroom audience capture Arendt and the judges in this way? Perhaps because the audience's response was a form of political action and, as Arendt tells us in her other work, when people act together in concert, they create power that resists compulsion and sustains new political realities.[43] It might seem counterintuitive to read the audience's silent response to Kovner's testimony as political action in the Arendtian sense—since we often associate Arendtian political action with heroic deeds and extraordinary founding moments[44]—but the audience's response bears many marks of how Arendt describes political action in *The Human Condition* and *On Revolution*: the audience's response was collective and "spontaneous,"[45] it revealed truth, it was unexpected, and it interrupted the compulsion of procedures.[46] Perhaps most important, the audience's action seemed to generate a new sense of possibility in the courtroom, or a "new reality," which is also characteristic of acting in concert on Arendt's account[47]—namely, the possibility of assessing Eichmann's individual responsibility for his deeds. Thus, we might speculate that the audience's riveted silence allowed Arendt and the judges to disregard the compulsion of legal procedures because it *empowered* them to do so.

This is not the only such moment in the book. Earlier, Arendt appreciatively describes another moment when the courtroom audience transgressed procedures and compelled the courtroom to attend to truth. However, in this moment, the audience does so through theatrical rather than riveted spectatorship, and the judges are compelled to formally incorporate the disclosed truth into the proceedings. This moment occurs during the testimony of Pinchas Freudiger, who "had been a prominent member of a *Judenrat*" (*EJ*, 124). Arendt tells us that "during his testimony the only serious incidents in the audience took place; people screamed at the witness in Hungarian and in Yiddish, and the court had to interrupt the session" (Ibid.). Arendt recounts this incident approvingly because the audience called attention to and passed judgment on the activities of the *Judenrat* that had thus far been left out of the trial. For Arendt, controversially, these activities were important to establishing the whole truth of Eichmann's actions—both because they showed that Eichmann's crimes could only have been committed in a "criminal state," that is, in the context of a state apparatus and society (including some Jews) that sanctioned or were complicit in them (*EJ*, 262) *and* because the story of the *Judenrat* punctured the prosecution's narrative of eternal anti-Semitism (Jewish complicity complicates a story of universal enmity between Jews and their enemies). In this instance, however, spectators did not simply compel the courtroom to attend to truth. Rather, Arendt suggests that the audience's actions also empowered the court to formally incorporate their questions into the proceedings. When the witness, Freudiger, replied to the crowd, "What could we have done? What could we have done?" Arendt writes that "the only response to this came from the presiding judge: 'I do not think this is an answer to the question'—*a question raised by the gallery but not by the court*" (*EJ*, my emphasis, 124). Rather than silence the audience, the judges were compelled to acknowledge its voice and to formally admit into the proceedings another truth about Eichmann's crimes—namely, that even though he must bear individual responsibility for those crimes, they were only possible in a situation of systematic complicity.

If Arendt were the juridical thinker that Felman paints her to be, she would have cast these two moments when the audience held sway in court as dangerous challenges to judicial authority. Yet Arendt's recounting portrays these moments differently: as moments of political action that, through challenging procedures, revealed truth. When we attend to Arendt's appreciation of the courtroom audience, an important tension in the text comes to light: namely, that Arendt's sympathy with the judges vis-à-vis the Israeli prosecution does not lead her to be *opposed* to the audience's dramatic resistance to the Court's procedural strictness. Rather, Arendt appreciates the Court *and* the audience's resistance to that Court. How should we read this double sympathy? We could read it as exemplary of the openness and flexibility necessary when addressing unprecedented crimes—an openness to both rule-deferent and rule-resistant approaches to the crimes at hand and the flexibility to affirm both when they help us see truth. This reading has some merit, but if we read Arendt in this way, then we seem to be confined to a choice between deferring to or resisting the rules,[48] between the rule and the exception[49]—a choice that does not accord with the complexity of the courtroom audience's actions in the trial as described by Arendt. While the audience resists legal constraints in these moments, they do so not on behalf of opposing law in general, but on behalf of *claiming* law—as embodied in the courtroom—as a site of truth. Rather than reflecting the need for a *choice* between rule-deferent or rule-challenging behavior, these moments may call attention to how law is beholden to political action that resists legal strictures. Indeed, as I will suggest in the next section, by returning to Arendt's call for an international tribunal, Arendt may not be asking us to choose from a menu of rule-resistant and rule-deferent behaviors, but rather may be calling on us to remember law's debt to initiatory, founding political action that law cannot control or predict.

ARENDT'S CALL FOR AN INTERNATIONAL TRIBUNAL: A "COULD HAVE BEEN" NARRATIVE

Arendt's call for an international tribunal is usually read as an outgrowth and fulfillment of her juridical approach to Eichmann's trial—specifically, as a call for a court that could do justice to Eichmann's crimes because it possesses the correct rule (crimes against humanity) and the correct jurisdiction (all of mankind). Arendt's call for such a court is certainly concerned in part with justice. Yet when we read Arendt's appeal to this court as a *solution* to the limits of the Eichmann trial in doing justice, we miss how she also portrays that court as a political problem—an institution that cannot exist and do its work unless it is generated through political action. Indeed, while Arendt argues that Eichmann's crimes against humanity "needed an international tribunal to do justice" to them (*EJ*, 269), her retroactive narrative of how this might have happened suggests that such a court could only have been founded through political demands and action.

Arendt's "might have been" narrative portrays justice in Eichmann's trial as a "lost cause" that could have been otherwise—that is, if Israel had called for an international tribunal after the Jerusalem Court handed down its verdict. Israel, she says, could have "waiv[ed] its right to carry out [Eichmann's] sentence once it had been handed down, in view of the unprecedented nature of the court's findings" (*EJ*, 269–270). Israel then, she says, could have gained "recourse to the United

Nations and demonstrated, with all the evidence at hand, that the need for an international criminal court was imperative, in view of these new crimes committed against mankind as a whole" (*EJ*, 270). Like the courtroom audience's shouted questions at Freudiger, Israel's call for an international court should have been theatrical: Israel should have " 'create[d] a wholesome disturbance,' by asking again and again just what it should do with this man whom it was holding prisoner" (Ibid.). Just as the theatrical questions in court solicited the attention of courtroom spectators, so also might Israel's theatrical questions have solicited a world public: Israel could have "*impressed on worldwide public opinion* the need for a permanent international criminal court" (my emphasis, Ibid.). Thus, like the courtroom audience Arendt describes, which resisted the compulsion of courtroom procedures and generated new possibilities of judgment, Arendt suggests that Israel's demands might have solicited a world public that resists the compulsion of existing institutional paths and generates a new legal possibility—a new court representing mankind.

Arendt's framing of justice via an international court as a "lost cause" invites the reader into an oblique temporal relationship with her call for an international court. The "might have been" character of her lost cause narrative portrays the lost cause of justice in Eichmann's case not as purely past (i.e., as something that simply did not happen), nor as purely something to be remedied by the future creation of an international court. Rather, this "might have been" narrative creates an alternative temporal trajectory that shoots off into another possible present—a present that is a mirror of the moment in which Arendt is writing, but with the crucial difference that (Israeli) political actors had (in this alternate present) demanded justice from an international court. Yet what changes in this "might have been" present is not necessarily the outcome of the trial—Arendt's "might have been" narrative makes no claims about whether an international court could or would actually have been established had Israel demanded it and called on world opinion in this way. Rather, what changes in Arendt's narrative is the presence of political demands and a solicitation of solidarity on behalf of justice.

Why foreground the importance of political action in concert in her "might have been" narrative, rather than the actual creation of an international court? One reason may be that Arendt aims to remind us that when (or if) we have an international court, that court will remain as indebted to political action and contestation as domestic courts—the need for political action on behalf of justice, in other words, does not disappear simply because a better institution has been created. Another reason may be, however, that Arendt is seeking to *solicit* and not just describe the kind of political action necessary to found a new court. Indeed, in staging her call for an international court as a "might have been" story, Arendt may be seeking to generate yearning for a "might have been" past that did not actually occur—a staging similar to what Arendt does in *On Revolution*, when she portrays the American past in a new (and fabulist) way in hopes of generating a different present and future.[50] Here, Arendt's narrative creates a longing for a "could have been" moment of international solidarity. In so doing, she addresses the public this past would have postulated—a world public that Arendt's appeal seeks, for a moment, to bring into being. Arendt herself supports this reading in the "Epilogue"—which she writes *after* the conclusion of the trial and punishment, and which, as she notes, "ceases to be simple reporting" (*EJ*, 287)—when she indicates the importance of future, rather than simply past, analysis and discussion of Eichmann's trial. She writes, "Hence, to the question most commonly asked about the Eichmann trial: What good does it do?, there is but one possible answer: It *will* do justice" (*EJ*, my emphasis, 253). For Arendt, Eichmann's trial is important not only as an exemplar of law's failure to do justice, but also as an event that, perhaps through her own recounting, could enable responsiveness—namely, the *political* work of soliciting a future world public that will demand better.

Arendt's appeal to an international court does not, then, have to be read as part of a juridical (moral-universal) approach to law, as Benhabib suggests, but may also be read as a criticism of that approach and an expression of an alternative approach: one that foregrounds law's indebtedness to politics and the importance of political solidarity on behalf of justice for its own sake. This distinction may seem small—since Arendt in any event is calling for an international court—but it has large stakes. Benhabib's reading focuses on the importance of an international court's fidelity to universal morality—a reading that casts political action as promising by virtue of its connection to moral norms (i.e., democratic iterations *of* such norms). By contrast, if we see Arendt's call for an international court as I have suggested—as displaying that court's dependence on political action—then we are pushed to attend to political action as constitutive of legal stability. Consequently, not moral norms, but activities of contestation and initiation that claim law in new ways or that found new institutions are in the forefront as the "grounds" of law—a foregrounding that reminds us of the import of engagement in such activities, even and *especially* when there is no concrete legal or moral referent by which they are guided.

Arendt's affirmation of law's dependence on political action suggests that her analysis of Eichmann's trial may point toward an *agonistic* (not juridical) understanding of law—that is, an understanding that sees political contestation and action as the condition of law's stabilizing force in human affairs.[51] In contrast to a juridical view of law, which may engender a sense of helplessness among citizens and legal actors when faced with new crimes, dangers, and rights abuses not captured by the standards that liberal and democratic thinkers advocate, an agonistic approach to law emphasizes law's dependence on that which juridical thinkers believe law must first regulate—political activities of contestation. While an agonistic approach to law does not thus offer a better standard to secure law's regulating function, it reveals a wider terrain of possibility for calling law to account and rendering it responsive to new crimes—that is, the terrain of political action, contestation, and the imaginative and creative power of people acting in concert. Certainly, people acting together can go astray, but so, too, can legal agents and institutions—and as Arendt warns us in *Eichmann in Jerusalem*, it is dangerous to assume that legal agents and not citizens are better agents of response to new dangers and problems.

Of course, this dependence of law on political action is not just promising; it is also a problem. The spontaneity and open-endedness of the political action that Arendt theorizes and calls for as an enabling condition of law leaves such action vulnerable to betrayal, and it is this openness to betrayal to which I suspect her juridical readers are reacting when they cast *Eichmann in Jerusalem* as primarily concerned with justice and standards of right. While Arendt theorizes law's deep dependence on political action in "Civil Disobedience,"[52] and *On Revolution*,[53] readers like Benhabib seem to want her to be saying in *Eichmann in Jerusalem* that at some point—perhaps at the point when crimes against humanity appear—law must be able to draw a line in the sand that politics does not touch, a line that Benhabib calls the "supreme crime against humanity," genocide.[54] This is an understandable yearning, but in casting *Eichmann in Jerusalem* as a juridical text, these readers obscure the importance of the human capacities to resist legal compulsion and to found new institutions, which Arendt sees as paramount in addressing new horrific crimes. For Arendt, *especially* at the moment when crimes against humanity appear, we must acknowledge law's indebtedness to political action. While the open-endedness and spontaneity of political action mean that it may go astray, it is this same open-endedness and spontaneity that make possible new legal institutions, as well as new ways of claiming law.

Given the risks that (unpredictable) political action poses to law and moral norms, it may be tempting to flee from these risks to the supposedly secure ground of law and procedure. Yet this supposedly secure ground is itself performatively produced—in court, as we have seen, through the actions of judges, prosecutors, witnesses, and the courtroom audience. Rather than papering over the tension between law and the political activities that sustain it, Arendt's example suggests that we should embrace the risky political claiming and contestation of law—an activity whose risks will not be resolved through legal regulation or moral norms, but rather can only be responded to through ongoing political action and engagement in our political-legal world.

PUBLIC OPINION AND PUBLIC SPIRIT

However, Arendt's publication of *Eichmann in Jerusalem* failed to produce the public she called for. Instead, her book solicited (and continues to solicit) a public that viewed *Eichmann in Jerusalem* as anti-Israel and, to some extent, even anti-Semitic. In response to this democratic failure, Arendt did not acknowledge that failure is an inevitable risk of democratic politics that demands further response and negotiation. Instead, she responded to her critics in a juridical register—framing some forms of contestation (such as her own) as "authentic," or exemplary of "true" democracy and the kind of independent judgment necessary to justice, and others (such as those of her critics) as inauthentic and detrimental to democracy and justice. For example, in response to Gershom Scholem's criticism of *Eichmann in Jerusalem*, such as his claim that Arendt "blur[red] the distinction between torturer and victim,"[55]

Arendt responds by claiming that Scholem's judgment was not properly formed:

> It is a pity that you did not read the book before the present cam-
> paign of misrepresentation against it go under way from the side
> of the Jewish "establishment" in Israel and America. There are,
> unfortunately, very few people who are able to withstand the
> influence of such campaigns. It seems to me highly unlikely that
> without being influenced you could possibly have misunderstood
> certain statements. *Public opinion, especially when it has been carefully
> manipulated, as in this case, is a very powerful thing.*[56]

Arendt's claim that Scholem's judgment is derivative and inauthentic is
not a legalistic one—as was the Jerusalem Court's juridical approach.
However, it works in a juridical register insofar as Arendt does not *only*
respond to Scholem's criticism substantively, but also through classify-
ing it as improperly formed in any case: she suggests that Scholem's
judgment, in order to *be* a true judgment, must work according to
proper criteria that he has here violated—specifically, by direct encounter with the text and without influence from "public opinion."

In her broader response to the controversy around her book, Arendt
portrays not just Scholem, but her critics in general, as forming improper
judgments insofar as they are influenced by public opinion. In reply to
a set of questions about *Eichmann in Jerusalem* from Samuel Grafton
(for an article in *Look* magazine that was never written or published),
Arendt, explicitly referencing her recently published *On Revolution*,
portrays "public opinion" in the controversy as a perverse imitation
of what she calls "authentic public spirit."[57] She draws specific attention in her answers to Grafton to a section of *On Revolution* where she
describes "public spirit" in terms of the revolutionaries' concern "with
the stability and durability of a purely secular, worldly realm"[58] that
is "constituted by an exchange of opinion between equals."[59] When
this durable public realm falls into decline—as Arendt suggests is the
case in contemporary politics—public opinion appears as a substitute
for public spirit, offering the solace of unanimity in the absence of a
durable public realm constituted by an exchange of diverse opinion.[60]
This substitute, however, ends up further deadening the possibility for
the exchange of opinions that could reconstitute the durable public
realm and perhaps hasten the emergence of true public spirit. This is

because, for Arendt, individuals are only able to form true opinions through encounter with the "multitude of opinions held by others":[61] "opinions are formed and tested in a process of exchange of opinion against opinion."[62] The "rule of public opinion" crushes the possibility of this process of testing because it dissolves contexts where diverse opinions are formulated and made known and, thus, where individuals can authentically form their own opinions through contestatory discussion with others. Consequently, in a society deferent to "public opinion," an individual's opinion is not his or her own, but instead reflects submission to the rule of the unanimous "nobody" of public opinion.

In *On Revolution*, Arendt examines how "public spirit" transformed into "public opinion" and identifies past and present resources and precedents that might enable a resurgence of "public spirit," capable of contesting the deference of the contemporary American public to "public opinion."[63] Similarly, in *Eichmann in Jerusalem*—where Arendt is worried about the problem of the Court's and the state's deference to a rule-bound approach to justice—Arendt fleshes out the reasons for this deference, substantively engages many of its proponents, and actively contests and offers alternatives to this vision of the trial. However, in response to the controversy over *Eichmann in Jerusalem*, Arendt does not deeply examine why or how public opinion dominates; nor does she offer resources for responding to what she clearly sees, in the public's response to her book, as a moment of democratic failure. Rather, she dismisses her critics' points as inauthentic and improper—and, excepting Scholem, as almost not worthy of response—and does not substantively examine, address, or contest their claims. In contrast, then, to the agonistic approach to law that we find in *Eichmann in Jerusalem*— which encourages attentiveness to how juridical approaches to law may dampen capacities for open-ended action that are necessary to encourage legal responsiveness to new crimes—Arendt's writings on the controversy over her book display a juridical approach to democracy: that is, an approach to democratic contestation that is focused on distinguishing between proper and improper forms of political action/ contestation and that encourages dismissal of, rather than engagement with, democratic actors who see things differently. This shift in perspective leads Arendt to be insufficiently attentive to the complex realities of contestation over her book—where critics ranged in their degree of sympathy for her position, as well as in their reasons for critique—and to paint her critics as a uniform mass, deferent to a "public opinion" that none of them actually created.

Given Arendt's worries about how the Court's juridical approach in *Eichmann in Jerusalem* left them unable to address the complex reality of the crimes they were trying to judge, why would she invoke a juridical distinction between proper and improper forms of contestation in her response to the Eichmann controversy that obscured the complicated reality of the debate? It may be that Arendt's dismissal of those who disagreed with her is her way of following the advice that she gave retrospectively to Clemenceau in *Origins* (discussed in the previous chapter): namely, to claim only those who agreed with her as the "true people," thus avoiding the "error" that she says Clemenceau made of confusing the people with the mob, an "error" that hastened his loss of faith in "the people" and his sense of the superiority of his own judgment.

Indeed, Arendt herself ties the two affairs (the Dreyfus Affair and the Eichmann controversy) together, both implicitly and directly. In a letter to Mary McCarthy, Arendt implicitly compares the "public opinion" at work during the Eichmann controversy to the "mob" of the Dreyfus Affair when she uses the language of "the mob" to describe the actions of her critics: "one can say that the mob—intellectual or otherwise—has been successfully mobilized."[64] Further and even more strikingly, in a July 20, 1963, letter to Jaspers, Arendt draws a direct comparison between the Eichmann controversy and the Dreyfus Affair. Arendt writes that "[i]t is quite instructive to see what can be achieved by manipulating public opinion and how many people, often on a high intellectual level, can be manipulated. Among the Jews themselves there are very many who retain their independent judgment, but the reactions have taken such a turn (with rabbis who preach from the pulpit) that a friend said it's like the time of the Dreyfus affair. Families are split down the middle!"[65] Just as her analysis of the Affair portrays it as a contest between the "people" and the "mob," so, too, here: public opinion stands in conflict with the true people of public spirit "who retain their independent judgment." Finally, just as Arendt portrays the true people during the Dreyfus Affair as a "heterogenous minority"[66] who were linked by nothing except their independently formed opinion on the Affair, so, too, does she portray those who agreed with her during the Eichmann controversy as united only by their judgments (not by identity): "By and large the Jews who support my book are just like me—Jews with no strong connections to the Jewish community, for whom, however, the fact of their Jewishness is not a matter of indifference."[67] Those who agree with her, in other words, exemplify public spirit. In contrast, her critics exemplify the taste for deception (image) and the desire to be ruled—or to defer to the opinions of others—that is characteristic of the mob and of public opinion.

Arendt's clean separation of judgment formed by public spirit (those who agree with her) from judgment formed by public opinion (those who do not) has the virtue of allowing her to retain her faith in "the people" and their ability to make independent judgments on behalf of justice.[68] Yet Arendt's framing of those who agreed with her as the public of "public spirit" also seems to obscure, or at least fail to foreground, the possibility for public change and transformation upon which she relies and for which she calls in *Eichmann in Jerusalem*—that is, that the "public opinion" of today can, if felicitously solicited, become the "public spirit" of tomorrow, that the nationally oriented publics of today can, if felicitously solicited, become part of a world public of tomorrow that will call for fuller justice for crimes against humanity. In other words, Arendt's affirmation of those who agree with her as the "true people" obscures how the justice and legal transformation for which she calls in *Eichmann in Jerusalem* may depend not on our ability to distinguish between the people and the mob—between public spirit and public opinion—but rather on resistance to juridical approaches to democracy that fatalistically assume that one part (or all) of the population is irrational and incapable of judgment.

I will suggest in the next section that Arendt herself offers resources for resisting this juridical approach to democracy, and for approaching the victory of public opinion as an occasion for responsiveness rather than resignation. Specifically, in her review of the fiction of Nathalie Sarraute, published at the height of the controversy over *Eichmann in Jerusalem* in the *New York Review of Books*, Arendt portrays the victory of public opinion as a political problem that does not call for resignation, but rather for response through practices of laughter and comedy. Such practices cast the supposed absoluteness and unanimity of public opinion into relief and make space for claims on behalf a plural "we."

COMEDY: INTERVENING IN THE "THEY"

In her review essay of Nathalie Sarraute's fiction published on March 5, 1964, Arendt suggests that the comedy of Sarraute's fiction—especially *The Golden Fruits*—allows the reader to laughingly acknowledge the distortive power of "the they" without succumbing to it. Arendt admired Sarraute, one of the originators (along with Alain Grille-Robert, Marguerite Duras, and others) of the French "New Novel" in the 1950s and 1960s.[69] In particular, Arendt admires what she calls Sarraute's two comic novels—*The Planetarium* and *The Golden Fruits*—which switched from a focus on the family (the site of her earlier novels) to "Society, which is 'artificial' in comparison to the family and even more artificial in this case as it is the society of the literary clique."[70] These novels, especially *The Golden Fruits*, inhabit the world of "the they." The characters of *The Planetarium*, Arendt writes, "are not true protagonists, but more like members of a chorus that has lost its protagonist, the almost accidentally chosen figures of the 'they.' "[71] Like the public in the realm of "public opinion," these protagonists defer to an authority that is itself nonexistent—an image of unanimity and conformity (and expertise), rather than actual authorities or rules.

Sarraute's *The Golden Fruits* concerns, as Arendt writes, "another book, a novel just published and called 'The Golden Fruits,' from its initial spectacular success to its quiet downfall into oblivion, and it ends with an outlook into the book's uncertain future."[72] We know nothing of the book, itself, but rather only see the dialogue of "the they" (along with the interior dialogue/thoughts of individuals that compose "the they"). Thus, "this is the story of Everybook that has the misfortune to fall into the hands of the literate Everybody, whose whispers and shouts last until Everything has been said."[73] One could say (although Arendt does not say it explicitly) that it is thus also the story of *Eichmann in Jerusalem*—told, however, in the narrative arc of success to failure, rather than in the narrative of the scandalous controversy over a book with a denouement into misunderstanding.

Arendt reads *The Golden Fruits* as a comedy because of its irony: that it reveals "the they" to be dependent or parasitic on the opposite of what it appears or claims to be. First, the book reveals the supposedly authoritative opinions of "the they" as the result not of actual judgment (formed through an exchange of diverse opinions), but rather of the attempt to maintain the *image* of authority—primarily through broad, mutual coercion of diverse individuals to hold the same opinion because "everyone" else holds it, too. Indeed, for Arendt, what makes the book so funny in part is the convincing depiction of familiar literary "types" and "talk" without any actual referent. Their behavior, in other words, is predictable *regardless* of the content of the novel, and Sarraute's novel reveals this predictability in sharp form:

> "[E]verybody is present: The critic; the *maître*: and the admiring ladies; 'the culprit' who once had 'fallen from grace' by offending impeccable taste, but has been 'disinfected long ago'; the husband who is suspected of not having discovered 'The Golden Fruits' by himself, but he has, he has, says his wife"—and we might add, once *The Golden Fruits* has fallen from favor, the same wife insists her husband always knew it wasn't any good—"the provincial who far from 'them' had found the novel full of platitudes (but it was done 'on purpose,' and he is convinced); the scholars ('heads heavy with learning') who, having grouped the dead 'according to category, lesser, average, great,' find a place for the newest arrival; even the doubter, 'mad, exalted creature who goes about the world, barefooted and in rages' disturbing its peace; even 'the foreigner, the pariah' (but 'you are one of us,' there 'can be no question of excluding you'). As they exhaust all aspects, all arguments and outdo each other with superlatives until they all know: 'There will be those who came before and those who came after 'The Golden Fruits'."[74]

Second, and connectedly, Arendt suggests that the book reveals the supposed expertise and absolute authority of "the they" as dependent on contingent, worldly concerns. Those intellectuals, scholars, and "pundits" who are supposed to be the most "inner-directed" are revealed as completely "outer-directed"—as being filled with meaning and importance from outside admiration and affirmation, rather than finding meaning in offering their independent judgment or opinion to the world.

In contrast to her sharp opposition of public opinion and public spirit in her writings on the Eichmann controversy, Arendt's review of Sarraute suggests that the comedic approach to "the they" reveals connections between "public opinion" (the realm of "the they") and individuals' desire for "public spirit." Specifically, Arendt argues that *The Golden Fruits* reveals that individuals are driven to embrace the opinion of "the they" out of a desire for its opposite, namely, for the true realm of public spirit where they could be acknowledged for their independent opinions and form those opinions in relation to others. She says that individuals are driven to defer to "the they" because they are "lonely": "Each one of them has come out of hell and is afraid of being returned there, remembering only too well how it was when he was still alone, a 'poor devil, obscure little fellow, unknown author,' always trying to be admitted and invariably beaten down."[75] The realm of "the they," in other words, feeds on and perverts the authentic human desire to be acknowledged, and to have one's opinions acknowledged and considered—the authentic desire that Arendt sees as finding a home in the durable public realm valued by authentic public spirit. In short, "public opinion" and "public spirit" are not only opposites, but also are entwined in individuals' desires for public discussion and exchange of opinions.

This diagnosis of entwinement in turn leads to a possibility occluded by Arendt's opposition between public opinion and public spirit that I discussed in the previous section: namely, that things could be and could have been otherwise, that the desires which lead individuals to "the they" are not dead ends for democracy, but may also lead them toward democratic solidarity. Indeed, Arendt suggests that Sarraute's comedic narration of "the they" reveals opportunities for democratic responsiveness to the oppressiveness of public opinion that might otherwise remain hidden. Arendt notes that "[s]hortly before the end" of *The Golden Fruits*, "Nathalie Sarraute turns from the 'they' and the 'I' to the 'we,' the old We of author and reader.[76] It is the reader who speaks: 'We are so frail and they so strong. Or perhaps. . . we, you and I, are the stronger, even now.' "[77] Here, Arendt suggests that the novel's comedic treatment of "the they" opens onto a new possibility: judgment not in the name of the (lonely) "I" or the (oppressive) "they," but in the name of the "We." This possibility seems to emerge through an acknowledgment of common oppression by "the they," which becomes an act of solidarity. The "we" of "We are so frail and they so strong" opens onto "perhaps. . . we, you and I, are the stronger, even now."

How does this passage happen—from the "I" versus "the they," to "We"? Likely through ironic laughter. Indeed, on Arendt's reading, the "we" here is the "we" of author and reader—that is, of Sarraute and ourselves, who have just jarringly seen the emptiness of "the they." We have shared, in other words, the experience of ironic laughter that Arendt, in an earlier essay, identifies with Lessing—the laughter that allows us to acknowledge reality without "selling one's soul" to it. In that essay, Arendt says that while "Lessing's kind of anger, reveals and exposes the world," "Lessing's kind of laughter in *Minna von Barnhelm* seeks to bring about reconciliation with the world."[78] For Arendt, laughter can reconcile us with things as they are, not as we would like them to be (via the lens of some ideology), because "[s]uch laughter helps one to find a place in the world, but ironically, which is to say, without selling one's soul to it."[79] Laughter, in other words, allows the laugher to feel grounded in the world—to locate oneself among a community of laughers, who are also acknowledging the reality revealed by our laughter. However, because one is laughing, one also occupies an ironic distance to the world that allows the laugher to not be overtaken (or ruled) by it.[80]

Arendt's review of Sarraute thus reveals the democratic failure of the rule of public opinion not as cause for resignation, as it appears in Arendt's own writings on the Eichmann controversy, but as an occasion for responsiveness through comedy and laughter. If we read Arendt's review of Sarraute's novels in terms of the victory of public opinion in the Eichmann controversy in particular, that victory no longer appears as the end of the story—as exemplifying the decline of democracy as such—but rather as a site that calls for comedic narration and a community of laughers that might reinvigorate our capacities for democratic solidarity (the plural "we") and independent judgment. These, of course, are the same democratic capacities to which Arendt appealed in *Eichmann in Jerusalem* on behalf of justice. Thus, while Arendt does not directly connect her review of Sarraute to *Eichmann in Jerusalem*, we might nonetheless read that review as offering a lost cause narrative of the public's response to *Eichmann in Jerusalem*—that is, as a victory of public opinion that could have been otherwise, that could have been rebuffed through a comedic and laughing response to "the they" and turned into an occasion for a plural "we" pursuing justice.

Of course, laughter and comedy may seem like ill-suited companions to Arendt's claims on behalf of justice in *Eichmann in Jerusalem*. Justice, after all, seems to call for seriousness and solemnity that display respect for the weightiness of the issues and human stakes involved—especially in a case like Eichmann's, which involves such terrible, unprecedented crimes. Yet I will suggest in the next section that Arendt's own embrace of laughter and comedy within *Eichmann in Jerusalem* may gesture toward the importance of challenging the centrality of seriousness and solemnity, and the respect for rules and precedents these comportments involve.

COMEDY AND JUSTICE

In her reply to Gunter Gauss's comment in a 1964 interview that many criticisms of *Eichmann in Jerusalem* "are based on the tone in which many passages are written," Arendt suggests that her ironic tone in the book is simply an expression of her (often laughing) judgment of Eichmann:

> Well, that is another matter. What can I say? Besides, I don't want to say anything. If people think that one can only write about these things in a solemn tone of voice.. . . Look, there are people who take it amiss—and I can understand that in a sense—that, for instance, I can still laugh. But I was really of the opinion that Eichmann was a buffoon. I'll tell you this: I read the transcript of his police investigation, thirty-six hundred pages, read it, and read it very carefully, and I do not know how many times I laughed— laughed out loud! People took this reaction in a bad way. I cannot do anything about that. But I know one thing: Three minutes before certain death, I probably still would laugh. And that, they say, is the tone of voice. That the tone of voice is predominantly ironic is completely true. The tone of voice in this case is really the person. When people reproach me with accusing the Jewish people, that is a malignant lie and propaganda and nothing else. The tone of voice, however, is an objection against me personally. And I cannot do anything about that.[81]

When Gauss replies, "You are prepared to bear that?" Arendt says, "Yes, willingly. What is one to do? I cannot say to people: You misunderstand me, and in truth this or that is going on in my heart. That's ridiculous."[82] Arendt thus frames her laughter at Eichmann as a marker

of the independence of her judgment, but also—as in her discussion
of Lessing—as a way of reconciling herself to the reality of a person
(Eichmann) who otherwise seems incomprehensible.

Within *Eichmann in Jerusalem*, Arendt references many aspects of
the trial as comedic.[83] However, as Yasco Horsman argues, "what
Arendt singles out as the main source of humor during the trial" is
"Eichmann's peculiar use of language, more precisely his incapacity to
speak in terms other than banalities or clichés"[84]—a use of language
that exemplifies Eichmann's "thoughtlessness." For example, in only
one of the many instances when Arendt refers to the comedic aspects
of Eichmann's thoughtlessness, she says that "[t]he German text of the
taped police examination, conducted from May 29, 1960, to January
17, 1961, each page corrected and approved by Eichmann, constitutes
a veritable gold mine for a psychologist—provided he is wise enough
to understand that *the horrible can be not only ludicrous but outright funny*"
(my emphasis, *EJ*, 48).[85] Arendt implies that "the horrible" is "outright
funny" here because of the incongruity between the sheer emptiness
of a man, Eichmann, and the massive scale of his crimes. For Arendt,
this "macabre humor" reaches its pitch when we see the death camps
through Eichmann's eyes—when he tells a story, for example, of how
he went to try to help a Jewish functionary with whom he had worked
who had been sent to Auschwitz.[86] Eichmann says to him, "Well, my
dear old friend, we certainly got it! What rotten luck!" (*EJ*, 51) and
then asks Hoss to get him a lighter workload (clearing a path of gravel).
Then to his Jewish functionary "friend," Eichmann says,

> "'Will that be all right, Mr. Storfer? Will that suit you?'
> Whereupon he was very pleased, and we shook hands, and then
> he was given the broom and sat down on his bench. It was a great
> inner joy to me that I could at least see the man with whom I had
> worked for so many long years, and that we could speak with each
> other." Six weeks after this normal human encounter, Storfer was
> dead—not gassed, apparently, but shot. (*EJ*, 51)

Why does Arendt frame this horrible anecdote for the reader as "macabre comedy"? Perhaps because it allows her to highlight how her own
attempt to grapple with the mismatch between Eichmann's person
and his deeds was made possible by a willingness to encounter him
in the register of comedy. Whereas a comportment of solemnity may

have simply led Arendt to see Eichmann's story as another instance of his evil disposition—thinking he was "helping" Storfer when in fact he was ensuring his death—her willingness to laugh at the horror of Eichmann's story allows her to grapple with the incongruity contained therein: namely, between Eichmann's use of ordinary workplace language and euphemisms—seeming to think that he was offering assistance to a subordinate to lessen his workload—and the extraordinary, horrific situation in reference to which he uses them, where the question of whether or not Mr. Storfer could have a lighter workload was jarringly irrelevant to the system of mass execution that stared Eichmann in the face, but that he failed to truly see and judge.

Horsman argues that we should read Arendt's laughter at these moments as "testif[ying] to the breakdown of her capacity to understand, which occurs when Eichmann's banality stares her, as he puts it, in the face."[87] In other words, Arendt's laughter identifies, but cannot adequately describe or comprehend "a moment of *nonunderstanding*, which occurs precisely when we seek to apply our faculty of judgment and are confronted with its failure."[88] For Horsman, then, Arendt's laughing, ironic tone serves as a visceral marker of her experience of the shocking character of Eichmann's deeds and person—a shocking character that cannot be fully comprehended, but only marked:

> Because the stumbling can be experienced only in the first person, every attempt at explaining it would necessarily entail an explaining away of its shocking impact. The lesson of the trial, I would therefore argue, comes across though [*sic*] her ironical tone. It is performed through the "laughter" that permeates her book. This laughter, which scandalized her critics, is an attempt to render the *skandala* at the heart of the trial without resolving its scandalizing nature.[89]

Horsman's reading suggests that Arendt's laughter and ironical tone can be rendered compatible, rather than in a dissonant relation, with justice because laughter marks that which exceeds our attempts to bring formal legal or cognitive closure to the event and which still cries out for justice. For Horsman, this means that Arendt's laughter must be a purely individual, or subjective experience—as Felman reads K-Zetnik's fainting—that serves as a marker of a failure of closure, but that cannot be fully shared with or communicated to others. Indeed,

Horsman argues that the "stumbling block" of Eichmann's "banality of evil"—which "makes it impossible to understand him in a human way "—cannot be "phrased in the third person, without explaining away the stupefying and thought-defying aspect of it."[90] Rather, "the stumbling block can be experienced only in the first person, every attempt at explaining it would necessarily entail an explaining away of its shocking impact."[91] Thus, all we can do, when we experience Arendt's first-person experience, is to also experience it that way ourselves, without being able to put it into a third-person formulation. For Horsman, Arendt's laughter interrupts, but it does not constitute anew.

Yet Horsman's split between the third and first person leaves out a crucial possibility: the possibility of responding to Arendt's laughter neither in the first or third person (the "I" or the "they"), but in the register of the "we"—that is, in the register of solidarity. If Lessing's ironic laughter allows us to acknowledge reality without forgoing judgment of it, then perhaps Arendt's ironic laughter during the Eichmann trial opens a possibility of acknowledging the (almost incomprehensible) reality of Eichmann's deeds and "thoughtlessness," while also enabling an opening for independent judgment and solidarity—perhaps in the register of the "world public" discussed earlier. In other words, Arendt's ironic laughter may reveal the reality of Eichmann's deeds in such a way that a possibility of a "we" opens up where there was not one before—namely, in the claim for justice, for a new institution (an international court) that would adequately address "crimes against humanity."

Of course, laughter does not always enable the unsettling of the "they" and the formation of a new "we"—a plural "we" of public spirit. It may also reinforce the power of "the they" and dissolve attempts to form a "we." Arendt herself notes an example of this kind of laughter in her introduction to Bernd Naumann's *Auschwitz*—a report on the Frankfurt trial of lower level Nazi guards at Auschwitz in 1964. There, Arendt notes the truthful statement of the prosecution that *"The majority of the German people do not want to conduct any more trials against the Nazi criminals"*[92] and she says that "[a]mong the many awful truths with which this book confronts us is the perplexing fact that German public opinion in this matter was able to survive the revelations of the Auschwitz trial."[93] For Arendt, this climate of public opinion—which insisted on the importance of Germans "stick[ing] together"—was "manifest in the behavior of the defendants—*in their laughing, smiling, smirking impertinence toward prosecution and witnesses*, their lack of respect for the court, their 'disdainful and threatening' glances toward the public in the rare instances when gasps of horror were heard. Only once does one hear a lonely voice shouting back, Why don't you kill him and get it over with?"[94] In this scene, the predictable, disciplinary laughter of the defendants reflects and shores up the power of "the they," leaving the voice of resistance a lonely "I" rather than a potential "we."

Laughter, then—like law, and like politics—has an ambiguous relationship with justice. On the one hand, ironic laughter can unsettle the power of rule-deferent judgment—according to legal rules, or in deference to the "they"—and allow us to grapple with truth in the company of a community of other laughers with whom we may claim solidarity on behalf of justice. Yet on the other hand, laughter can reinforce the power of "the they" on behalf of injustice. Arendt's ambivalent portrayal of laughter thus does not direct us to try to engage in a correct form of laughter,[95] nor to spark such a correct form of laughter in an audience—an attempt which, like other appeals to publics, is destined to always at least partially go awry—but rather may encourage us to be attuned to the possibility of laughter's capacity to reveal truth and to help us reconcile ourselves with reality, as well as its possible generation of a "we" on behalf of justice. That is, Arendt's comments on laughter and comedy gesture toward the importance of cultivating a sensibility where we see plural forms of democratic receptivity—laughter as well as seriousness and solemnity—as opening avenues for political solidarity on behalf of justice.

To return to and reframe the agonistic understanding of law that I drew out of *Eichmann in Jerusalem*, we might say that law's stability and responsiveness depends not only on agonistic contestation of its rules, standards, and institutions, but also on cultivating diverse forms of democratic receptivity to democratic failure—for example, to not only view solemnity, mourning, and despair as appropriate responses to failure and injustice, but also comedy and laughter. Indeed, Arendt's own laughter during the Eichmann trial may have allowed her to grapple with an incongruity between Eichmann and his crimes that approaching him via a comportment of a solemnity, with a respect for rules and precedent, might have obscured. Through pluralizing our understanding of "proper" democratic comportments to failure, democratic actors and theorists might be better able to see supposed democratic successes or achievements as containing aspects of failure, and to see democratic goods in supposed moments of failure. A public that is able to see laughter, as well as seriousness, as an appropriate democratic comportment vis-à-vis justice may be better equipped to seek justice in new, ever-changing circumstances, where we will be confronted with new crimes, and where we must demand new forms of justice.

TOWARD A
DEMOCRATIC
CONCEPTION OF
JUSTICE

Put the car away; when life fails,
What's the good of going to Wales?
Here am I, here are you:
But what does it mean? What are we going to do?
—W. H. Auden, "It's No Use Raising a Shout"

In the past four chapters, I have developed an understanding of lost cause narratives as offering productive reformulations of democratic failure—framing them as occasions for responsiveness rather than resignation, as democratic failings (weaknesses) rather than failures of democracy (fatal flaws). I have suggested that lost cause narratives are importantly distinct from fatalistic narratives of democratic failure that tend to dominate political theory and practice. Where fatalistic narratives portray democratic failure as revealing the (possible) failure of democracy as such and call for civic deference to elites and rules, lost cause narratives portray democratic failure as a contingent event that could have been otherwise. By emphasizing how things could have been different in past democratic failures, lost cause narratives suggest that the future is similarly contingent, and they appeal to a belated public that could seek justice for the past and in the present. Rather than calling the demos to defer to rules or experts for the sake of its survival, lost cause narratives call for the demos to transform its character, habits, self-understandings, and/or tastes so as to be more capable of acknowledging and responding to its own failures, past, present, and future.

Yet I have also shown how the politics of lost causes is vulnerable to fatalist narration or reception—how Burke, Zola, and Arendt all fall prey to the temptation to despair of democracy altogether and to play the expert to the mob. In this sense, the lost cause narratives that I have examined do not point toward excising fatalism from democracy, since such an attempt would simply obscure its periodic resurgence. Instead, they resituate fatalism as a persistent democratic temptation to which we must be alert. While democratic failure may always tempt us to despair of democracy and to turn to rules or elites (perhaps to ourselves as elites), the politics of lost causes foregrounds the dangers of such submissiveness (and the elite rule that it supports) and calls for more diffuse democratic agency, practices of solidarity, and collective action.

In short, the politics of lost causes calls for a democratic conception of justice: that is, a conception focused on democratic resistance to persistent injustice, not one focused on making rules to assure justice. The latter is important, but it is not sufficient to democratic needs. Democratic resistance to injustice may involve (as it does in the writings of Burke, Zola, and Arendt) calls for better rules, but such a conception is aware of the limitations of rules as solutions to the problem of justice. Thus, a democratic conception of justice decenters rule-making, focusing instead on the democratic political practices that sustain, chasten, challenge, or defer to those rules. In particular, such a conception highlights the import of resisting rule-deferent habits in favor of a more active, agentive relation to law that may in some instances call for deference to or even active support of law, but which may also demand collective resistance to rules, or to legal officials' use and interpretation of those rules.

In the remainder of the conclusion, I further develop this democratic conception of justice in three ways. First, I discuss the particular form of democratic agency called for by lost cause narratives: the belated public. Second, I show how the sensibility cultivated by the politics of lost causes—an agonistic sensibility toward failure—may re-orient us to contemporary failures as occasions for action, not resignation. In this part of the chapter, I focus on what I argue is a contemporary public trials moment: the trials (or lack thereof) for detainees accused of terrorist activities, in particular, for Khalid Sheikh Mohammed. Finally, I discuss an "art of losing causes" that may enable democratic political actors to resist the temptation to democratic fatalism.

THE BELATED PUBLIC

The lost cause narratives that I examine all solicit a belated public as the animating figure of the pursuit of democratic justice—that is, a public called to seek justice for a cause that is lost and, in so doing, to address contemporary injustices, as well. In this section, I unpack this somewhat enigmatic figure of democratic agency, showing that the solicitation of a belated public can be heard in at least two ways: as calling a public to address the continued presence of past injustice *and/or* as calling a public to acknowledge the belatedness, and hence insufficiency, of all attempts to do full justice. Yet in both these instances, the solicitation of a belated public reminds us of the import of democratic action that does not (and perhaps cannot) arrive in time, to forestall injustice and assure justice. Belated publics create chains and webs of resistance to injustice that forge contexts for continued political action on behalf of justice.

When lost cause narratives solicit a belated public, they are in part calling that public to attend to the continued persistence in the present of a particular form of (seemingly) past injustice. Burke's writings on the Hastings impeachment call a future public to attend to and resist imperial injustice that persists in their present. Zola's writings on the Dreyfus Affair solicit a public that would address the perseverance of anti-Semitism into the present. Arendt's writings on the Eichmann trial press us to address the continued failure to adequately address crimes against humanity. These narratives of the past are political acts that rejuvenate democratic responses to past injustice. Lawrie Balfour makes a similar argument about W. E. B. DuBois in her recent book, *Democracy's Reconstruction*. Specifically, Balfour argues that the work of DuBois is valuable because it counters the contemporary tendency to memorialize past injustice at the expense of addressing present injustice: "Du Bois's scathing indictment of his contemporaries and predecessors who rushed to locate slavery as 'the past' just as neo-slavery was on the rise warns against a similar impulse to assert the inauguration of a "postracial" era and unsettles the view that appeals for redress of racial injustice are exclusively backward-looking."[1] In other words, the re-narration of the past as unfinished, as still unfolding its legacy in our present, is one important way of resisting triumphalist narratives of a "postracial" era that insist that racial injustice is wholly in the past. For Balfour, DuBois is an exemplary narrator of this "present-past" because his "reworking of received historical narratives. . . reminds us that the constitution of the past is itself a political question."[2] Similarly, in their focus on the failure to fully assure justice to imperial oppression, anti-Semitism, and crimes against humanity, the lost cause narratives I examine here re-politicize them to present readers with issues that remain unfinished, that persist and require response through democratic action.

In addition to calling future publics to address the persistence of past injustice in the present, however, lost cause narratives, similar to the writings of Balfour's DuBois, also call a belated public to acknowledge and address the wrongs of dominant state and collective narratives that fail to capture and respond to injustice. In this sense, lost cause narratives are similar to, but ultimately are distinct from, "the project of critique," as Wendy Brown has recently described it. Brown argues that the project of critique consists in "set[ting] the times right again by discerning and repairing a tear in justice through practices that are themselves exemplary of the justice that has been rent."[3] This is certainly one aspect of lost cause narratives' calls to a belated public: these narratives enact forms of resistance that serve as enabling precedents for the belated public they solicit. Yet where Brown argues that critique is incited by and "engages" moments of political crisis—moments when there is "a rupture in a political imaginary,"[4] when "the times are unhinged, running off course," when "time itself lacks its capacity to contain us and conjoin us"[5]—the import of lost cause narratives lies in their claim that there *is* a tear in justice that calls for response. In other words, lost cause narratives do not respond to a crisis that everyone already acknowledges, but rather *claim* there is crisis (hitherto unacknowledged or in dispute): framing Britain's government in India as a national crisis, rather than a successful imperial project; framing France's crisis during the Dreyfus Affair to be one of its own ideals rather than an alien intrusion; framing the Eichmann trial as revealing an international crisis of how to do justice to crimes against humanity; and so on. Lost cause narratives do not simply attempt to repair a tear in time; they also claim a disjuncture of time, a rip in collective self-understandings and collective navigation.

Lost cause narratives thus call the belated public not only to address the persistence of injustice, but also to dwell in this rip in collective time on behalf of orienting the polity in a new direction. Indeed, if the belated public responded to past injustice through the terms of dominant narratives—as Balfour argues that many contemporary "apologies" for slavery do when they position its injustice in the past— that public would simply cover over the injustice again. Or to put the point differently, the public would no longer be belated, since it would assume that it could (finally) be on time, that it could adequately and fully address the injustice done. This is precisely what lost cause narratives resist when they criticize public judgments and actions that defer to dominant narratives and laws. In this sense, lost cause narratives try to call belated publics into being, in the hope that they will not only address the persistence of injustice, but also, through re-occupying the rip in collective understandings in the past, record the insufficiency of present collective understandings and laws.

Belated public action is thus animated by two demands that may stand in tension with each other. On the one hand, the belated public must address the persistence of past injustice, perhaps through turning to the state and courts as potential allies. On the other hand, the belated public is called to be alert to the insufficiencies of, and injustices sanctioned by, state and legal narratives of justice. We can find an example of this tension in Arendt's writings on the Eichmann trial, where both she and (as she notes in *Eichmann in Jerusalem*) the Israeli prosecutor respond to the problem of justice in the Eichmann trial through addressing themselves, at the same time, to Zola's diagnosis of injustice during the Dreyfus Affair. She notes that the prosecutor, Hausner, invokes "J'Accuse!" in his opening speech during the trial on behalf of all the victims of the Holocaust who cannot utter it themselves. Hausner thus frames Eichmann's trial as a successor instance to the Dreyfus Affair—a moment when Jews will be able to utter

"J'Accuse!" themselves and secure the justice (here, against Eichmann) that was never fully done in the Dreyfus Affair. Zola's call for justice in the Dreyfus Affair—his solicitation of a belated public—is here fulfilled by Hausner, who claims to be able to find justice for suffering Jews in a formal court of law, which was not achieved for Dreyfus.

Arendt, however, claims that Hausner's invocation of Zola is not convincing because Hausner misunderstands—or at least partially misunderstands—the nature of Zola's invocation of "J'Accuse!" For Arendt, the reason that Zola's "J'Accuse!" has become a paradigmatic demand for justice is that it was uttered *not* by an agent of the state, but by someone who was forced, due to the insufficiencies of the state, to take the law into his own hands in order to restore law to the project of justice. Hausner, in other words, mishears Zola's "J'Accuse!" as a call to *complete* Zola's attempt to achieve justice through the state, rather than as a form of resistance to the state's claim to be the bearer of justice in Dreyfus's case. Hausner's interpretation is not unreasonable. The state did fail in the Dreyfus case, and Hausner may have thought that to do better in this case, the state would have to succeed. Yet Arendt sees things differently. Inhabiting the moment of democratic failure diagnosed by Zola and the tear in collective self-understanding that it enacts, Arendt argues that a more convincing exemplar of a "J'Accuse!" moment lies in the Shalom Schwartzbard trial in 1927, where Schwartzbard was charged with shooting a Ukrainian leader responsible for mass pogroms, but whom the state refused to bring to justice. Schwartzbard immediately turned himself in to stand trial (as Zola offered himself up for a libel trial)—thus signaling that his act was not aimed at simply breaking the law, but also at *restoring* and at the same time *transforming* the law through the verdict of his peers on his act. So, Arendt says, "the J'accuse, so indispensable from the viewpoint of the victim, sounds, of course, much more convincing in the mouth of a man who has been forced to take the law into his own hands than in the voice of a government-appointed agent who risks nothing" (*EJ*, 266). In the voice of Hausner, the "J'Accuse!" sounds to Arendt like an attempt to mask the exercise of state-building happening in the trial by portraying that state as still a victim, an heir of Zola, unable to have its claims heard in court. Yet in the Eichmann trial, the court is hearing the state and the state has built the court. Thus, for Arendt, the Eichmann trial has not finally fulfilled Zola's demand for justice, but rather stages again the need for a belated public to resist state narratives of justice done—both during the Dreyfus Affair, and to Eichmann's "crimes against humanity."

In this exchange that Arendt creates between herself, Hausner, Schwartzbard, and Zola, "J'Accuse!" appears as democratically important not only or primarily in terms of its concrete results (which were ambivalent), but also insofar as it offers an exemplary call to a future, belated public to address the injustice done during the Dreyfus Affair. Yet Hausner and Arendt hear this call differently. Hausner hears it as a call to a state that only just came into being in time to do justice for a people historically wronged by unjust states. For Arendt, as I read her, Hausner's claim that he—and the state of Israel—can finally be "on time" in doing justice to Eichmann masks the way in which the pursuit of full justice may always be belated, insofar as it is agonistically related to the dominant categories and narratives that frame our understanding of timeliness. Or to put the point differently, where Hausner sees Zola's "J'Accuse!" as revealing the continued presence of past injustice, Arendt sees it as calling us to inhabit a more general agonistic sensibility toward dominant claims of democratic success and failure, as well as toward the collective narratives that structure those distinctions.

Their differences matter, but Arendt and Hausner are both right: Zola's solicitation to a belated public calls us in both ways. To hear Zola only as calling us to inhabit an agonistic relationship with existing standards, laws, and values would obscure how he also calls to address the continued presence of past injustice—of anti-Semitism and military illegal treatment of detainees, among others. Yet, at the same time, to see Zola as *only* drawing attention to the continued presence of past injustice obscures how attempts to secure justice for Jews may partake of the same strategies used by the French state that Zola accused of injustice—namely, the mythical claim to be on the side of justice at the cost of neglecting truth and, hence, failing to do full justice (which is precisely Arendt's critique of the Eichmann trial).

Lost cause narratives, then, call a belated public to remedy or respond to a particular persistent injustice, but they also call that belated public to relate to narratives of democratic success and failure agonistically— to see them as contestable, contingent, insufficient, and perhaps even implicated in the wrongs they purport to address. Attending to the (unfinished) chain of responsiveness and solicitations to belated publics staged in lost cause narratives shifts our theoretical focus: moving attention away from the project of assessing outcomes and pressing us instead toward the task of identifying the meaningfulness of belated democratic action that may not attain the outcome it seeks. If, as Jason Frank argues, the prospective orientation of democratic claims made in the future perfect (claims that "it will have been"), cultivates an "orientation enlivened by a sensitivity to the unanticipated and emergent,"[6] then the "could have been" claims of lost cause narratives cultivate an orientation animated by regard for the significance of belated political action, demands, and claims-making—action that comes too late and can never fully assure the justice it seeks. Such an orientation reveals democratic action as important not just as an outcome-achieving, but also as a meaning-making, practice: a practice of responsiveness on behalf of goods that might never be fully achieved, but that still creates meaning and the conditions for the possible birth of other belated publics in the future.

In the next part of the conclusion, I make an argument for the contemporary import of the re-orientation to democratic failure offered by lost cause narratives by discussing it in relation to the trial(s) of Khalid Sheik Mohammed. Examining the debates surrounding the trial through the double lens (reparative *and* agonistic) offered by lost cause narratives, I make a case for seeing the Mohammed trial as a public trials moment—that is, a moment when both law and the people have failed to assure justice. This reframing in turn opens up alternative possibilities for democratic responsiveness to this failure—some of which have been pursued by contemporary public intellectuals, such as David Cole and Slavoj Zizek. However, I argue that their framings of the trial insufficiently highlight the import of democratic support and action—both in the failure to assure justice, and in possible narratives of how it might have been otherwise. In contrast, I find in the recent film *Zero Dark Thirty* a compelling lost cause narrative of the American treatment of detainees. *Zero Dark Thirty*, I argue, reveals the contingency and contestability of our post-9/11 approach to terrorism *and* diagnoses a tear in our collective self-understanding that it also calls on us to inhabit on behalf of re-orienting ourselves for the future.

THE TRIAL(S) OF KHALID SHEIKH MOHAMMED AS PUBLIC TRIAL

On November 13, 2009, Eric Holder held a press conference to announce that he would pursue indictments against Khalid Sheikh Mohammed, the alleged "mastermind" of the 9/11 attacks, and his co-conspirators in federal court in Manhattan. Holder said, "After eight years of delay, those allegedly responsible for the attacks of September 11 will finally face justice. They will be brought to New York—to *New York*—to answer for their alleged crimes in a courthouse just blocks away from where the twin towers once stood."[7] While Holder did not directly refer to Bush-era policies for detaining and trying detainees, he did stress the importance of following legal procedure even when dealing with devastating crimes. Holder said, "For over 200 years, our nation has relied on a faithful adherence to the rule of law to bring criminals to justice and provide accountability to victims. Once again, we will ask our legal system. . . to rise to that challenge. I am confident that it will answer the call of fairness with justice."[8] Holder's call to finally do justice to Mohammed, in other words, was also an attempt to restore the rule of law in the United States.

Conservative critics immediately lambasted the plan, arguing that federal courts were inappropriate venues to try "enemy combatants."[9] Writers such as Andrew McCarthy and William Shawcross defended the Bush-era argument that some detainees are simply not subject to *any* legal protections, due to their status as "unlawful enemy combatants."[10] For these critics, alleged terrorists should not be treated as criminals entitled to legal rights, but instead as sources of information that might prevent future attacks. In the words of Shawcross, "[c]riminal justice is reactive, fighting terrorism is proactive. Intelligence—information—is the most important goal."[11]

Holder's critics won this argument. Khalid Sheikh Mohammed will undergo trial in a Guantanamo military commission—a less public venue with less legal protection and more active censorship of the proceedings than would have been possible in a federal court. How should we view this failure to try Khalid Sheikh Mohammed in federal court? The arguments of Holder and his conservative critics frame Mohammed's trial as exemplifying a conflict between the rule of law and exigency. In this framing, the failure to try Mohammed in federal court looks like a victory for a politics of emergency over a politics of law—a victory that calls (if you support the conservative narrative) for further deference to military elites or (if you support Holder's narrative) for further attempts to bring military commissions back under the purview of the "normal" rule of law. This view of the Mohammed trial and its stakes reiterates some of the key issues in debates over the War on Terror, but it also seems to force us into a false choice between law and "decisionism" that obscures the shortcomings of dominant narratives of Mohammed's trial and, in turn, hinders us from exploring alternative forms of responsiveness to the trial. In contrast, if we approach the trial via the double—reparative and agonistic—lens offered by lost cause narratives, we will be better equipped to attend to the insufficiencies of both conservative and liberal views of the trial and to identify alternative possibilities for political response. First, the agonistic sensibility cultivated by lost cause narratives immediately calls us to question the sufficiency of the two narratives operating in the debate: on the one hand, the conservative narrative of exigency, in which law must be subordinated in times of emergency to the decisions of military experts; and, on the other hand, Holder's narratives of the trial as a forum for redressing the injustices of the Bush era and reasserting the rule of law.

Conservatives' framing of the trial in the context of a narrative of emergency demands deference to the elites who claim to be able to save our democracy from terrorist violence. Putting the survival and security of the United States at the center of their narrative, conservatives appear to render their claims uncontestable—that is, since contesting them would appear to threaten our very survival. Yet when put in the context of the lost cause narratives examined here, this conservative narrative appears more contestable. Specifically, the narrative of emergency appears as only the latest instance of elite assertions of exigency that seek to cultivate popular deference on behalf of releasing elites from legal and popular accountability. Like Hastings in the eighteenth century and the French Army officers of the Dreyfus Affair, Holder's critics argue that exigency demands that military and paramilitary officers be less constrained, or unconstrained, by law. The problem with these claims, as diagnosed by Burke and Zola, is twofold. First, they serve as cover for aggrandizement and scapegoating, which ultimately undermines the rule of law, freedom, and equality that they claim to preserve. Second, they cultivate a politics of deference to elites that leaves citizens less able to resist injustice in the future.

In this context, and from a perspective concerned with reparation for past injustice, Holder's attempt to try Mohammed in federal court appears as an important belated response to injustice: an attempt to redress the broad range of injustices done by the Bush (and now Obama) administration in the name of exigency, as well as past military attempts to evade legal accountability more generally. In the trial of Mohammed, in other words, Holder was attempting to finally be "on time" in doing justice to military detainees, and in resisting military unaccountability as such. Yet if Holder enacted one important belated response to injustice—attempting to redress the presence of supposedly past injustice—lost cause narratives also call us to relate to Holder's state-based narrative of justice agonistically, to interrogate its adequacy in seeking justice, as well. That is, even if deferring to courts may have been (as Holder says) a boon for justice in this instance, might Holder's narrative of justice, and the role of law in achieving it, also be complicit in the wrongs that he claims to be addressing? Indeed, while Holder's federal trial would have symbolically reasserted the rule of law over Bush-era policies based in claims of exigency, this symbolic reassertion likely would have come at the cost of addressing the use of torture and other illegal, coercive interrogation techniques on Khalid Sheikh Mohammed and his co-conspirators. Holder claimed in his press conference that he had assembled a case against Mohammed that did not depend at all on information extracted through torture or other coercive techniques. This strategy could have publicly delivered a guilty verdict according to law—surely an improvement on the secretive, more legally lax military commissions. Yet this very obfuscation of the torture of Mohammed—this fantastical image of America treating him only according to law—would have threatened to symbolically reinstate a rule of law that remains beholden to, and complicit in, practices of illegal torture that it claims to regulate and transcend.[12]

It is not surprising that Holder (and Obama) would seek to avoid, rather than address, these practices of torture. After all, the enmeshment of the rule of law that Holder sought to save in illegal practices of torture would seem to raise the specter of arbitrariness that he was trying to defeat. Put differently, from Holder's (and the courts') perspective, justice can only be assured if law is impartial, if it is not implicated in the wrongs it must address. Yet what if we viewed law's implication in torture from the standpoint of a *democratic* conception of justice? That is, what if we viewed justice as something that can never be fully assured through rule-making, but that always also demands democratic resistance to persistent injustice? From this perspective, diagnosing the likely failure of the courts to fully address the torture and illegal interrogation techniques done to Mohammed and others— an injustice not only to Mohammed, but also a broader social injustice that threatens the rule of law and citizens' rights in general—appears not as a threat to, but an integral part of, the project of justice.

The importance of popular action in the pursuit of justice has been generally obscured in law/exigency framings that operate according to fatalistic reasoning: presenting justice or success in Mohammed's trial as only possible if military officials or courts make the decisions. In contrast, an approach informed by lost cause narratives foregrounds the import of popular challenges to injustice and identifies possible practices or sites through which such challenges might emerge. For example, we might do better (if not full) justice to Mohammed—and set a better precedent for future judgments of detainees—if the United States more forthrightly acknowledges and addresses its own practices of torture, perhaps through the creation of a truth commission analogous to those established in situations of transitional justice. Such a commission would make more room for democratic (not just elite or legal) responsiveness to Bush era practices of torture *and* would create a space to address democratic complicity in those practices. Of course, elites would never create such a commission if they were not pressured to do so. The people would have to demand it and, more generally, to demand justice in addressing illegal, criminal treatment of detainees— a demand that so far has been lacking. The Mohammed trial, in other words, represents not just a moment of legal failure, but of democratic failure—a moment when not only law, but also the people have failed to assure justice.

Attending to the insufficiencies of liberal and conservative narratives while also foregrounding the import of popular action and demands-making (which has thus far been lacking), my analysis reframes the Mohammed trial as not simply presenting a victory of exigency over law—a framing that seems to force liberal democrats to simply call for more law as an antidote to "decisionism." Rather, the Mohammed trial appears as moment of democratic failure that cannot be fully addressed by law, and that demands response by a people who also bear some measure of responsibility for their failure thus far to demand justice and accountability. In turn, narrated in this way, that event looks less like a dead end for democracy or a harbinger of democracy's failure as such—a moment of legal failure that simply must be hidden in order for democracy and the rule of law to regain traction—and more like a failure that calls out for, and demands, diffuse democratic response and action.

Contemporary commentators on the Mohammed trial have largely operated within the law-exigency framework established by Holder and his critics. However, a few have offered alternative narrations that reveal possibilities for democratic action. One such important alternative narration can be found in the work of the incisive and prolific critic of the Bush (and now Obama) administration, David Cole. In his writings on the Mohammed trial at the time of Holder's announcement, Cole uncritically affirms Holder's decision as correct.[13] Yet Cole later argues that *any* trial of Mohammed will result in a failure of justice if American practices of torture and rendition (and other illegal practices) are not addressed and officials are not called to account for their part in authorizing them. In his introduction to a collection of the memos by John Yoo and others in the Office of Legal Counsel authorizing torture, Cole calls for a commission to hold Yoo and others to account for their actions.[14] Further, in a later essay on Guantanamo in the *New York Review of Books*, Cole argues for the import of "some form of official accountability for the torture we inflicted on others."[15] Cole ties his call for accountability to the administration's failed bid to hold the Mohammed trial in federal court. Arguing that the administration *could have* succeeded in holding the trial in federal court if it had made it a priority,[16] Cole argues that so, too, could the administration pursue justice now in the form of accountability for torture. In other words, Cole reframes the Obama administration's failure to assure justice in Mohammed's trial as a failure that could have been otherwise and thus as a failure that calls for further pursuit of justice—in the form of accountability for torture—in the present.

Like the lost cause narratives I have examined, Cole's narrative of the administration's failure to hold Mohammed's trial in federal court stresses the agency of loss—that is, that Obama could have acted differently to pursue justice. However, Cole's narrative is not insistently focused on the public action that could or should have been taken. Instead, Cole focuses on the failure of elites, specifically, of the president and his advisors: "Some will say that even if he had fought, he could not have won on these issues—that was almost certainly Rahm Emanuel's calculation. *But you never know until you try.* And the administration's success in defeating Senator Graham's bill in 2009 suggests that such an effort is by no means quixotic" (my emphasis). Cole's critique of Obama and his advisors suggests there would have been dignity and meaning in such a fight, even if it resulted in a loss—a critique that resonates with a politics of lost causes, where the outcome of political action is not the only or primary determinant of that action's meaning. Yet Cole's critique makes not the public, but elites—Obama and his administration—the source of a romantic "could have been" story and thus positions the public as only spectators of, rather than also agents, in the story of justice yet to be written and forged. Letting the public off the hook for its complicity in Bush era practices of torture,[17] Cole runs the same risk that Zola did in soliciting a mythical sovereign public—namely, that this public (if it appeared) might support justice in this case without addressing its broader practice of scapegoating (the very practice that Cole criticizes, incidentally, in *Enemy Aliens*). Cole's narrative of the Mohammed trial thus productively reframes the failure of the Mohammed trial as an occasion for responsiveness. However, his narrative encourages the public to blame democratic failure on leaders and institutions, rather than acknowledging their own complicity in injustice and, hence, their responsibility to enact and press leaders to pursue other forms of responsiveness to injustice.

Like Cole, Slavoj Zizek has re-narrated the Mohammed trial as an event that will smack of injustice unless practices of torture are addressed and remedied. In a 2007 opinion piece on Mohammed in the *New York Times*, Zizek argues that new revelations about the illegal interrogation techniques used on Mohammed means that "any legal trial and punishment of Mr. Mohammed is now impossible—no court that operates within the frames of Western legal systems can deal with illegal detentions, confessions obtained by torture and the like."[18] Yet unlike Cole, Zizek emphasizes public complicity in that failure of justice. However, he does not argue that this complicity could have been otherwise. Rather, he regards it as symptomatic of broader democratic decline. In his 2008 book, *In Defense of Lost Causes*—wherein he repeats some of the same points about the torture of Khalid Sheikh Mohammed—Zizek argues that our society's comfort with the torture debates stems, ironically, from our contemporary obsession with happiness and the avoidance of suffering: "One of the great ironies of our predicament is that this same biomorality, focused on happiness and on preventing suffering, is today invoked as the underlying principle for the justification of torture: we should torture—impose pain and suffering—in order to prevent more suffering."[19] Our society's turn away from Western moral norms of freedom and equality, and toward happiness, has allowed torture to become a normal tactic of assuring that happiness. For Zizek, the failure to do justice in Mohammed's trial thus exemplifies the broader failure and decline of liberal democracy. Zizek writes, "the greatest victims of torture-as-usual are the rest of us, the informed public. *A precious part of our collective identity has been irretrievably lost.* We are in the middle of a process of moral corruption: those in power are literally trying to break a part of our ethical backbone, to dampen and undo what is arguably our civilization's greatest achievement, the growth of our spontaneous moral sensitivity."[20] The normalization of torture does not reveal one particular moment of democratic failure, but rather the failure of democracy as such.

Zizek's narrative focuses on the democratic failure implicit in the Mohammed trial, but obscured by most news outlets and commentators. However, his claim that public and official complicity in torture is due to a broader process of democratic decline is fatalistic and strangely relieves the public (and officials) of responsibility for that failure. This keeps Zizek's narrative from being a "lost cause narrative" in the way I have used that term in this book (notwithstanding the title of his own book)—that is, as a narrative that reveals the democratic agency of loss and in turn reveals that loss as an occasion for belated public response by revealing how things could have been otherwise and may yet be so. Zizek frames the failure of Mohammed's trial as an event that should return us to the importance of pursuing "lost causes," but by that he means returning to revolutionary ideals of fundamentally transforming society that may have failed in practice, but that should be pursued with more commitment in the future. In particular, Zizek defends revolutionary excesses on behalf of freedom and equality that we usually classify as failures (the prime example here is the Terror of the French Revolution) because they resist the domestication of the revolution- ary event—the return of the political moment into the police (he uses Rancière's terms).[21] These ideals of utopian social transformation, of carrying the revolution into the everyday—and not specific instances of injustice, such as Mohammed's trial—are the lost causes that Zizek seeks to defend. To put the point differently, Zizek does not call for a belated public, but rather for a public that would, in deferring to the judgment of elites like him, finally be "on time"—that would finally instantiate revolutionary ideals, rather than seeing them as impractical or dangerous.

Zizek's approach to lost causes is thus fundamentally different from mine. Whereas I have argued for lost cause narratives that reveal the ambivalence of democratic failure—as both a site of democratic prob- lems and promise—Zizek examines the "lost" part of "lost cause" primarily in order to say that we should try not to lose it. As Judith Halberstam puts it, Zizek does not examine the ambivalence or prom- ise of failure, but rather "situates failure as a stopping point on the way to success."[22] For him, the important thing is not the democratic practice of and response to failure and loss, but rather the revolution- ary cause, about which we learn almost nothing by seeing its failure in practice, except that we need to try again—and harder and better.[23] Zizek's fatalistic narrative of democratic failure in the Mohammed case thus issues in a fatalistic democratic politics—calling the public to defer to those who can redirect them to true democracy.

I see Zizek's re-narration of Mohammed's trial as democratically disempowering and Cole's as too elitist in scope, but there is no doubt that their writings have contributed to a vibrant public discussion of the trial and American practices of torture in general—a discussion which, I have been implicitly suggesting here, is itself valuable. In the next section, I offer a lost cause narrative of the Mohammed trial that (I will suggest) portrays the American approach to terrorism and detain- ees in general to be a democratic failure. Perhaps surprisingly, I find this narrative in Kathryn Bigelow's recent film, *Zero Dark Thirty*—a film that Zizek critiques as entrenching the normalization of torture in the West. The film has also been criticized by many on the Left, such as Jane Mayer and Steve Coll, for supposedly misleading audiences about the efficacy of torture. I will argue in contrast that *Zero Dark*

Thirty ultimately reveals the complicity of the public in the instrumental logic of torture and, in turn, reframes democratic failure as an occasion for response—soliciting its audience to imagine committing to a non-instrumental value (perhaps justice) to orient their actions.

ZERO DARK THIRTY AS LOST CAUSE NARRATIVE

At the outset of the movie, the ostensible "hero" of *Zero Dark Thirty*, Maya, walks into a dirty room with her CIA mentor, Dan. In the room, Maya watches while Dan waterboards the nephew of Khalid Sheikh Mohammed. Eventually, with Maya's help, Dan extracts useful intelligence from the detainee about Osama bin Laden's courier. Later, Maya watches, halfway participates in, and directs the torture and abuse of detainees. In one notable scene, where she is trying to cull information about this courier, she watches multiple tapes of detainees offering information in various poses of being tortured and under duress.

Much of the public discussion about *Zero Dark Thirty* has asked whether this "normalization" of torture (in Zizek's words) conveys a message for or against it. If *Zero Dark Thirty* portrays torture as generating the information that leads to the capture of bin Laden, is it "pro-torture"? In my view, this framing of the question misses what is most important and compelling about *Zero Dark Thirty*: it reveals that the calculus of torture (Does it work? What kind of information, or situation, justifies torture?) is only one part of a broader post-9/11 American worldview in which the capture, detention, sometimes torture, and killing of terrorists has become its own *raison d'être*—animated not by any deeper or higher principle, but its own empty momentum, its appearance of being animated by a higher purpose, and a seldom acknowledged public, libidinal desire for violent revenge. (At one point, one of Maya's bosses screams, "Do your job! I want targets! Bring me people to kill!"—a statement that encapsulates the movie's general portrayal of the outlook of Americans.) I will suggest that the import of torture, as depicted in *Zero Dark Thirty*, lies not in it actually achieving "results," but rather in the myth of "results" and forward progress that torture provides and that is propelled by, even as it obscures, a public desire for revenge. Thus, asking whether the movie "condones" torture obscures its more radical challenge to Americans' self-understanding: its diagnosis that the debate over whether torture "works" is itself a way of avoiding the public's implication in a cycle of violent revenge that the practice of torture supposedly helps to arrest.

Many critics of the film have argued that the lead character, Maya, who ultimately is responsible for pressing the CIA to track down bin Laden's courier and to raid the house to which she and her colleagues trace him, should be read as the "hero" whose actions we are invited to applaud and cheer on. In contrast, Steven Johnston argues for seeing her as the protagonist in a "revenge fantasy" that goes wrong.[24] But there is a third option for understanding the character, pitched less in the register of judgment and more on the register of interpellation or identification—one that asks, to what perspective are we enlisted by the film? I argue here that the film invites us to see Maya as a mirror of the post-9/11 American public—a public that in a moment of democratic failure thoughtlessly endorsed torture but that might (through the reframing that the film ultimately offers) yet respond to their own failure.

The film invites us to see Maya as the mirror of the public when it contrasts Maya and her senior colleague, Dan. Dan, whom Maya observes torturing a detainee in the opening scene of the movie, was in the CIA before 9/11 and seems to represent an older America—one that has to put aside its morals and principles in order to engage in torture and other abuse. In this older America, there is still a distinction between the "animalistic" behavior of torture and the "principled" normal life of the United States. We see this in several ways in Dan's character. First and most obviously, when Dan is in the Middle East, he wears a beard—taking on the appearance of the "animal" that he actually turns into when torturing detainees. In D.C., he is clean-shaven. The film's portrayal of Dan as animalistic while in Pakistan is compounded by his strange (and otherwise inexplicable) affinity with, and care for, a group of monkeys kept in cages at the base ("my monkeys," he says to Maya). After he tells Maya that he needs to go back to D.C., he claims that the monkeys have been killed, suggesting that Dan's animalistic (torturing) self has also been killed. Finally, and most obviously, Dan—unlike anyone else in the movie—shows signs of realizing that torture is morally wrong, or at least that it is *seen* as morally wrong. He tells Maya, for example, that he is feeling stressed out from his encounters with detainees and that he needs to go back to "normal" life in D.C. While Dan may certainly bring back to D.C. some of the "animalistic" traits he exhibits in Pakistan—and while that animalism may be simply hiding under the clean-shaven surface—the distinction between immorality and morality (or at least his acknowledgment of that distinction) seems to remain intact in his character, even as he behaves immorally.

In contrast, Maya is portrayed as having been born *out of* 9/11: she tells the CIA director (played by James Gandolfini) that she was recruited out of high school and that hunting bin Laden is "all she's ever done." 9/11 is the founding event that is the structuring principle of her life. In contrast to Dan's apparent enjoyment of and, later, disgust with torture, Maya seems to have literally no emotions—except, sometimes, anger at her superiors for not moving fast enough to capture bin Laden. There is no sense of morality, feelings of compassion, or any other kind of emotion that crosses her face. This is especially the case in her encounters with and involvement in torture. While she initially seems to feel some instinctual disgust or repulsion at practices of torture (we see her wincing in the opening scene), she adapts and never says anything about torture. We could take this to suggest that Maya therefore represents the post-9/11 CIA and not, as I am suggesting, the public. However, as Steve Coll and Ali Soufan have shown, agents were not impassive in the use of torture.[25] Rather, some of them were disgusted by the CIA's use of torture and contested it, while others (like Dan) seemed sometimes to enjoy it. Soufan and Cole therefore argue that the movie misleads audiences when it portrays Maya as impassive (when few agents actually were). But we have another option. Maya may not represent the CIA at all. Since she never participates in torture but is more often a spectator at a distance, she may arguably better be said to represent the American public—a public that for 10 years after 9/11 (and still) is aware of the torture done in its name, but is always removed from its actual practice, complicit in and supportive of it from afar.

If we read Maya as a mirror of the post-9/11 American public (rather than as an exemplar of the actual, historical actions of the CIA, or as a hero whose actions we should identify with),[26] we are positioned to see the film's depiction of torture differently: not as condoning torture and misleading its audiences about torture's effectiveness,[27] but rather as revealing, and shaking us into awareness of, our own impassive complicity in torture. This is not complicity in occasional uses of torture in a regime where torture is illegal and abhorred. Rather, the film jarringly awakens its audience to its complicity in a culture of torture, where the use of torture by government officials and agents is an open secret. In this culture of torture, the need for "results" bars discussion of the costs of achieving them, there is no shame in the use of torture, and those who perpetrate it are neither apprehended nor punished.[28] By revealing the public's complicity in torture, the film opens up a different set of questions about torture (that Zizek asks to a certain degree, even as he reads *Zero Dark Thirty* as part of the normalization of torture): namely, questions about how and why much of the public came to see torture and other paramilitary (alegal or illegal) actions as a normal and often acceptable response to terrorism, and how we might intervene in and respond to that complicity now. That is, is there a way to exit the culture of torture?

Zero Dark Thirty offers a response to these questions in the last two scenes of the movie, which follow the raid on bin Laden's house (scenes edited to offer no emotional indication—through music or expressions of the characters—of how the audience is "supposed to" react).[29] In these scenes, we see Maya identifying bin Laden's body and then departing on a carrier (alone) back to the United States. I want to suggest that these scenes follow the trajectory of sexual climax and the morning after. First, after the Special Forces team returns to the base with bin Laden's body, Maya walks slowly through the crowd of Special Forces agents to see the body bag in which she hopes she will find the corpse of Osama bin Laden (she is charged with identifying the body). Upon finding it to be him, the previously impassive Maya has a moment of near ecstasy (deep breathing, inhaling and exhaling), followed by the camera moving in on bin Laden's face, of which only a bloody nose is visible. We need not recur to old motifs of the nose as a penis to see something jarringly sexual in this scene.[30] Indeed, the earlier parts of the film position us to view it that way. Maya has no intimate human-to-human relationships in the film, let alone romantic ones. She tells her colleague, who tries to inquire into her romantic attachments, that "I'm not that girl who fucks"—and she doesn't. Rather, she fantasizes. . . about killing bin Laden (she tells the Special Forces agents that she wants them to "kill bin Laden for [her]") and then experiences pleasure for the only time in this film when she comes face to face with his dead body.

How should we read Maya's heavy breathing? Do we witness here the desire for (and love of) violence and killing implicit in the mass celebrations in the United States following the announcement of bin Laden's assassination? If we read the film as a narrative of democratic failure, there is another possibility. Maya's strange moment with the corpse might reveal that public complicity in the new culture of torture is not rooted primarily in some rational calculation of what we need to do to prevent the next attack, but rather in unacknowledged desire: specifically, the desire for killing, torture, violence. Does Maya's pseudo-orgasmic moment with the corpse, in other words, reveal that the public's impassivity about torture has its roots in a forbidden love for the "war against terror"—that is, not in love for the homeland itself, but rather the vengeful and bloody pursuit of an enemy? ("Protect the homeland!" says Maya's station chief, who is in favor of searching for the next attack rather than bin Laden, but Maya argues that the only way to prevent the next attack is to find bin Laden; she knows, in other words, what our goal "really is" here—which is to say, to have an enemy and to fantasize, and then carry out, its killing.)

Yet like all desires (at least on Lacan's account), Maya's is disappointed when it is seemingly fulfilled. When Maya's fantasy of killing bin Laden is consummated and appears in the form of a body bag, that fantasy of bloody revenge appears as what it is—not the triumph of the United States, but a dead man, the continuation of a cycle of torture and violence. Indeed, after this climax, Maya walks out into the night, where she exhales and opens her eyes. In the next scene, we see Maya returning to the United States. This is the morning after, temporally, but also iconically, marked as such by her solitariness (she is the only one on the aircraft carrier) and her sudden emotionality (for the first time in the movie, we see a tear come down Maya's face). What induces this emotion in Maya is a question asked by her pilot, who remarks on the fact that she is alone. He says, "Where do you want to go?"

Why does that question induce Maya's tear? Does it simply reflect the inevitable let-down after one's goal—indeed, Maya's entire life goal? There may be let-down, but there is something more. For the pilot's question, whatever else it is, is a democratic question. Do we want to stay in the torture culture? Or do we want to go somewhere else? By interjecting that question between Maya's viewing of the corpse and her tears, *Zero Dark Thirty* interjects space between the instrumental logic of torture to which the public has become affectively attached (before and during the movie) and the meaning or destination of such a logic. The film, we might say, creates a rift in time, in our collective self-understanding. Maya's tear may suggest that this question demands mourning rather than a substantive answer—and as Burke has shown us, mourning can itself be an important form of democratic responsiveness to failure. That is, the introduction of the question of what end the whole paramilitary hunt for terrorists serves may press us to reflect on the *absence* of such an end and, hence, to mourn the violence and injustice that has been inflicted in its name. Yet this question, and Maya's response of a single tear, may also serve a different purpose: it presses the audience to answer it themselves. That is, Maya's mute response may solicit a public, the movie's audience, to answer in her place—to *take* her place as she flies away on the aircraft carrier (this character who has served as their mirror) and to answer on her behalf. Where do you want to go?[31]

This question does not solicit a public on behalf of a particular goal—justice, freedom, equality, security—but instead invites the audience, which has come face to face with the consequences of their love relationship with torture and killing, to experiment with thinking non-instrumentally. It invites the public to put the instrumentality of torture and the broader logic of the war on terror into the context of values that exceed, and perhaps shed critical light on, instrumentality. In this sense, *Zero Dark Thirty* does not offer a judgment on torture in the way that Burke, Zola, and Arendt offer judgments on the democratic failures they experienced. *Zero Dark Thirty* does not make a claim about the proper way forward. We could read this as a disadvantage to the film—that it does not contribute to rebuilding the context of plural judgments that Arendt sees as crucial to our ability to form independent judgment. Yet, on the other hand, this vexing refusal to name *which* value should guide us is a solicitation to the public—Where do you want to go?[32]

This solicitation could, of course, go astray—and it has. As one critical reviewer of *Zero Dark Thirty* put it, "To all the people defending the movie, what do you think Dick Cheney's review is going to be? Isn't it just a crazy coincidence that he's probably going to love it?"[33] That may be. But the message is there to be heard and, more important, to get under the public's skin in a subtle way. No moralizing film could call a public into being against torture. We are too attached to it and the claims of its proponents that violence can be justified by "results." To be able to be effective in constituting a new public, worn out by and complicit in torture, a film has to depict its pleasures and terrors, its victories and dissatisfaction. If this means the unsubtle Cheney can find affirmation in it, this is less an indictment of the film than of Cheney, surely, because the sort of film he could *not* mistake for affirmation—a moralistic or legalistic denigration of torture—would also be uneffective in jarring a public into recognition of, and responsiveness to, the democratic failure of post-9/11 United States.

"Where do you want to go?" The response may not be what we would like, but there may be more responses to come. At least *Zero Dark Thirty* has revealed democratic complicity in torture neither as something that reveals democracy's failure in general (Zizek) nor as something that must be obscured if the people are to press for accountability and justice. Instead, it reveals that failure as something that, if our liberal democracy is to maintain its rule of law and commitment to justice and freedom, must be addressed and called to account in ourselves, as well as in elected officials, judges, and intelligence agencies.

Yet even as *Zero Dark Thirty* sparked (and continues to spark) a wide-ranging, broad conversation about torture, law, justice, and the role of art vis-à-vis history and facts, the military commission trial of Khalid Sheikh Mohammed and others has been, at the time of this writing, undergoing pretrial motions in Guantanamo Bay, with a censoring mechanism in place to prevent any mention by detainees or lawyers of torture from leaking into the public record.[34] The solicitations to a public of independent judgment by *Zero Dark Thirty*, and to a public on behalf of justice by David Cole and others (like Jane Mayer), have certainly generated response, but the majority of the American people have not mobilized against torture or on behalf of justice. Rather, we are faced—as in the trials faced by Burke, Zola, and Arendt—with another democratic failure. And even when lost cause narratives portray democratic failure as an occasion for responsiveness rather than a dead end, they may not solicit the belated public that they envisioned.

Even in the context of ongoing democratic failure, though—and perhaps *especially* in that context—lost cause narratives still have much to offer us. In particular, by narrating democratic failure in the register of responsiveness, lost cause narratives that stress the democratic agency of loss suggest that failure need not spell the end of democracy, but rather may stand as yet another occasion for responsiveness. In other words, by conceiving failure in the register of responsiveness, lost cause narratives better equip us to resist fatalism and the practices of deference it cultivates. Indeed, even if *Zero Dark Thirty* has not solicited the public that would remedy the injustice of torture, it has nonetheless sparked broad public discussion and debate on how to respond to this democratic failure—a discussion that itself creates a public context in which further democratic responsiveness begins to make sense. Lost cause narratives keep democratic possibility in view, alongside the persistence of failure, as part of our political horizon.

THE ART OF LOSING CAUSES

This aspect of lost cause narratives—that they offer a way of understanding and addressing democratic failure that resists fatalistic thinking—may be particularly important in times of persistent democratic failure like our own. Specifically, lost cause narratives postulate what we might call an "art of losing causes"[35] through which democratic actors and theorists might resist the temptation to understand democratic failure fatalistically, as ushering in democracy's death. Such an art of losing causes bears affinities with thinkers of the "ethical turn" in political theory, such as Judith Butler and Stephen White, who also seek to redeem and find democratic resources in moments of democratic loss or finitude. Yet where Butler and White seek ethical resources from outside democratic practice—for example, in the common experience of shared loss and/or suffering (Butler) or in our shared experience of finitude (White)—I seek resources from experiences of political and, in particular, democratic failure. As Ella Myers has argued, thinkers of the ethical turn often focus on the self as the site of ethical work and rehabilitation.[36] In contrast, the art of losing causes addresses the peculiarly democratic predicament of the failure of others to respond to our call for justice, and it is cultivated primarily through political interactions with others, rather than through solitary or dyadic work on the self. [37] In conclusion, then, I discuss the outlines of what such an art might look like, and how we might cultivate it in ourselves.

The art of losing causes negotiates democratic actors' inability to control the actions and beliefs of others with whom they share a world. Other people may consistently fail to respond to lost cause narratives, claims of democratic failure, and other claims for democratic goods. In the context of democratic failure, such an art of losing causes can be as important as the art of winning them. While one could cull many principles for such an art from the examples of lost cause narratives that I have examined, I here offer five principles to get us started.

First, *create a place for despair, mourning, and loss as part of democratic life*. The experience of democratic failure often induces disappointment and despair. That experience may appear opposed to democracy, a political regime that is usually portrayed as forward-moving, willing, legislating, or enacting, rather than as composed of experiences of blockage and shortcoming. Yet as many theorists have recently reminded us, mourning and disappointment may productively orient us to the tragic dimensions of democratic life[38]—usefully interrupting the forward movement of modern democracy and attuning democratic actors to the costs (in human life, equality, and freedom) of such forward motion and ideological adherence to it. Also, as I suggested in Chapter 2, mourning may itself be a productive democratic practice of responsiveness to democratic failure.

Rather than seeing despair as an individual experience incapable of expression in collective life, politicize despair: through public writing, or through creating new groups and associations—as women created consciousness-raising groups in the 1960s to politicize supposedly individual feelings of despair,[39] or like punk musicians and teenage girls brought Riot Grrrl groups into being in the 1990s as a way to politicize and resist supposedly individual fears and traumas.[40] Or in Bonnie Honig's words, move from a politics of *mourning* to a *politics* of mourning by seeking out fellow conspirators to resist public prohibitions on collective enactments of despair.[41] A key example for Honig is ACT UP, a group that displayed individuals' despair over the AIDS crisis as a theatrical enactment of, and a call to, political action. Insist, together, on the politicality of failure—that it be displayed in public for the sake

of democratically resisting injustice, rather than obscured on behalf of
a politics of deference.

Second, *seek out and create plural monuments*. As I noted in Chapter 3,
on Zola, we often think of democracy as being given its orientation by singular monuments of founding, such as the Declaration
of Independence or the Constitution. Yet the politics of lost causes
teaches us to be suspicious of singular monuments of events that,
as Alan Keenan shows in his discussion of democratic founding,
often simultaneously enshrine and obscure an injustice, exclusion,
or closure.[42] Rather than thinking of future democratic action and
response to events as guided by only one dominant narration of the
democratic failure we experience, democratic actors should seek
to pluralize monuments—soliciting future belated publics through
alternative narratives of events that reveal how things could have
been otherwise. We might also respond to dominant "monuments"
of events through practices of de-monumentalizing and even (para-
doxically) of monumentalizing the practice of de-monumentalizing.
If political actors are to negotiate and respond to democratic failure
without despairing of democracy, they must write and narrate events
otherwise, pluralizing the meaning of events, as well as the publics
that might respond to them.

Third, *create a dissident "little platoon."* The "little platoon" is the term
Edmund Burke uses to describe the "subdivision" we belong to in
society—that is, our family, friends, or like-minded colleagues—that
he calls the "first germ" by which we proceed to a love of our society
and country. Being part of a "little platoon" in Burke's sense can be
dangerous insofar as it leads us to love, and acquiesce in, societal identities and narratives that sanction injustice, but creating a *dissident* "little
platoon" in response to democratic failure can allow democratic actors
to cultivate and maintain alternative stories, practices, and identities in
what Arendt calls "dark times." This is how Michael Warner discusses
queer publics in times of oppression, which were generated through
poesis and created novel, freer ways of speaking, acting, and associat-
ing.[43] Creating and maintaining a dissident "little platoon," democratic
actors keep alternative narratives of injustice alive and available for
moments when broader public resistance again seems possible—when
the "little platoon" could help to germinate broader societal identity
rather than being subsumed by it.

Fourth, *solicit belated publics*. While failures of the public to respond to calls for justice and other democratic goods may appear to spell the end of democracy, see such failures in the context of the belated public—past, present, and future. At the end of his life, for example, Burke was almost deserted by those he had formerly counted among his friends and supporters—his calls for justice in the Hastings trial fell on deaf ears. Yet rather than despair of the public, Burke turned to the future—to posterity—in the hope that through "bearing" his sorrow at the injustice of the trial, some new public might be birthed. While Burke has in fact been heard—by many different belated publics—his turn to that public would have been meaningful regardless, insofar as it enacted a sense of democratic possibility alongside failure that helps to form the broad web of responsiveness into which democratic actors might act, and respond, and respond again. When one re-narrates democratic failure to a belated public, or responds to an injustice while claiming to be part of such a public, that failure is reconceived as a site of democratic possibility rather than quiescence.

Fifth, *situate democratic failure in a web of responsiveness*. Write or enact democratic action and failure as part of a chain of lost causes and responses to them over time—for example, as Occupy Wall Street enacted itself as a response to the Arab Spring, which was itself claimed as an iteration of the Prague Spring, which was in turn in part a response to the failure of the Paris Commune, which was of course a response to the failures of the French Revolution, which was conceived in part as a response to the decline of the Roman republic, which understood its founding as a response to the fall of Troy, and so on. Through enacting contemporary democracy action and failure as part of a broad chain of responsiveness, we can reveal the significance of such action even when it fails—namely, in creating meaningful precedents for future resistance and in producing meaning and freedom for those who participate in them. In turn, creating such connections generates hope—not the kind of Kantian hope that depends on behaving "as if" we were already part of a perfect democracy, nor the hope of the Melians whose hope in Thucydides' history works to shield them from their inevitable destruction by the Athenians (though of course any exercise of hope may end this way). Rather, locating present failures and responsiveness in a web of lost cause narratives generates, and enacts, the hope of responsiveness—that is, that failures in our present may be responded to by future publics, just as we respond to the failures narrated in the lost cause narratives of the past.

Through cultivating this art of losing causes, democratic actors and theorists might resist to a certain degree the temptation in the face of losing and failure, to turn away from the cause pursued and, out of despair, reject the people who failed you (as Arendt says Clemenceau did and as Arendt herself did, to a certain degree). While many have likely succumbed to this temptation, turning away from democracy may be more of a true failure than the lost cause itself. Indeed, such turning away may leave the lost cause un-narrated for others, without a story of what might have or should have been, or an elegy, or an expression of laughing despair or ironic bewilderment. In contrast, through making a place for despair in public life, creating plural monuments, forming a dissident "little platoon," soliciting belated publics, and enacting democratic failure as part of a web of lost causes and responsiveness to them, we might plant seeds of solidarity and responsiveness for the future that may never find its audience, but which also might, like Zola's miners working furiously underground, germinate until the day its proper harvesters find it, harvest it, and perhaps practice the art of losing causes all over again.

NOTES

Chapter 1

1. Emile Zola, *The Dreyfus Affair: J'Accuse and Other Writings*, trans. Eleanor Levieux, ed. Alain Pagès (New Haven, CT: Yale University Press, 1996), p. 52.

2. Ibid., p. 43.

3. Ibid., p. 116.

4. Plato, *The Apology*, in *Four Texts on Socrates*, trans. Thomas G. West and Grace Starry West (Ithaca, NY: Cornell University Press, 1984, 1998), p. 83.

5. This reading is not incompatible with readings of the *Apology* that emphasize the democratic possibilities implicit in Socrates' activity as a "gadfly." As J. Peter Euben puts it, "[h]ere Socrates is portrayed as walking the streets talking to anyone he meets (including women and slaves) in a common language about the actions and thoughts of their everyday lives. Though he speaks to all, he is especially concerned with his fellow citizens since who they are and what they do create the community in which he lives his life as an Athenian and a philosopher. That is why he is so incredulous when his accusers claim that he is purposefully corrupting the young" (in "Reading Democracy: 'Socratic' Dialogues and the Political Education of Democratic Citizens," in *Demokratia: A Conversation on Democracies, Ancient and Modern*, ed. Josiah Ober and Charles Hedrick, Princeton, NJ: Princeton University Press, 1996, p. 329). In *Socratic Citizenship*, Dana Villa similarly argues that "Socrates invented a form of philosophical or dissident citizenship" that allowed him to be "an irritating moral and intellectual conscience to his city" (Princeton, NJ: Princeton University Press, 2001, p. xi, xii). Yet while I agree that the model of Socratic citizenship that Villa especially, and Euben to a certain degree, find in Socrates may reveal Socrates as (in Euben's words) a "sympathetic if critical friend of democracy" (p. 333), I am interested in the narrative of democratic failure implicit in (Plato's) Socrates' practice and explicit in his speeches. It is premised on the notion that, left to themselves, democratic citizens will *inevitably* fail to be just and free—that to save themselves they require guidance and intervention from philosopher experts like Socrates. This is fatalistic reasoning that encourages deferent behavior to experts (e.g., Socrates' conversation "partners" most often seem to feel like they have been rendered subservient through the "dialogue" rather than being an equal partner in it).

6. Rousseau, Jean-Jacques, *On the Social Contract*, trans. Maurice Cranston (New York: Penguin, 1968), p. 83.

7. Holmes makes this argument through comparing the demos to Ulysses in *The Odyssey*, where he rationally binds himself to the ship in order to prevent himself from

later (when he is "Ulysses Drunk") going to the Sirens. Stephen Holmes, *Passions and Constraint: On the Theory of Liberal Democracy* (Chicago: University of Chicago Press, 1995).

8. Seyla Benhabib, "Deliberative Rationality and Models of Legitimacy," *Constellations* 1(1994):1, 26–52, 30.

9. In particular, the deliberative approach seeks to reconcile legitimacy (the *fact* that the demos consents to a government—a consent which could be manufactured by propaganda and/or a charismatic leader) and rationality by showing legitimacy as necessarily dependent on a rational procedure of democratic deliberation. On this point, see Seyla Benhabib's "Toward a Deliberative Model of Democratic Legitimacy," in *Democracy and Difference* (Princeton, NJ: Princeton University Press, 1996), p. 80.

10. The language of "sluices" is Jürgen Habermas's in *Between Facts and Norms*, trans. William Rehg (Cambridge, MA: MIT Press, 1998).

11. Habermas offers such a progress narrative in "Constitutional Democracy: A Paradoxical Union of Contradictory Principles?" *Political Theory* 29(2001):6, 766–781. For a diagnosis and critique of that narrative, see Bonnie Honig's "Dead Rights, Live Futures: A Reply to Habermas's 'Constitutional Democracy," *Political Theory* 29(2001):6, 792–805.

12. On this point, see Bonnie Honig's "Between Decision and Deliberation: Political Paradox in Democratic Theory," *The American Political Science Review* 101(2007):1, 1–17.

13. Carl Schmitt is usually viewed as the primary proponent of emergency politics—that is, politics that gains its vitality from the moment of "exception" or "decision" rather than the norm. See his *Political Theology: Four Chapters on the Concept of Sovereignty*, trans. George Schwab (Chicago: University of Chicago Press, 2006). For nuanced critiques of the turn to "emergency politics," see Bonnie Honig's *Emergency Politics* (Princeton, NJ: Princeton University Press, 2009); Jason Frank's "'Unauthorized Propositions': The Federalist Papers and Constituent Power," *diacritics* 37(2007):2–3, 103–120; and Leonard Feldman's "Judging Necessity: Democracy and Extra-Legalism," *Political Theory* 36(2008):4, 550–577.

14. Jeffrey Toobin, "Edward Snowden Is No Hero," *The New Yorker*. June 10, 2013. Web. http://www.newyorker.com/online/blogs/comment/2013/06/edward-snowden-nsa-leaker-is-no-hero.html. Accessed February 13, 2014.

15. Steven Johnston. "Snowden's Real Crime," *The Contemporary Condition*. October 24, 2013. Web. http://contemporarycondition.blogspot.com/2013/10/snowdens-real-crime.html. Accessed February 13, 2014.

16. Ibid.

17. See the Introduction to Honig's *Emergency Politics*.

18. James Tully, *Public Philosophy in a New Key, Volume I: Democracy and Civic Freedom* (Cambridge: Cambridge University Press, 2008), p. 143.

19. Judith Halberstam shows how moments of supposed failure can reveal problems with existing standards of success *and* offer forms of meaning not captured within those standards in *The Queer Art of Failure* (Durham, NC: Duke University Press, 2011).

20. Patchen Markell, "The Rule of the People: Arendt, Árche, and Democracy," *American Political Science Review* 100(2006):1, 1–14, 13.

21. Aletta Norval, "Democratic Identification: A Wittgensteinian Approach," *Political Theory* 34(2006):2, 229–255.

22. For example, see Lawrie Balfour's chapter on John Brown in *Democracy's Reconstruction: Thinking Politically with W.E.B. DuBois* (New York: Oxford University Press, 2011).

23. Kathi Weeks turns to the "wages for housework" movement in *The Problem with Work* (Durham: Duke University Press, 2011) as an invigorating and exemplary—if

also problematic—precedent for a contemporary movement that would demand a basic income.

24. On the political import of demands for reparation, see Lawrie Balfour's "Reparations after Identity Politics," *Political Theory* 33(2005):6, 768–811, and Martha Minow's chapter on "Reparations" in *Between Vengeance and Forgiveness: Facing History after Genocide and Mass Violence* (Boston: Beacon Press, 1998).

25. On the militancy of the suffragettes, see Linda Ford's *Iron-Jawed Angels: The Suffrage Militancy of the National Women's Party, 1912–1920* (Lanham, MD: University Press of America, 1991).

26. See Lauren Berlant's *Cruel Optimism* (Chicago: University of Chicago Press, 2011) and Ann Cvetkovich's *Depression: A Public Feeling* (Durham, NC: Duke University Press, 2012).

27. Michael McCann, *Rights at Work: Pay Equity Reform and the Politics of Legal Mobilization* (Chicago: University of Chicago Press, 1994), pp. 57–58.

28. Ibid., p. 68.

29. Ibid., p. 69.

30. Ibid., my emphasis, p. 86.

31. See, for example, Robert Ferguson's *The Trial in American Life* (Chicago: University of Chicago Press, 2008) and Lynn Chancer's *High-Profile Crimes: When Legal Cases Become Social Causes* (Chicago: University of Chicago Press, 2005).

32. Emile Zola, *The Experimental Novel and Other Essays*, trans. Belle Sherman (New York: Haskell House, 1964), p. 287.

33. Chancer, *High-Profile Crimes*, p. 5.

34. An important exception can be found in Andrew Murphy's recent work on trials. In his essay, "Trial Transcript as Political Theory: Principles and Performance in the Penn-Mead Case," *Political Theory* 41(2013):6, 775–808, Murphy argues for the political theoretical benefits of examining trial transcripts. He writes, "What we find in these and other like cases are dramatic presentations of the exercise of (and resistance to) political power, episodes in which claims and counterclaims are enacted in the midst of interpersonal conflict and debate, in which political argument commingles with theatricality, performance, and gesture as citizens contesting the political with each other, with market actors, and with the state. All of these types of texts share an experiential element, in which political theory maintains a constant presence outside the bounds of canonical treatises and traditional venues" (p. 799).

35. Uday Mehta, *Liberalism and Empire* (Chicago: University of Chicago Press, 1999).

36. Seyla Benhabib, *The Reluctant Modernism of Hannah Arendt* (Lanham, MD: Rowman & Littlefield, 2003), p. 185.

37. See, for example, John Rawls's discussion of the Supreme Court as the "institutional exemplar" of public reason in *Political Liberalism* (New York: Columbia University Press, 1993, p. 235) and Ronald Dworkin's claim in *Law's Empire* (Cambridge: Harvard University Press, 1986) that the reasoning of courts best teaches us about what it means to be subjects of law's empire. While "[c]itizens and politicians and law teachers also worry and argue about what the law is" (p. 14), "the structure of judicial argument is typically more explicit, and judicial reasoning has an influence over other forms of legal discourse that is not fully reciprocal" (p. 15).

38. Rousseau, *On the Social Contract*, Book II, Chapter 4.

39. Wendy Brown, *States of Injury: Power and Freedom in Late Modernity* (Princeton, NJ: Princeton University Press, 1995), p. 66.

40. Sheldon Wolin also often sees law and regulation as agents of de-politicization. See his "Fugitive Democracy," *Constellations* 1(1994):1, 11–25. We can see a similar

suspicion of law in Michael Warner's critique of the gay marriage movement: the turn to legal marriage normalizes what could have been an emancipatory movement for a more equitable distribution for everyone (see Warner's *The Trouble with Normal: Sex, Politics and the Ethics of Queer Life* [Cambridge, MA: Harvard University Press, 2000]). In an insightful essay on the Arab Spring, Roxanne Euben has recently shown how Western narratives of the Benghazi protests as a "clash of rights" de-politicize and flatten the issues involved—allowing American citizens to hold on to a clichéd affirmation of the "right to free speech" rather than engaging in the harder work of politically examining the complexity of the conflict. See Roxanne Euben, "In Praise of Disorder: The Untidy Terrain of Islamist Political Thought," in *Radical Futures Past: Untimely Essays in Political Theory*, ed. Romand Coles, Mark Reinhardt, and George Shulman (Lexington: University of Kentucky Press, 2014).

    41. Sonali Chakravarti, *Sing the Rage: Listening to Anger after Mass Violence* (Chicago: University of Chicago Press, 2014). On the insufficiency of legal forms to do justice in transitional justice, see (among many others) Priscilla Hayner's *Unspeakable Truths: Transitional Justice and the Challenge of Truth Commissions* (New York: Routledge, 2011), Martha Minow's *Between Vengeance and Forgiveness* (Boston: Beacon Press, 1999), and Margaret Urban Walker's *Moral Repair: Reconstructing Moral Relations after Wrongdoing* (Cambridge: Cambridge University Press, 2006).

    42. Some scholars have argued that *all* political trials are subservient to the demands of exigency and thus represent only a corruption of ordinary legal practice. See, for example, Michael Belknap's "Introduction" to *American Political Trials* (Westport, CT: Greenwood Press, 1981, p. 16). Similarly, while Barbara Falk argues that political trials, "[a]s concentrated legal narratives and expressions of political activity,. . . are neither entirely pejorative nor positive," she also suggests that understanding the criteria by which we can recognize political trials will allow us to understand "how and under what conditions justice is politicized"—in particular, in the current War on Terror (*Making Sense of Political Trials: Causes and Categories*, Toronto: Munk Centre for International Studies, 2008, p. 1). However, most scholars typologize—offering a typology of acceptable political trials (capable of doing justice) from those that are unacceptable. For example, Ronald Christenson seeks to distinguish between what he calls "partisan trials"—trials (such as those held under Nazism and Stalinism and that Kirchheimer calls "show trials") that are "totally unsupported by laws" and defined by absolute "expediency"—and political trials that *"within the rule of law* juggle both the legal and the political agendas" and, in so doing, display existing political and legal problems in sharper and more theatrical fashion for the public (my emphasis, "A Political Theory of Political Trials," *The Journal of Criminal Law and Criminology* 74(1983):2, 547–577, 552, 554). Similarly, Lawrence Douglas, in his study of Holocaust trials, argues that trials can serve as an important source of education and remembrance about the Holocaust—a source of what he calls "didactic legality." Yet in order for such trials to be acceptable tools of didactic legality, they must maintain a commitment to the procedural restraint and protections of the rule of law (*The Memory of Judgment: Making Law and History in the Trials of the Holocaust*, New Haven, CT: Yale University, 2000, p. 3). Eric Posner also seeks to distinguish between legitimate and illegitimate political trials, suggesting that political trials mounted for the sake of public liberty and security are acceptable ("Political Trials in Domestic and International Law," *Duke Law Journal*, 55(2005):75, 75–152.

    43. Judith Shklar, *Legalism* (Cambridge, MA: Harvard University Press, 1964), p. 1. Grounded in the "fear of the arbitrary" (p. 15), legalists view law as apolitical and aimed only at justice, as opposed to politics, which is the realm of expediency (p. 111).

    44. Ibid., p. 160.

45. Ibid., p. 143.

46. Ibid., p. 143. In the case of Nuremberg, Shklar believes that it served "liberal ends" for two reasons: because it "promote[d] legalistic values in such a way as to contribute to constitutional politics and to a decent legal system" (p. 145) *and* because it pursued the "fundamental value" of "the prospect of a tolerant society" in a postwar Germany— namely, because it put the charge of "crimes against humanity" at the center of the trial (p. 151). If the trial had been justified on this basis, Shklar argues it would have been more convincing and offered a more solid and coherent basis for rebuilding postwar Germany.

47. Michael Walzer. "Introduction" to *Regicide and Revolution: Speeches at the Trial of Louis XVI* (New York: Columbia University Press, 1992), p. 79. For Walzer, the trial pointed the way to everyday justice because it staged the core values of the new republic in a dramatic way: equality under the law (Louis is made into a citizen), freedom to make your own defense, the right to a trial, and the right to counsel (among others). Walzer thus does not think that *any* "compromise with corruption" (p. 75) would be beneficial to the new republic; rather, he only sees means as permissible that, in the example they set, establish principles of justice for the future republic (Ibid.)

48. This is why, for example, she sees the breaks with procedural protections in the Eichmann trial as inappropriate. Shklar, p. 154.

49. For example, Maihle—the deputy who delivered the Gironde speech arguing for the Convention's ability to legally try Louis—argued that the National Convention could decide to subject Louis to a trial because "the nation was not bound by the Constitution. It retains, inalienably, the right to alter its Constitution" (p. 99). Indeed, Maihle argues that while "[i]n the ordinary course of events, judicial procedure may be considered the safeguard of the fortune, liberty and life of citizens," "all the complicated apparatus of legal procedure would plainly not be needed if society itself passed sentence on the crimes of its members. For a society which makes its own laws must surely know the principles of justice by which it wishes to be ruled, and must know as well, that to wrong its members through disorderly passion is to wrong itself" (p. 106). Here, Maihle draws a connection between the capacity for self-rule (through law-making) and the knowledge of principles of justice, or the capacity for judgment. The implication seems to be that since an autonomous people is a law-making people—to rule oneself otherwise is to rule arbitrarily and through the passions and thus is not legitimate rule at all—it has to have knowledge of the principles of justice that are implicitly or explicitly present within the laws that they make. A truly autonomous people, in other words, is inherently the best judge of matters of justice because it has the truest knowledge of justice. Thus, in a case of an unprecedented crime like that of Louis, the best possible route to take is to have the people craft legal procedures out of their principles of justice and judge according to them—or, in this case, to have their representatives do so. Yet Maihle's argument also suggests that the people's true knowledge of justice is *always* superior to and grounding of the formal rule of law—that is why he says that the "complicated apparatus of legal procedure" would be unnecessary if the people were able to judge cases directly.

Another prominent member of the Gironde, Vergniaud—who argued for the Gironde on behalf of appealing the verdict of death to popular vote—argues that to deny this appeal to the people is "to take sovereignty from them, to transfer it, by a usurpation nothing short of criminal, to the hands of the representatives chosen by the people, to transform their representatives into kings or tyrants" (p. 195). If the National Convention executes Louis without appeal to the people, "the people would be able to present only sterile and empty challenges" (p. 196)—i.e., because Louis would be dead. Echoing Maihle's argument earlier that law depends on popular judgment and action for its capacity to do justice, he says, "[w]hen one seeks to make a revolution against tyranny, it is necessary to veil the statue of the law which consecrates or protects tyranny. *But when you veil the statue of the law which consecrates the sovereignty of the people—you start a revolution which will turn to the tyrant's profit*" (my emphasis, p. 203). In other words, for Vergniaud, as for Maihle, law's—and justice's—connection to the people is not something to be hidden, but rather to be celebrated. Yet Vergniaud is also making a further point here—namely, that when elites behave as though popularly sanctioned legality can be disregarded in the people's name (as Robespierre does), you open the door to tyranny because, first, you open the door to claims that the people can legitimately act without regard to law *and* to claims that the people's will can be represented (by elites) without reference to law.

50. Aletta Norval, *Aversive Democracy* (Cambridge: Cambridge University Press, 2007), p. 191.

51. Ibid., p. 209.

52. Linda Zerilli, "We Feel Our Freedom: Imagination and Judgment in the Thought of Hannah Arendt," *Political Theory* 33(2005):2, 158–188, 171.

53. Jacques Rancière, *Dis-agreement*, trans. Julie Rose (Minneapolis: University of Minnesota Press, 2004), p. 29.

54. Ibid., p. 30.

55. For example, Habermas says that in the late eighteenth century, "[a] political consciousness developed in the public sphere of civil society which, in opposition to absolute sovereignty, articulated the concept of and demand for general and abstract laws and which ultimately came to assert itself (i.e. public opinion) as the only legitimate source of this law" (Jürgen Habermas, *The Structural Transformation of the Public Sphere*, Cambridge, MA: MIT Press, 1991, p. 54). This public opinion, which was viewed as the marker of legitimacy, was constituted through "private people in their capacity as owners of commodities communicat[ing] through rational-critical debate in the political realm, concerning the regulation of their private sphere" (pp. 55–56).

56. Habermas says that "only during this phase"—the close of eighteenth century in Britain—"was civil society as the private sphere emancipated from the directives of public authority to such an extent that at that time the political public sphere could attain its full development in the bourgeois constitutional state" (Habermas, *Structural Transformation*, p. 79). Many have criticized Habermas's narrative of the public sphere on historical and other grounds. See, for example, Craig Calhoun's ed. volume, *Habermas and the Public Sphere* (Cambridge, MA: MIT Press, 1993). Jason Frank also offers an important cautionary note about accepting the dominant Habermasian narrative in "'Besides Our Selves': An Essay on Enthusiastic Politics and Civil Subjectivity," *Public Culture* 17(2005):3, 371–392. Also see Jodi Dean's compelling critique in *Publicity's Secret: How Technoculture Capitalizes on Democracy* (Ithaca, NY: Cornell University Press, 2002).

57. Michael Warner, *Public and Counterpublics* (New York: Zone Books, 2005), pp. 12, 67.

58. Ibid., my emphasis, p. 114.

59. For example, see Jennifer Culbert's *Dead Certainty: The Death Penalty and the Problem of Judgment* (Palo Alto, CA: Stanford University Press, 2008); Michael McCann's *Rights at Work*; Lawrence Douglas's *The Memory of Judgment*; Jason Frank's *Constituent Moments*; Bonnie Honig's *Emergency Politics*; Karen Zivi's *Making Rights Claims: A Practice of Democratic Citizenship* (Oxford: Oxford University Press, 2012); and Leonard Feldman's "Judging Necessity: Democracy and Extra-Legalism."

60. Popular constitutionalists, like me, are worried about rule- and court-deferent behavior by citizens, but they argue for seeing such deference as *opposed* to, rather than *part* of, democracy—a move that leads to seeing rules and courts as oppressing/victimizing the

people (and thus portrays the people as fairly powerless to stop it), rather than acknowledging the people's responsibility for their own failures—an acknowledgment that is necessary for justice, and that also reveals that the people have the power to change things. See, for example, Larry Kramer's *The People Themselves: Popular Constitutionalism and Judicial Review* (Oxford: Oxford University Press, 2005) and "Popular Constitutionalism, circa 2004," *California Law Review* 94(2004), 959–1011; Robert Post and Reva Siegel, "*Roe* Rage: Democratic Constitutionalism and Backlash," *Harvard Civil Rights-Civil Liberties Law Review* 42(2007), 373–433; Tom Donnelly, "Making Popular Constitutionalism Work," *Wisconsin Law Review* 159(2012), 159–194.

61. Lawrie Balfour makes an analogous move in her recent work on reparations. For example, in "Un-thinking Racial Realism: A Future for Reparations?" Balfour argues: "in contrast to much of the reparations scholarship, *I focus on the demands of democracy rather than justice*. Doing so, I argue, both helps to evade some of the technical questions that have prevented full consideration of the political work of reparations and indicates how a commitment to reparations could serve the unfinished task of democratic reconstruction. Countering the historical and ongoing devaluation of black citizenship, reparations provide a vehicle for redefining both governmental and civic responsibility in the shadow of slavery and Jim Crow" (my emphasis, DuBois Review: *Social Science Research on Race*, available on CJO2014. doi:10.1017/S1742058X14000058.).

62. Rancière, p. 5.

63. Ibid., p. 18.

64. Jacques Derrida. "The Force of Law: the Mystical Foundations of Authority," *Cardozo Law Review* 11(1989–1990), 920–1046, 965. For Derrida, such an infinite idea of justice demands that we interrogate all our existing laws and principles of right [*droit*] to see if they are themselves just—an interrogation which leads, Derrida says, to the discovery that the foundation of *droit* inevitably lies in a "performative and therefore interpretive violence that in itself is neither just nor unjust and that no justice and no previous law with its founding anterior moment could guarantee or contradict or invalidate" (Ibid., pp. 941, 943). This structure—where, as Derrida says, the authority of law ultimately appears to be founded in "the mystical" silence as to the justice or injustice of the founding act (Ibid., p. 943)—means that claims to the authority of law to do justice in the present must always depend on something which is *not* (or not certainly) justice for precisely this authority. For Derrida, that something is violence or force: "there is no law without enforceability, and no applicability or enforceability of the law without force" (pp. 925, 927).

65. Ibid., p. 957.

66. Ibid.

67. Jason Frank, *Constituent Moments: Enacting the People in Post-Revolutionary America* (Durham, NC: Duke University Press, 2009), p. 33.

68. William Connolly, *The Terms of Political Discourse* (Princeton, NJ: Princeton University Press, 1983).

69. For an elaboration of this concept, see my "Toward an Agonistic Understanding of Law: Law and Politics in Hannah Arendt's *Eichmann in Jerusalem*," *Contemporary Political Theory* 11(2011):1, 88–108. See also Andrew Schaap's edited volume, *Law and Agonistic Politics* (Farnham, UK: Ashgate, 2009).

70. James Tully, *Public Philosophy in a New Key, Volume 1*, p. 147.

71. Hannah Arendt, "Truth and Politics," in *Between Past and Future* (New York: Penguin, [1961] 1993), pp. 261–262.On Arendt's conception of storytelling, seeLisa Disch's *Hannah Arendt and the Limits of Philosophy* (Ithaca, NY: Cornell University Press, 1994).

72. Shoshana Felman, *The Juridical Unconscious: Trials and Trauma in the Twentieth Century* (Cambridge, MA: Harvard University Press, 2002), p. 110. Indeed, Arendt's

success in shaping debate of the Eichmann trial is likely why writers critical of Arendt continue to try to dispute her account today. For example, see Deborah Lipstadt's *The Eichmann Trial* (New York: Schocken Books, 2011).

73. Hannah Arendt, *Men in Dark Times* (New York: Harcourt Brace, 1968), p. viii.

74. Ibid.

Chapter 2

1. Jennifer Pitts, *A Turn to Empire: the Rise of Imperial Liberalism in Britain and France* (Princeton, NJ: Princeton University Press, 2005). On other critics of empire in the eighteenth century, see Sankar Muthu's *Enlightenment Against Empire* (Princeton, NJ: Princeton University Press, 2003).

2. Or, as Stephen White puts it, long-standing divisions in scholarship on Burke reflect attempts to "capture a true Burke" from a host of competing images. Stephen White, *Edmund Burke: Modernity, Politics, Aesthetics* (Lanham, MD: Rowman & Littlefield, 2002), p. xx.

3. For this reading, see Peter Stanlis's *Edmund Burke and Natural Law* (Piscataway, NJ: Transaction Publishers, 2003) and James Conniff's "Burke and India: The Failure of the Theory of Trusteeship," *Political Research Quarterly* 46(1993):2, 291–309.

4. Pitts, *A Turn to Empire.*

5. Uday Mehta, *Liberalism and Empire* (Chicago: University of Chicago Press, 1999).

6. Nicholas Dirks, *The Scandal of Empire: India and the Creation of Imperial Britain* (Cambridge, MA: Harvard University Press, 2008). Sara Suleri offers a similar reading in *The Rhetoric of English India* (New York: Penguin, 2005). Margaret Kohn and Daniel O'Neill, in "A Tale of Two Indias: Burke and Mill on Empire and Slavery in the West Indies and America," claim that Burke's critique of Hastings should be read as a defense of traditional hierarchies in both Britain and India (*Political Theory* 34(2006):2, 192–228).

7. Mehta, *Liberalism and Empire*, p. 22. Both Mehta and Pitts reads Burkean sympathy as a failure in practice, but a success in principle. Pitts says, for example, that "British conduct in India in the 1770s and 1780s demonstrated to Burke that sympathy can fail, that spectators incapable of achieving an imaginative substitution of others' concerns for their own, *can* be indifferent witnesses to others' suffering" while at the same time claiming that his call to his "British audience to exercise moral imagination and to extend sympathy beyond their traditional circle of moral concern" exemplifies a "peculiar universalism" that offers "a morally powerful, and philosophically rich, vision of a humane international and colonial politics" that, unfortunately, went unheeded in practice (*A Turn to Empire*, pp. 72, 71, 243).

8. On the East India Company and British Empire in the eighteenth century, see (to name just a very few) David Armitage's *Ideological Origins of the British Empire* (Cambridge: Cambridge University Press, 2000); Philip Stern's *The Company-State: Corporate Sovereignty and the Early Modern Foundations of the British Empire in India* (Oxford: Oxford University Press, 2011): Robert Travers's *Ideology and Empire in Eighteenth-Century India: The British in Bengal* (Cambridge: Cambridge University Press, 2007); P. J. Marshall's "Britain and the World in the Eighteenth Century: Reshaping the Empire," *Transactions of the Royal Historical Society*, 6th ser., 8 (1998), 1–18; and P. J. Marshall's *The Impeachment of Warren Hastings* (Oxford: Oxford University Press, 1965).

9. The Company, on Burke's account, originally conducted "Trade with India. . . upon the common Principles of Commerce" (Edmund Burke, *Writings and Speeches*, Oxford: Clarendon Press, 1981–2000, Vol. 5, p. 222)—by exchanging goods or silver from Britain for goods from India. This trade, Burke argues was mutually beneficial, "encouraged

Industry" in India, "and promoted Cultivation in a high Degree" (Ibid.). This purely commercial relationship changed when the East India Company acquired "the Territorial Revenues" (223) of Bengal—that is, when the East India Company made a treaty with the Mughal emperor to acquire the monetary tribute paid by subjects (via local officials, or *zamindars*) to the ruler.

Once the East India Company acquired the Diwan, Burke suggests that its commercial dealings with India became perverted because the Company began using the revenue acquired through the Diwan to purchase goods from Indians. "Bullion was no longer regularly exported by the English East India Company to Bengal, or any Part of Hindostan" and a "new Way of supplying the Market of Europe, by Means of the British Power and Influence, was invented; a Species of Trade (if such it may be called) by which it is absolutely impossible that India should not be radically and irretrievably ruined" (Ibid.). Rather than sending silver to India in exchange for goods, the East India Company then essentially *took* goods from India to send to Britain, offering nothing in exchange. Consequently, the "commerce" of the East India Company no longer involved exchange, but instead amounted to a "continual Drain" of India's wealth (226).

10. Edmund Burke, *Writings and Speeches* (Oxford: Clarendon Press, 1981–2000), Vol. 6, p. 273. Hereafter I will cite the *Writings and Speeches* parenthetically in the text as *WS* accompanied by volume and page number. Sara Suleri calls this the "economy of guilt" that circulates among spectators of empire—the sense that one is complicit in despotism, and benefits from it, but also is somewhat helpless to exert a check on it. Suleri sees the impeachment of Hastings as an *extension* of this economy of guilt, given Hastings's ultimate acquittal, but she also sees the impeachment as a "symbolic success" in extending consciousness of this complicity (Suleri, *The Rhetoric of British India*, p. 56).

11. Edmund Burke, *The Correspondence of Edmund Burke*, Vol. 5, ed. Thomas P. Copeland (Chicago: University of Chicago Press, 1968), p. 240. Hereafter cited parenthetically in the text as *C* with volume and page number.

12. Burke argues that the Company's evolution, which "began in commerce and ended in Empire," "is totally different from what has happened in all other ordinary affairs, and from what has happened in all the remote mysteries of politicians, or been dreamed of in the world" (*WS* 6:283). Indeed, the East India Company's assumption of political power happened through its acquisition of "the Territorial Revenues" (*WS* 5:223) of Bengal—that is, when the East India Company (in the person of Clive) made a treaty with the Mughal emperor to acquire the *Diwan* of Bengal, or the monetary tribute paid by subjects (via local officials, or *zamindars*) to the ruler.

13. Such an uprooting of native customs and laws must invariably be felt as despotic: "that which creates tyranny is the imposition of a form of government contrary to the will of the governed"—and thus "even a free and equal plan of government, would be considered as despotic by those who desired to have their old laws and ancient system" (*WS* 5:140–141).

14. Uday Mehta, *Liberalism and Empire*, p. 173.

15. Burke argues that the dominance of profit as the Company's motive even when acting in its political capacity rendered all (British or Indian) legal checks on the Company's power useless and futile. For example, Burke discusses how in the early days of Clive, the servants of the Company used their special "passport" (giving them lower duties on trade) without compunction and without respect to the official limits to this privilege. They did this, Burke says, because they had the same attitude as the Company, which "considered itself still as a Trader in the Territories of a Foreign Potentate, in the Prosperity of whose Country it had neither Interest nor Duty" (*WS* 5:244). In other words, the servants, like the Company, did not grasp that they, now holding political power, should have

responsibilities besides profit. Thus, they used their political power only for gain. This became clear when, in response to this unrestrained abuse of their passports, "Cossim Ali Khan, the Second of the Nabobs whom they had set up," attempted to rectify the situation by "annul[ing] all the Duties on Trade, setting it equally free to Subjects and to Foreigners" (*WS* 5:245). The servants' preoccupation with profit (emboldened by coincidence with sovereign power) led them to throw aside and render ineffectual all political and legal checks on their power.

On Burke's account, this kind of disregard for law was prevalent at all levels of the Company's hierarchy. For example, Burke describes in great detail how Hastings continually ignored directives from the Court of Directors, which existed by virtue of Parliamentary legislation as his superior.

16. Stephen White, *Edmund Burke*, p. 17.

17. For an interesting discussion of Pitt's decision to support the impeachment, see P. J. Marshall's *The Impeachment of Warren Hastings*.

18. Thanks to Jason Frank for helpfully suggesting the language of "dynamic" reflective judgment.

19. See, for example, Peter Stanlis's *Edmund Burke and the Natural Law* (Piscataway, NJ: Transaction Publishers, 1958, 2003), Russell Kirk's *The Conservative Mind: From Burke to Eliot* (Washington, D.C.: Regency Publishers, 2001), and James Conniff's "Burke and India: The Failure of the Theory of Trusteeship," *Political Research Quarterly* 46(1993):2, 291–309).

20. Mehta, *Liberalism and Empire*, p. 123.

21. Fanny Burney, *Journals and Letters*. New York: Penguin, 2001, my emphasis, p. 264.

22. John Scott, *A Third Letter from Major Scott to Mr. Fox, on the Story of Deby Sing; Two Letters Relative to the Expences attending the Trial of Warren Hastings, Esquire; and a Letter to Mr. Burke* (London: John Stockdale, 1789), p. 39. Similarly, an anonymous writer, writing in verse, claimed that Burke and his co-managers were pursuing the impeachment simply on behalf of fame and partisan power:

> Of Patriots, Gen'rals, Ministers of State,
> Some form a short and random estimate:
> In one department does their fav'rite shine;
> Give him but Eloquence, –he's all divine.
> Judg'd by this rule, his fame is roar'd aloud,
> And tickles *purely* the astonish'd croud.
> Thus many a party-chief emerg'd to fame,
> And bore in peace the patriot's sacred name;
> Thus Burke and Sheridan first learn'd to please,
> And shone quite Stars and Demi-Deities.

In *Reflexions on Impeaching and Impeachers: Addressed to Warren Hastings, Esq* (London: John Stockdale, 1788), p. 5. The same author later accuses Burke and his co-managers of "Seek[ing] ev'ry quirk, evasion, trick, and flaw; To make right wrong, and foul the source of Law" and portrays the impeachment proceedings as a vehicle for the revenge of Philip Francis, who the author claims is leading Burke, Fox, and Sheridan: "Thy' [Francis'] *great revenge had stomach* to devour; Poor Hastings at a snap;—but lack'd the pow'r. Forearm'd and sharpen' in the legal strife; With ev'ry passion hostile to his life, Couldst thou, O Francis, partial at the best, Sit the accuser of thy Foe profest? Come then with knife and scales, exact thy due." *Reflexions on Impeachers and Impeaching*, p. 16.

23. Pitts, p. 97.

24. Ibid., p. 68.

25. Ibid., p. 97.

26. Ibid., p. 99.

27. Ibid., p. 97.

28. Ibid., p. 99.

29. On the problem of reflective judgment, see Linda Zerilli's "'We Feel Our Freedom': Imagination and Judgment in the Thought of Hannah Arendt," *Political Theory* 33(2005):2, 158–188.

30. On justification and "vindication," see Bonnie Honig's "Between Decision and Deliberation," *The American Political Science Review* 101(2007):1, 1–17.

31. His interest in appealing to public opinion is visible even well before the trial, in his communications with Philip Francis about crafting the charges of impeachment. There, he argues that they must display all of Hastings's crimes in the charges (rather than focusing on just a few) because "the people at large would not consider one or two acts, however striking, perhaps not three or four, as sufficient to call forth the reserved justice of the State" (*C* 5:242).

32. Most conservative readers of Burke fall into this camp. For example, see Harvey Mansfield's *Statesmanship and Party Government*; Francis Canavan's *The Political Reason of Edmund Burke* (Durham, NC: Duke University Press, 1960); and Peter Stanlis's *Burke and the Natural Law*. On the other hand, liberal and democratic critics of Burke also fail to emphasize this aspect of his thought. For example, see Michael Freeman's *Edmund Burke and the Critique of Political Radicalism* (Chicago: University of Chicago Press, 1980) and, more recently, Corey Robin's *The Reactionary Mind* (Oxford: Oxford University Press, 2011).

33. On Burke's invocations of the "swinish multitude" as a form of contempt, see Don Herzog's excellent *Poisoning the Minds of the Lower Orders* (Princeton, NJ: Princeton University Press, 2000).

34. My reading here departs from Harvey Mansfield's reading of the "Thoughts on the Present Discontents." Mansfield reads the "Thoughts" as a straightforward defense of elite rule, or trusteeship, that can refine the claims and feelings of the people into practical laws and regulations. (For Burke's famous theory of trusteeship, see his "Speech at the Conclusion of the Poll" [*WS*, 3:63–70]). Mansfield argues that these elites, unlike ordinary citizens, are capable of "sort[ing] out" the "natural feeling" within the discontents of the people from other, more dangerous and disorderly sorts of feelings, or "popular passions," that arise in a given society. This "sorting out" maintains those complex, "natural" distances between various hierachical and cultural groups in society that, in turn, enables the maintenance of freedom (*Statesmanship and Party Government*, Chicago: University of Chicago Press, 1965, p. 195). While Mansfield is correct that Burke portrays elites as more capable than the public of discerning the public good, Mansfield fails to adequately grapple with Burke's consistent claim in the "Thoughts" that elite wisdom sometimes falls short of this goal and is incapable of saving itself from the morass of private interest and influence into which it has fallen. I emphasize this part of the "Thoughts" in my reading and, in turn, Burke's solicitation of the public as the ultimate safeguard of the public good in such moments of elite failure.

35. Burke suggests several possible ways that the people can intervene and press MPs to attend to the common good. "Until a confidence in Government is reestablished, the people ought to be excited to a more strict and detailed attention to the conduct of their Representatives" (*WS* 2:312). Further, Burke suggests that the project of settling standards by which representatives' conduct should be judged should *itself* be a task of public discussion. "Standards, for judging more systematically upon their conduct ought to be settled in the meetings of counties and corporations" (*WS* 2:312). Burke also wanted

"[f]requent and correct lists of the [Parliamentary] voters in all important questions" (*WS* 2:312) to be publicly available to Britons, thus suggesting that making them available to the public would spur public discussion and interposition on behalf of accountability. "By such means," Burke says, "something may be done" (*WS* 2:312).

36. Isaac Kramnick has argued for reading this tension as rooted in a tension in Burke's self: between his love of deference (to father figures and the aristocracy) and his rage against the infantalization this love requires (that itself emerges from his own position as a "new man," a member of the rising bourgeoisie). See Kramnick's *The Rage of Edmund Burke: Portrait of an Ambivalent Conservative* (New York: Basic Books, 1977).

37. Edmund Burke, "An Appeal from the New to the Old Whigs," in *Further Reflections on the Revolution in France*, ed. Ritchie (Indianapolis: Liberty Fund, 1992), p. 168.

38. Hanna Pitkin, *The Concept of Representation* (Berkeley: University of California Press, 1972).

39. As she puts it, "[i]f a group has serious, substantive grievances which are not being met in Parliament, this is taken as evidence that its interest is not being protected there, and hence that it has a unique interest not shared by any of the places that do send members" (Pitkin, *The Concept of Representation*, p. 178).

40. "When great multitudes act together, under that discipline of nature"—that is, with both a soul and a body as just outlined—"I recognize the PEOPLE" and "[i]n all things this grand chorus of national harmony ought to have a mighty and decisive influence." (Burke, "Appeal from the New to the Old Whigs," p. 163).

41. There is a case to be made that Burke's writings on the French revolution call on the public in a similar way—to choose between competing groups of elites who claim to be representing the public good. For example, Burke writes in the "First Letter on a Regicide Peace" that the elite "natural representative" of the British people (whom he defines here narrowly) do not have consensus of opinion on the French revolution: "It cannot be concealed. We are a divided people" (*WS* 9:223).

42. Edmund Burke, *Reflections on the Revolution in France* (New York: Penguin, 1986), p. 135.

43. Ibid., my emphasis, p. 315.

44. Indeed, Burke's argument on behalf of actual representation for Irish Catholics portrays actual representation not as necessary only or primarily because the vote alone will help Catholics better show that their interests were not sufficiently represented, but because it connects Catholics and Protestants in relationships of obligation that should induce them to see each other as proper objects of state and societal care. He says:

"There is a relation in mutual obligation. Gratitude may not always have a very lasting power; but the frequent recurrency for favours will revive and refresh it, and will necessarily produce some degree of mutual attention. It will produce, at least, acquaintance; the several descriptions of people will not be kept so much apart as they now are, as if they were not only separate nations, but separate species. The stigma and reproach, the hideous mask will be taken off, and men will see each other as they are. Sure I am, that there have been thousands in Ireland, who have never conversed with a Roman Catholic in their whole lives, unless they happened to talk to their gardiner's workmen. . ." (9:629–630).

In other words, what is important about actual representation is not simply the power to vote for a representative, but rather engagement in relationships of obligation with others in the community, including their representative. Through such relationships, acquaintance with each other's needs develops that would otherwise remain absent, a victim of prejudice. The representative's attention to the public good is figured here, in the "Letter on Langrishe," as it is in the "Thoughts," as dependent on the representative being compelled by the public to tether himself to the networks of obligation that emerge in ordinary life and that are best known by the members of the public themselves.

45. Similarly, in India, Burke argues that the Company's transformation of Company concerns with profit into public concerns has rendered the meaning of the public good indeterminate, if not meaningless. As Burke puts it, while before the incursion of the East India Company into the Carnatic, "[a]ll ranks of people had their place in the public concern, and their share in the common stock and common prosperity," with the advent of British rule, "[i]t was their policy to consider hoards of money as crimes; to regard moderate rents as frauds on the sovereign; and to view, in the lesser princes, any claim of exemption from more than settled tribute, as an act of rebellion. Accordingly all the castles were, one after the other, plundered and destroyed. The native princes were expelled; the hospitals fell to ruin; the reservoirs of water went to decay; the merchants, bankers, and manufacturers disappeared; and sterility, indigence, and depopulation, overspread the face of these once flourishing provinces" (WS 5:423)

46. On this point, see Kohn and O'Neill, "A Tale of Two Indias."

47. On sentimentalism in eighteenth-century Britain, see John Mullan's *Sentiment and Sociability: The Language of Feeling in the Eighteenth Century* (Oxford: Clarendon Press, 1988); Markman Ellis's *The Politics of Sensibility: Race, Gender, and Commerce in the Sentimental Novel* (Cambridge: Cambridge University Press, 1996); and Michael Frazer's *The Enlightenment of Sympathy: Justice and the Moral Sentiments in the Eighteenth Century and Today* (Oxford: Oxford University Press, 2010).

48. Kathleen Wilson, *The Sense of the People: Politics, Culture, and Imperialism in England, 1715–1785* (Cambridge: Cambridge University Press, 1998), p. 3.

49. Ibid., p. 17.

50. While most often, as Wilson argues, "the political public represented by and through the press was being staked out as the preserve of the masculine, commercial and middling classes,"—and this is how Burke himself portrays it—"the public being created by print was becoming more inclusive," including women, literate laborers, etc. (pp. 46–47). Readers and discussers of public affairs exceeded, in other words, the construction of the public assumed and constructed by the press. Further, as H. T. Dickinson shows in *The Politics of the People in Eighteenth-Century Britain* (New York: St. Martin's Press, 1995), one of the most important topics and contested foci of the eighteenth-century "public" was the question of its own constitution—especially in the context of debates over who is the proper subject of representation by Parliament (in the late eighteenth century, only property-owning men were able to vote, the criteria for voting varied by location, and representation was not allocated according to population). Some Britons argued for equal representation for all property-owning men and others argued for the franchise for all men who paid taxes to a specified amount (p. 178). Still more radically, others argued for universal male suffrage (pp. 178, 181) or that the vote must be regulated by educational qualifications (p. 181), and some (Thomas Spence) even claimed that women should be given the right to vote (p. 185). Spence also argued for the nationalization of land to create economic equality, which alone, on his account, could equalize political influence (p. 189). Perhaps most interestingly, "Cartwright's fellow radical John Jebb" envisioned "a permanent, national association of delegates elected by universal suffrage" that "would function as a kind of 'counter-parliament' (some radicals in fact spoke of an 'out-of-doors Parliament') to pressure the government into implementing electoral reform" (Melton, p. 38). Dickinson also shows that successful action by "the public" in seeking to influence public affairs was not always pursued by those assumed to be its legitimate (white, male, propertied) participants. For example, "woolen manfuacturers who were based in towns with no direct representation in parliament," mounted

successful campaigns to protect their interests (Dickinson, p. 70). Similarly, the forms of public action taken by members of the public did not take one form (such as voting). While one form of claiming representation as "the public" happened via voting—and the forms of demanding representation of interests that the people could claim from their representatives and their sponsors—other forms included pressure campaigns (petitions, lobbying of MPs, etc.), local government and associations, and crowd action and riots.

51. In his first "Letter on a Regicide Peace" (written after the conclusion of the Hastings trial), Burke defines the "British publick" as consisting in those individuals who are able to obtain information (likely through reading) about public affairs, have the leisure to engage in discussions about it, and are independent (as evidenced by being economically independent):

"I have often endeavoured to compute and to class those who, in any political view, are to be called the people. Without doing something of this sort we must proceed absurdly. We should not be much wiser, if we pretended to very great accuracy in our estimate. But I think, in the calculation I have made, the error cannot be very material. In England and Scotland, I compute *that those of adult age, not declining in life, of tolerable leisure for such discussions, and of some means of information, more or less, and who are above menial dependence, (or what virtually is such) may amount to about four hundred thousand.* There is such a thing as a natural representative of the people. This body is that representative; and on this body, more than on the legal constituent, the artificial representative depends. *This is the British publick*; and it is a publick very numerous. The rest, when feeble, are the objects of protection; when strong, the means of force" (my emphasis, *WS* 9:223)

52. Paddy Bullard argues in *Edmund Burke and the Art of Rhetoric* (Cambridge: Cambridge University Press, 2011) that the standard Burke is using here is the standard of "decorum," or propriety, such as the notion of propriety invoked by Adam Smith in *Theory of Moral Sentiments*. Burke is certainly invoking a proper notion of public behavior here—especially in response to the serious accusations leveled at Hastings—but Bullard insufficiently attends to Burke's argument that standards of propriety themselves gain legitimacy because of their basis in natural feelings of sympathy (pp. 134–136).

53. David Hume, *A Treatise of Human Nature*, ed. David Fate Norton and Mary J. Norton (Oxford: Oxford University Press, 2000), p. 235.

54. Adam Smith, *The Theory of Moral Sentiments* (Amherst, MA: Prometheus Books, 2000), p. 23.

55. Hume, *Treatise of Human Nature*, pp. 320–321.

56. Ibid., p. 321.

57. Ibid., my emphasis, p. 370.

58. Siraj Ahmed, "The Theater of the Civilized Self: Edmund Burke and the East India Trials," *Representations* 78(2002):Spring, 28–55, 44.

59. On the fruitfulness of a "second nature" paradigm for political theory, see *Second Nature: Rethinking the Natural through Politics*, ed. Crina Archer, Laura Ephraim, and Lida Maxwell (New York: Fordham University Press, 2013).

60. Ahmed, p. 41.

61. Brycchan Carey, *British Abolitionism and the Rhetoric of Sensibility: Writing, Sentiment, and Slavery 1760–1807* (London: Palgrave Macmillan, 2005), p. 19.

62. While the eighteenth century has been described as the century of politeness and sentimentalism—a period when new norms of politeness and appeals to the heart allowed a rising bourgeois class to negotiate its relationships with the upper classes—Simon Dickie has recently challenged this broad characterization in his book, *Cruelty and Laughter: Forgotten Comic Literature and the Unsentimental Eighteenth Century* (Chicago: University of Chicago Press, 2011).

63. Carey, p. 20.

64. The injuries described by Burke are taken from a report by John Paterson that Paterson himself later claimed to be in error, or at least not entirely true.

65. Ahmed, p. 44.

66. Mehta, p. 170.

67. Mehta, p. 20. Burke's cosmopolitan project assumes mutual unfamiliarity, and thus the necessity of "a conversation between *two* strangers" (p. 22). Burke assumes mutual unfamiliarity because he assumes that there is no ultimate, universal standard to which both cultures can be subjected. Rather, for Burke, "territory or *place*, is a fundamental condition of collective and individual political identity" (p. 123), in the sense that "a certain shared order on the ground" (p. 161) inevitably helps to constitute individual and communal sentiments, opinions, laws, and norms. Consequently, from a Burkean perspective, cosmopolitanism—the ideal of understanding and dialogue between individuals and nations of different cultures—depends not on subsuming both cultures under a universal standard, which is really an exercise in cultural domination, but instead on the "conversation between *two* strangers" where an acknowledgement of "possible estrangement"—that is, that full understanding may *not* be possible due to cultural difference or other factors—"lies the possibility of *mutual* understanding, *mutual* influence, and *mutual* recognition" (p. 23). This "cosmopolitanism of sentiments. . . holds out the possibility, and even the hope, that through the conversation, which has as its purpose the understanding of the sentiments that give meaning to people's lives, wider bonds of sympathy can be forged" (p. 22).

68. David Stewart Erskine, Earl of Buchan *Letters of Albanicus to the People of England: On the Partiality and Injustice of the Charges Brought Against Warren Hastings, Esq; Late Governor General of Bengal*, J. Debrett, opposite Burlington-House, Piccadilly, 1786, p. 96.

69. On this problem in Western women's attempts to represent the concerns of non-Western women, see, for example, Uma Narayan's "The Project of Feminist Epistemology: Perspectives from a Nonwestern Feminist," in *Gender, Body, and Knowledge: Feminist Reconstructions of Being and Knowing*, ed. Allison Jaggar and Susan Bordo (New Brunswick, NJ: Rutgers University Press, 1989). On the problem of white women claiming sympathy with women of color, see bell hooks's *Feminist Theory: From Margin to Center* (Boston: South End Press, 1984).

70. Lauren Berlant, "The Subject of True Feeling," in *Cultural Pluralism, Identity Politics, and the Law*, ed. Austin Sarat and Thomas R. Kearns (Ann Arbor: University of Michigan Press, 1999), p. 53.

71. Amit Rai, *The Rule of Sympathy: Sentiment, Race, and Power 1750–1850* (London: Palgrave Macmillan, 2003), p. 42.

72. Ibid., xix.

73. Toward the end of the book, Rai does argue that "[t]here are moments were sympathy seems to spill beyond good policy, embodying an entirely different strategy" (Ibid., 167)—i.e., when its proponents question the very civilization and economies which seem to limit it (for example, through the figure of the "impartial spectator" in Smith, which for Rai stands in as the figure of the civilized man). Rai gestures toward this excess in his closing as a potential site of resistance to normalizing humanitarian sympathy (in which we still traffic). Yet he does not develop what such a resistant sympathy might look like.

74. In his writings on the impeachment, Burke himself seems to understand that sympathy may be an impossible goal, even though he does not seem to see the tensions inherent in his own appeal to it. Specifically, Burke marks to a certain degree the limits of the attempt to pursue sympathy across national boundaries—namely, in moments when

he suggests that full sympathy between Indians and Britons may be impossible because of cultural differences between the two peoples. For example, Burke argues that we are "so little acquainted with Indian details; the instruments of oppression under which the people suffer are so hard to be understood; and even the very names of the sufferers are so uncouth and strange to our ears, *that it is very difficult for our sympathy to fix upon these objects*" (my emphasis, *WS* 5:404). Similarly, Burke argues in his opening speech that full sympathy between Britons and Indians is unlikely because of the insurmountable geographical and cultural divide between the two nations—that is, the "great gulf, created by manners, opinions, and laws" between Britain and India that prevents communication between them (*WS* 6:302). Further, while Burke suggests in one moment that Britons have a greater capacity than Indians to understand and sympathize with other cultures, he also suggests that the point may be moot because Indians do not want to communicate with Britons.

Elsewhere in his writings, Burke portrays both Hindus and Muslims as incapable of understanding or adjusting to British laws and practices because of their rootedness in their land: they "have stood firm in their own country and cast their roots deep in their native soil. . . and fixed their opinions in their native soil, and bound them together" (*WS* 6:305). In the *Treatise*, Hume similarly suggests that such differences between people hinders the cultivation of sympathy between them—namely, because sympathy is easier to achieve when one can, through identification of resemblance between oneself and the sufferer, easily envision oneself in the place of the sufferer: "There is a very remarkable resemblance, which preserves itself amidst all their variety; and this resemblance must very much contribute to make us enter into the sentiments of others, and embrace them with facility and pleasure. Accordingly we find, that where, beside the general resemblance of our natures, there is any peculiar similarity in our manners, or character, or country, or language, it facilitates the sympathy. The stronger the relation is betwixt ourselves and any object, the more easily does the imagination make the transition, and convey to the related idea the vivacity of conception, with which we always form the idea of our own person" (Hume, *A Treatise of Human Nature*, p. 207). Thus, Hume argues, like Burke, that "[t]he sentiments of others have little influence, when far remov'd from us, and require the relation of contiguity"—spatial closeness to us—"to make them communicate themselves entirely" (Ibid.).

Sometimes, Burke seems to suggest that Britons might be able to overcome this "great gulf"—and feel sympathy for Indians—in ways that Indians cannot. For example, Burke argues that due to the Indian inability to accommodate British culture, Britons must "extend ours [our ideas] to take in theirs; because to say that that people shall change their maxims, lives and opinions, is what cannot be" (*WS* 6:302). Burke links this potential ability of Britons to their navigation of the sea. While Indians have no practice on "the sea"—that is, "that very element which, while appearing to disconnect, unites mankind" (*WS* 6:302)—Britons, as a seafaring people, are more familiar with diverse customs and thus are more flexible and capable of adapting their maxims and principles to accommodate Indian culture. Thus, the Lords must not try to "force nature" into the "circle of municipal justice," but rather "enlarge the circle of justice to the necessities of the Empire that we have obtained" (*WS* 6:279; cf. 6:307).

However, Burke also portrays this task of sympathy across deep difference as impossible even for the most enlightened Lord or member of the public due to Indian unwillingness to communicate with *them*. Burke claims that this unwillingness is due to cultural specificity: because Indians are so rooted in their soil—and unable to travel in their perspective—and "because their laws forbid them to mix with us, this nation," "we can have no immediate communication with them" (*WS* 6:302). However, we might also read this passage as Burke's way of attempting to soften or explain why a people subject to imperialism would not want to, or be able to, have a frank dialogue with the imperialists. Regardless of his justification, Burke's sense that Britons and Indians cannot have a direct conversation with each other leads him to suggest that some kind of analogy must be employed for Britons to approximate an understanding of India at all. For example, in his speech on Fox's East India Bill, Burke argues that Britons should employ Germany as a "middle term" by which "India might be approximated to our understanding and if possible to our feelings; *in order to awaken something of sympathy for the unfortunate natives,* of which I am afraid we are not perfectly susceptible, whilst we look at this very remote object through a false and cloudy medium" (my emphasis, *WS* 5:340). This suggests that British understandings of India will invariably be mediated and viewed through a European cultural lens that—even when attempting to understand India through analogy—inevitably distorts, even as it may amplify, Indian culture and law. After all, however much comparing Germany to India may allow Britons to grasp the nature of India (its importance, its size, its government, etc.), India is certainly not Germany. Sympathy for India that develops out of this analogy, then, will always be imperfect—creating sympathy that will always be to some degree misdirected and insufficient.

Burke's recognition of the likely impossibility of full sympathy, at least across national boundaries, is not a major theme of the impeachment speeches. However, its presence in those writings—however fleeting—should give us pause about seeing Burkean sympathy as *pure* fantasy and instrument of private or imperial interest as Rai portrays it.

75. Edmund Burke, *Selected Letters of Edmund Burke*, ed. Harvey Mansfield (Chicago: Chicago University Press, 1984), p. 397. Hereafter cited in the text as *SL*.

76. Both Uday Mehta (in *Liberalism and Empire*) and Harvey Mansfield (in *Selected Letters of Edmund Burke*) do so.

77. "Here I am in the last retreat of hunted infirmity. I am indeed aux abois: But, as the thro the whole of a various and long Life I have been more indebted than thankful to Providence, so I am now. Singularly so, in being dismissed, as hitherto I appear to be so gently from Life and set to follow, those who in Course ought to have followd me [Burke's son, Richard Burke, had recently died], whom, I trust, I shall yet, in some inconceivable manner, see and know; and by whom I shall be seen and known" (*SL*, 397).

78. Indeed, Burke's will specifically asked that no great physical monument be erected after his death to memorialize him. As quoted in an 1834 edition of his "Works," Burke's will stated: "I wish my funeral to be (without any punctiliousness in that respect) the same as that of my brother, and to exceed it as little as possible in point of charge, whether on account of my family or of any others who would go to a greater expense; and I desire, in the same manner and with the same qualifications, that no monument beyond a middle-sized tablet, with a small and simple inscription on the church-wall, or on the flag-stone, be erected. I say this, because I know the partial kindness to me of some of my friends. But I have had, in my life-time, but too much of noise and compliment." *The Works of the Right Honorable Edmund Burke: With a Biographical and Critical Introduction, and Portrait*, ed. Sir Joshua Reynolds (London: Holdsworth & Ball, 1834, p. xxxviii).

79. On funeral monuments in eighteenth-century Britain, see Nigel Llewellyn's *Funeral Monuments in Post-Reformation England* (Cambridge: Cambridge University Press, 2000); Ralph Houlbrooke's *Death, Religion, and the Family in England, 1480–1750* (Oxford: Clarendon Press, 1998); and David Bindman and Malcolm Baker's *Roubiliac and the Eighteenth-Century Monument* (New Haven, CT: Yale University Press, 1995).

80. Funeral monuments were also a contested part of the public sphere. In part, this was because, as David Bindman argues, the growing local tourism surrounding funeral monuments—as in Westminster Abbey—itself turned monuments into part of

the public sphere, that is, part of the space in which people met, engaged in discussion, and formed opinions (Bindman, p. 15). Further, however, funeral monuments were an object of contention in the press—especially in terms of the question about whether ostentatious funeral monuments served or detracted from the public good they were supposed to serve. For example, Samuel Johnson, in his "Essay on Epitaphs," condemns "the inclusion of all lighter or gayer ornaments" in epitaphs meant to "perpetuate the examples of virtue" and "supply the want" of the dead man's presence (in *The Idler*, 1767, pp. 290, 292).

81. Llewellyn, pp. 15–59; Holbrouke, pp. 331–371.

82. Bindman, p. 36.

83. Ibid., p. 35.

84. *The Spectator*, March 1970, no. 26, p. 3.

85. My emphasis. Henry Mackenzie, *The Man of Feeling* (New York: Oxford, 2009), p. 74.

86. Ibid., p. 98.

87. Ibid.

Chapter 3

1. Jacques Rancière, *The Ignorant Schoolmaster*, trans. Kristin Ross (Palo Alto, CA: Stanford University Press, 1991).

2. On the discourse of degeneration and its relationship to the rise of the mass public in nineteenth-century Europe, see Daniel Pick's *Faces of Degeneration: A European disorder, c. 1848–1918* (Cambridge: Cambridge University Press, 1989). On the discourses of crowd psychology in nineteenth-century France, also see Susanna Barrows's *Distorting Mirrors: Visions of the Crowd in Late Nineteenth-Century France* (New Haven, CT: Yale University Press, 1981).

3. In "Truth and Public Reason," Joshua Cohen attempts to articulate a "political conception of truth" consisting in common understandings of the nature of truth that can guide debates over truth in particular instances (*Philosophy and Public Affairs* 37(2009):1, 2–42). Similarly, Habermas has long argued that the question of truth in politics should be approached by finding criteria or procedures through which we can assess the truth of statements. See, for example, his *Truth and Justification*, trans. Barbara Fultner (Cambridge, MA: MIT Press, 2003).

4. Hannah Arendt, "Lying in Politics," in *Crises of the Republic* (New York: Harcourt Brace & Company, 1969), p. 45.

5. Michel Foucault, *Fearless Speech*, ed. Joseph Pearson (Los Angeles: Semiotext(e), 2001), p. 170.

6. For an important critique of Habermas's claim that the "force" of the better argument can be discerned through non-contradiction, see Davide Panagia's chapter on "The Force of Political Argument: Habermas, Hazlitt, and the Essay," in *The Poetics of Political Thinking* (Durham, NC: Duke University Press, 2006).

7. Foucault discusses this problem of tutelage as the Kantian problem of Enlightenment: "Having a book take the place of understanding (*Verstand*), having a director take the place of conscience (*Gewissen*), and having a doctor dictate one's diet are what characterize, exemplify, and concretely manifest what it is to be in the condition of tutelage" (*The Government of the Self and Others: Lectures at the College de France 1982–1983*, trans. Graham Burchell, New York: Picador, 2010, p. 30).

8. As Arendt puts it, "every claim in the sphere of human affairs to an absolute truth, whose validity needs no support from the side of opinion, strikes at the very roots of

all politics and all governments." Such claims are problematic because they presume a mode of assuring validity—independent of human opinion—that is at odds with political life, where opinions gain meaning and validity precisely by taking into account the opinions of others. Hannah Arendt, "Truth and Politics," in *Between Past and Future* (New York: Penguin, 1954, 1968), p. 233.

9. Jean Starobinski, *Jean-Jacques Rousseau: Transparency and Obstruction* (Chicago: University of Chicago Press, 1988).

10. Bernard Lazare, *Une Erreur Judiciare: l'Affaire Dreyfus*, ed. Philippe Oriol. (Paris: Allia, 1993).

11. In addition to the works explicitly cited throughout this chapter, my general historical knowledge of the Affair is indebted to Jean-Denis Bredin's *The Affair: The Case of Alfred Dreyfus*, trans. Jeffrey Mehlman (New York: George Braziller, 1987) and Ruth Harris's *Dreyfus: Politics, Emotion and the Scandal of the Century* (New York: Picador, 2011).

12. Arendt, "Truth and Politics," p. 260.

13. As Venita Datta notes, "the fin de siècle was a time of cultural crisis. The works of writers and artists of this period reflect the contemporary form of the manifestation of modernity, which included the emergence of mass democracy, the growth of cities, the rise of the working class, and the entry into public life of Jews and women. France in particular was haunted by the loss of national honor, in light of both the defeat in the Franco-Prussian War and the precipitous decline of the national birthrate" (*Birth of an Icon: The Literary Avant-Garde and the Origins of the Intellectual in France*, Albany: State University of New York Press, 1999, p. 63).

14. Louis Begley, *Why the Dreyfus Affair Matters* (New Haven, CT: Yale University Press, 2009), p. 48.

15. Emile Zola, *The Dreyfus Affair: "J'Accuse" and Other Writings*, trans. Eleanor Levieux, ed. Alain Pagés (New Haven, CT: Yale University Press, 1996), p. 61. Hereafter cited in the text as *DA*.

16. As Louis Begley has recently argued, there are more than a few parallels here between Dreyfus's trial and contemporary military tribunals in Guantanamo (Begley, "Introduction" to *Why the Dreyfus Affair Matters*).

17. Similarly, he says in "M. Scheurer-Kestner" that "any nation that did not base its sole *raison d'etre* on truth and justice would today be a nation doomed" (*DA*, 12) and in his speech to the jury in his libel trial, Zola says, "No nation can be wrought-up to this extent without the very core of its moral sense being endangered" (*DA*, 60).

18. Indeed, the Dreyfus Affair "reveals in broad daylight all the nasty politicking that goes on in smoke-filled back rooms; it besmirches the parliamentary system and will do it in" (*DA*, 40). Incidentally, this is also how Hannah Arendt sees the origins of the Dreyfus Affair in her analysis of it in *The Origins of Totalitarianism* (New York: World Publishing, 1958), pp. 95–99.

19. Gustave Le Bon. *The Crowd: A Study of the Popular Mind* (Mineola, NY: Dover Publishing, [1895] 2003).

20. Ibid., p. 15.

21. Ibid., p. 7.

22. Ibid., p. 6.

23. Barrows, *Distorting Mirrors*, p. 190.

24. Barrows argues that Zola's fiction similarly resists Le Bon's depiction of the crowd. While Zola portrayed the crowd as violent and bestial in his fiction (particularly in *Germinal*), Barrows argues that he also depicted this violent, bestial nature as *produced* by a bestial economic system that treated men like animals. In her words, "Zola's crowds, in short were not the faceless *canaille*; their desperate acts of violence were, in Zola's

eyes, a savage but comprehensible reaction to a dehumanizing, indeed immoral, system. Reducing men to beasts, he warned, made bestial retaliation inevitable" (p. 108). Zola, Barrows says, "included the crowd, a theme of Taine's 'persistent nightmares,' within the ranks of humanity, and he struggle to comprehend the political perspectives, the aspirations, and the fears of both rich and poor" (p. 113).

25. Similarly, Zola says that those who are worried about the republic must "group together! They must write; they must speak up!" in order to "enlighten the little people, the humble people who are being poisoned and forced into delirium" (DA, 42). Zola sees himself as embarked on such a task. And in a satirical essay on the supposed Jewish "syndicate" behind the Dreyfusard cause, Zola writes that "[o]urs is a syndicate to act on public opinion, to cure it of the frenzy into which the foul press has whipped it up, and to restore it to its age-old dignity and generosity. . . —of that syndicate I am a member, have no doubt about it! And I devoutly hope that every decent person in France will become a member!" (DA, 19). In order to beat back the forces of injustice, he says that he and other "sons who love you and honour you, France, have but one ardent duty in this gravest hour: to act powerfully on public opinion: to enlighten it and rescue it from the error towards which blind passions are steering it. There is no more useful, more sacrosanct task than this" (DA, 36).

26. In Zola's narrative, Paty de Clam bears a resemblance to the Romantic authors he critiques in his literary criticism. Zola argues that Paty de Clam, like Romantics infatuated with the medieval period, proceeded as if in "some fifteenth-century chronicle" and used "the methods that litter cheap novels" (DA, 45, 44). In his later "Statement to the Jury," Zola also calls the anti-Dreyfusard's story about Dreyfus a "legend" that is also "an old wives' tale" (DA, 58).

27. Henri Mitterand. "Histoire, mythe, et literature: La mesure de 'J'Accuse. . .!' " in Historical Reflections/Reflexions Historiques 24(1998):1, 21.

28. As Barthes puts it, "[a]s a total of linguistic signs, the meaning of the myth has its own value, it belongs to a history. . . : in the meaning, a signification is already built, and could very well be self-sufficient if myth did not take hold of it and did not turn it suddenly into an empty parasitical form" (Roland Barthes, Mythologies, trans. Annette Lavers, New York: Hill and Wang, 1972, p. 117).

29. Ibid., p. 116.

30. Ibid., p. 118.

31. Ibid., p. 116.

32. Ibid., p. 118.

33. "[T]he Negro who salutes is not the symbol of the French Empire: he has too much presence, he appears as a rich, fully experienced, spontaneous, innocent, indisputable image. But at the same time this presence is tamed, put at a distance, made almost transparent; it recedes a little, it becomes the accomplice of a concept which comes to it fully armed, French imperiality: once made use of, it becomes artificial." (Ibid.)

34. Emile Zola, The Experimental Novel, and Other Essays, trans. Belle Sherman (New York: Haskell House, 1964), p. 8. Hereafter cited in the text as EN.

35. Emile Zola, Germinal, trans. Peter Collier (New York: Oxford University Press, 1993), p. 213.

36. Zola, Germinal, my emphasis, p. 216.

37. Petrey offers an important and acute analysis of this same scene in Realism and Revolution: Balzac, Stendhal, Zola, and the Performances of History (Ithaca, NY: Cornell University Press, 1988, p. 168). Petrey's interest is, however, slightly different from mine. Petrey does not emphasize the incommensurability of perspective revealed in the scene as illustrative of Zola's conception of truth, but rather focuses on refuting Lukac's critique

of Zola (Lukacs argues that Zola's naturalism essentially over-naturalizes his description of the world as singular and objective, thus obscuring how capitalism generates different vantage points on the world and, in particular, how it generates the proletarian potential for revolt).

38. Walker, "Prophetic Myths in Zola," *Publications of the Modern Language Association of America* 74(1959):4, 444–452. Walker shows that in *La Faute de l'abbe Mouret*, *Germinal*, and *La debacle* (among others), Zola often repeats and transforms Christian and Greco-Roman myths and symbols of apocalypse and, in turn, rebirth.

39. Zola, *Germinal*, p. 524.

40. Yet on the other hand, *Germinal* (like the rest of Zola's fiction) emphasizes the importance of human action and struggle in propelling forward a process of rebirth. The mine, after all, would not have collapsed—at least not as soon as it did—were it not for Souvarine purposefully weakening its supports. And the mine would not have been vulnerable to that weakening were it not for the long strike carried out by the workers. Finally, were it not for Étienne's will to survive in the mine when all avenues for escape seemed cut off, he would not be able to carry the message of the strike—and the potential rebirth out of destruction—beyond Montsou. Zola's myth of degeneration and rebirth, in other words, does seem to fold existing social and political problems into a material-ist myth of degeneration and rebirth, but it also places the agency for that rebirth—at least in part—in human hands. As I will suggest in a moment, it is a myth that suggests that rebirth is only possible if individuals attend to their reality, and seek to redress and survive it.

41. Cited in Walker, "Prophetic Myths in Zola," p. 448.

42. Thanks to Sara Kippur for help with translating this passage.

43. Walker, "Prophetic Myths in Zola," p. 447.

44. Linda Zerilli, "Truth and Politics," *Theory and Event* 9(2006):4. DOI: 10.1353/tae.2007.0015.

45. In this diagnosis of the problems inhabiting mass spectatorship, Zola echoes com-mon late nineteenth-century criticisms of "the crowd" and "mob," made perhaps most famously by Le Bon—namely, that when individuals come together in mass situations, they become susceptible to contagion of emotions (Le Bon's *The Crowd*; cf. Barrows's *Distorting Mirrors.*). Yet unlike Le Bon, who believed that individuals lost social inhibi-tions when they become part of a crowd, Zola seems to be suggesting that mass specta-torship is contagious in a different way: social norms, conventions, and prudishness are reinforced. Thus, while the behavior of a crowd or a mob may grow out of control, Zola is suggesting that this happens most often on *behalf* of engrained prejudice rather than against it.

46. Jason Frank, *Constituent Moments: Enacting the People in Postrevolutionary America* (Durham, NC: Duke University Press, 2009), p. 3.

47. Arendt, *Origins of Totalitarianism*, p. 113.

48. In "J'Accuse!" Zola says, "the War Office employed every means imaginable—campaigns in the press, statements and innuendoes, every type of influence—to cover Esterhazy, in order to convict Dreyfus a second time. *The republican government should take a broom to that nest of Jesuits. . . and make a clean sweep!*" (my emphasis, *DA*, 50).

49. Arendt, *Origins of Totalitarianism*, p. 106.

50. Ibid., p. 95.

51. Ibid., p. 94.

52. Ibid., p. 110.

53. Ibid., my emphasis.

54. Ibid., p. 118.

55. Ibid.

56. Ibid., pp. 290–302. On Arendt's critique of human rights and her claim of the "right to have rights," see Ayten Gundogdu's "Perplexities of the Rights of Man: Arendt on the Aporias of Human Rights," *European Journal of Political Theory* 11(2012):1, 4–24.

57. Arendt, *Origins of Totalitarianism*, pp. 114, 115.

58. Ibid., pp. 115, 114, 114.

59. Arendt, *On Revolution* (New York: Penguin, 1965), p. 130.

60. As Louis Begley says, *Vérité* is not among Zola's best works (Begley, *Why the Dreyfus Affair Matters*, p. 187). However, the novel does give us a sense of how Zola saw the animating causes of the Affair and it offers a sense of how he ultimately saw full justice. As Murray Sachs puts it in a rare complementary article about the book, "[t]he advantage Zola gained by transposing the Dreyfus Affair into a domain of national importance—elementary education—is alone worth attention because it made starkly evident that the Dreyfus Affair was no minor misunderstanding among the military establishment that has been blown out of proportion, as many wished to believe, *but was a product of harmful forces and attitudes endemic in French civilization, which needed to be rooted out*" ("Emile Zola's Last Word: *Vérité* and the Dreyfus Affair," *Romance Quarterly* 45(1998)4: 203–210, my emphasis, p. 209).

61. In the Calas Affair, it was (as in Zola's novel) a young boy who was killed, and the supposed motive in the Calas Affair was also (as in the novel) that the child supposedly wanted to convert to Catholicism and thus was killed by his Jewish family. Voltaire famously wrote his *Treatise on Tolerance* (trans. Brian Masters, Cambridge: Cambridge University Press, 2000) in response. Voltaire, like Zola, blames the injustice on fanaticism and he portrays the emergence of fanaticism in Toulouse as a kind of *resurgence*, as a response to the advancement of Reason and Enlightenment: "And this in our own day! In an age when Enlightenment had made such progress!. . . Fanaticism, infuriated by the advance of Reason, is thus seen to thrash about in an agony of frustration and renewed spite" (p. 6). On the Calas Affair more generally, see David Bien's *The Calas Affair* (Princeton, NJ: Princeton University Press, 1960).

62. *Vérité*, trans. Ernest Alfred Vizetelly (New York: John Lane, 1903), p. 34.

63. Almost at the outset of the book, Marc—upon hearing of the crime—rushes to the Catholic school where Zephirin lodged and found a monk and priest there, one of whom clearly tampers with a crucial piece of evidence (a copy-slip, which has initials on it that are later claimed by handwriting "experts" to belong to Simon even though they clearly were not his initials [*Vérité*, p. 101]—the priest tampers with it by tearing off the corner of the slip where a stamp from the Brothers' school was embossed).

64. For example, Zola characterizes Froment's students (and their parents) as "the multitude, the heavy, inert mass, many of them worthy people no doubt, but none the less a mass of lead, which weighted the nation down to the ground, incapable as they were of leading a better life, of becoming free, just, and truly happy, because they were steeped in ignorance and poison" (*Vérité*, p. 61). Their "semi-education" in Church schools "was nowadays acquired without method, and which reposed on no serious scientific foundation" and "led simply to a poisoning of the brain, to a state of disquieting corruption" (*Vérité*, p. 61).

65. *Vérité*, my emphasis, p. 89. For example, Marc sees the deceit practiced by the judge at Rozan (during the new trial) as a "great social crime" [crime against society]; that deceit "was carried on in the darkness in which great social crimes take their course; all that appeared on the surface was some turbid ebullition, a kind of terror sweeping through the streets as through a city stricken with a pestilence" (*Vérité*, p. 400). And as it seemed more certain that Simon would be re-convicted, Marc says that "[a]ssuredly the

greatest crime of all was now in preparation" (*Vérité*, p. 405). And after the guilty verdict, "Marc felt a deadly chill in every vein. It was a frigid horror: the supreme iniquity, in which just minds had refused to believe, the crime of crimes, which had seemed impossible a few hours earlier, which reason had rejected, had suddenly become a monstrous reality" (*Vérité*, p. 415). And when Genevieve (Marc's estranged wife, who had been turned back to the church by her grandmother) returns to Marc, she shows that she has become rational again because she recognizes this as a crime. She writes to him: "I have read the whole of the inquiry, I have followed the trial. The most monstrous of crimes has been committed. Simon is innocent" (*Vérité*, p. 416). Similarly, Marc says, with despair: "The crime of crimes had been committed, and France did not rise against it!" (*Vérité*, p. 419).

66. Marc listens to another schoolmaster (embittered by poverty and humiliation) say, "Ah! they regard it as a fine opportunity to crush the freethinkers. A Communal schoolmaster guilty of abomination and murder! What a splendid battle-cry!" (*Vérité*, p. 74) Similarly, Delbos accepts the case because he sees "all the public powers, all the forces of reaction, which, in order to save the old rotten framework of society from destruction, were coalescing and striving to ruin a poor and guiltless man" (*Vérité*, p. 99).

67. *Vérité*, my emphasis, p. 156. In a sentence highly typical of the novel, Zola says, "The highest *role* and the noblest in a nascent democracy is that of the poor and scorned elementary schoolmaster, appointed to teach the scorned elementary schoolmaster, appointed to teach the humble, to train them to be happy citizens, the builders of the future City of Justice and Peace. Marc felt it was so, and he suddenly realized the exact sense of his mission, his apostleship of Truth, that fervent passion to acquire Truth, certain and positive, then cry it aloud and teach it to all, which had ever possessed him" (*Vérité*, p. 157). This kind of education is depicted by Zola in the novel as the best response to the crime against society committed by the Church and government—that is, by remedying the social ill (ignorance) that made it possible: "He [Marc] considered that it was a crime to poison a lad's brain with a belief in miracles, and to set brute force, assassination, and theft in the front rank as manly and patriotic duties. Such teaching could only produce imbecile inertia, sudden criminal frenzy, iniquity, and wretchedness" (*Vérité*, p. 466).

68. *Vérité*, my emphasis, pp. 467–468.

69. I will not go into detail about the long, slow process of social change that occurs in the novel—sparked by Marc's mode of education, which allows students to learn to think for themselves, but which proceeds through the state's withdrawal of support for the church and its schools, as well as an elevation of secular school teachers in the social hierarchy. However, for Marc, even as society progresses, it cannot achieve full progress unless it does justice in the Simon affair—"that everlasting Simon case, which, after the lapse of so many years, still remained like a cancer gnawing at the heart of the country. People might deny its existence, believe it to be dead, cease to speak of it, but nevertheless it still stealthily prosecuted its ravages, like some secret venom poisoning life" (*Vérité*, p. 488). However, the gradual progress of the French people—"the social evolution" from which "a new nation was coming" (*Vérité*, p. 489), whose members were "all were now acquiring a true consciousness of things, setting their ideal no longer in any mysticism, but in the proper regulation of human life, which needed to be all reason, truth, and justice in order that mankind might dwell together in peace, brotherliness, and happiness" (*Vérité*, p. 501)—enabled them to do justice to the Simon Affair.

70. "As for the Court of Cassation, which still smarted form the smack it had received at Rozan, it tried the case with extraordinary dispatch, purely and simply annulling the Rozan verdict without sending Simon before any other tribunal. *It was all, so to say, a mere*

formality; in three phrases everything was effaced, and justice was done at last" (*Vérité*, my emphasis, p. 519). In other words, the formal legal proceedings were almost unnoticeable or unimportant after the social evolution had taken place, creating a people that would do justice—it was, as Zola says, a "mere formality."

71. Zola writes that in Maillebois, after the rehabilitation, there was a widespread sentiment that "reparation was necessary" (*Vérité*, p. 520): "when a whole people has been guilty of such an abominable error, when it has turned a fellow-being into such a pitiable, suffering creature, it would be good that it should acknowledge its fault, and confer some triumph on that man by a great act of frankness, in which truth and justice would find recognition" (*Vérité*, p. 520). As one young man says to Marc, "His legal acquittal does not suffice; for us—the children and grandchildren of the persecutors—it is a duty to confess and efface the transgression of our forerunners" (*Vérité*, p. 532).

72. *Vérité*, p. 528.

73. It is "not a palace, but a modest, bright, cheerful dwelling, which might be offered to Simon, so that he might end his days in it encompassed by the respect and affection of everybody. The gift would have no great pecuniary value—it would simply represent delicate and brotherly homage" (*Vérité*, p. 533).

74. *Vérité*, p. 534.

75. *Vérité*, p. 564.

Chapter 4

1. Letter from Hannah Arendt to Karl Jaspers, October 20, 1963. In *Hannah Arendt Karl Jaspers Correspondence 1926–1969*, ed. Lotte Kohler and Hans Saner, trans. Robert and Rita Kimber (New York: Harcourt Brace Jovanovich, 1992), p. 525.

2. Hannah Arendt, *Eichmann in Jerusalem* (New York: Penguin, 1963), p. 280. Hereafter cited in the text as *EJ*.

3. James Tully, *Public Philosophy in a New Key*, Volume 1: *Democracy and Civic Freedom* (Cambridge: Cambridge University Press), p. 56. Other examples of this juridical reading can be found in the work of Dana Villa and Leora Bilsky. While Dana Villa portrays Arendt in *Arendt and Heidegger* (Princeton, NJ: Princeton University Press, 1996) as a thinker of the specificity of political action, he argues in *Politics, Philosophy, and Terror* that in *Eichmann in Jerusalem* Arendt "identified herself so completely with the demands of justice in a case where justice seemed, to many, either transindividual or a matter of secondary importance" (Princeton, NJ: Princeton University Press, 1999, p. 49). Villa tempers this juridical reading when he suggests that Arendt's identification with justice leads her to be critical of "traditional moral yardsticks" (p. 53), but Leora Bilsky suggests that Arendt's focus on justice leads her to seek new criteria for reflective judgment—oriented by "liberal ends"—by which courts and the public could better judge unprecedented crimes against humanity (*Transformative Justice: Israeli Identity on Trial*, Ann Arbor: University of Michigan Press, 2004, p. 135). This is not, of course, the only way that Arendt's work on judgment may be conceived. For an interpretation of Arendtian judgment as a practice of freedom (rather than being a practice of rule-following oriented to particular, "liberal ends"), see Linda Zerilli's "'We Feel Our Freedom': Imagination and Judgment in the Thought of Hannah Arendt," *Political Theory* 33 (April): 158–188, and *Feminism and the Abyss of Freedom* (Chicago: University of Chicago Press, 2005).

4. Shoshana Felman, *The Juridical Unconscious: Trials and Trauma in the Twentieth Century* (Cambridge, MA: Harvard University Press, 2002), p. 112.

5. Seyla Benhabib, "Arendt's *Eichmann in Jerusalem*," in *The Cambridge Companion to Hannah Arendt*, ed. Dana Villa (Cambridge: Cambridge University Press, 2000), pp. 79–80.

6. An important recent reading of *Eichmann in Jerusalem* in political terms can be found in Lori Marso's "Simone de Beauvoir and Hannah Arendt: Judgments in Dark Times," *Political Theory* 40(2012):2, 165–193. There, Marso contrasts Arendt's and Beauvoir's criticisms of Eichmann's and Brasillach's trials in specifically political terms, ultimately arguing on behalf of Beauvoir's analysis.

7. Tully, *Public Philosophy in a New Key*, p. 147.

8. On this point, see Villa's *Politics, Philosophy, and Terror*, p. 49.

9. On *Eichmann in Jerusalem* as a critique of Israel using the trial for purposes of state-building, see Bonnie Honig's "Another Cosmopolitanism? Law and Politics in the New Europe," in *Another Cosmopolitanism*, Seyla Benhabib (Oxford: Oxford University Press, 2007).

10. Hanna Yablonka's history of the Eichmann trial, *The State of Israel vs. Adolf Eichmann*, largely supports Arendt's depiction of Hausner's vision of the trial (New York: Schocken Books, 2004).

11. "Civil Disobedience," in *Crises of the Republic* (Orlando, FL: Harcourt & Brace, 1969), p. 99.

12. As Arendt notes in *The Origins of Totalitarianism* (Cleveland: World Publishing Company, [1951] 1967), the "inherent logicality" of ideology and its "coercive" consistency and explanatory power (p. 472)—its "self-compulsion" (p. 474)—keeps us from judging events and deeds in their specificity because our interpretation of them is given in advance by the "coercive" logic of ideology.

13. On this point, I align with Leora Bilsky's reading of Arendt in *Transformative Justice*, p. 119.

14. Seyla Benhabib, *The Reluctant Modernism of Hannah Arendt* (Lanham, MD: Rowman & Littlefield, 2000), pp. 184, 185.

15. Seyla Benhabib, *Another Cosmopolitanism*, p. 19.

16. Cited in Benhabib, *Another Cosmopolitanism*, p. 15.

17. Ibid.

18. Ibid., p. 18. On this point, also see Benhabib's "Arendt's 'Eichmann in Jerusalem,'" p. 193.

19. Benhabib, *Another Cosmopolitanism*, p. 158.

20. Ibid., p. 19.

21. Ibid., p. 48.

22. Seyla Benhabib, "Claiming Rights across Borders: International Human Rights and Democratic Sovereignty," *American Political Science Review* 103(2009):4, 691–704, 698.

23. Ibid.

24. Villa, *Politics, Philosophy, and Terror*, p. 53. Indeed, Arendt notes that those Germans who clung to old value systems were the happiest to exchange those values for those offered by the Nazis (*EJ*, 295).

25. Bilsky, *Transformative Justice*, pp. 265, 266. Reflective judgment for Bilsky consists in a narrative practice of judging the new through imagining oneself occupying the perspective of concrete others—a practice that naturally spills over into actual deliberation with those others and, in turn, a community that values and respects pluralism (p. 135). This is not the only way to understand Arendtian reflective judgment. While I do not have the time or space to delve into this set of debates here, Bilsky's account finds a strong challenger in Linda Zerilli's reading of Arendtian reflective judgment—a reading that

suggests (contra Bilsky) that Arendtian reflective judgment is not about *communication* (with concrete others) but about *communicability*—that is, the practice of making claims that open up a new community. As Zerilli puts it, reflective judgment "stimulates the imagination of judging spectators and expands their sense of what is communicable, what they will count as part of the common world" ("We Feel Our Freedom," p. 180). While I do not have time to develop the point here, Zerilli's emphasis on the world-expanding character of spectators' judgment seems more complementary to the reading of *Eichmann in Jerusalem* I am developing here than Bilsky's.

26. Leora Bilsky, "When Actor and Spectator Meet in the Courtroom: Reflections on Hannah Arendt's Concept of Judgment," in *Judgment, Imagination, and Politics: Themes from Kant and Arendt*, ed. Jennifer Nedelsky and Ronald Beiner (Lanham, MD: Rowman & Littlefield, 2001), p. 273.

27. Bilsky distinguishes between "politics" as politicization and "politics" as an opening up of an issue for deliberation. "An issue becomes political" in the proper sense "when it is contested across a range of different discursive arenas and among a range of different publics" (2004, p. 68).

28. Bilsky, "When Actor and Spectator Meet in the Courtroom," p. 270; and *Transformative Justice*, p. 13.

29. Bilsky, "When Actor and Spectator Meet in the Courtroom," p. 271.

30. Ibid., pp. 266–267.

31. Ibid., p. 273.

32. Bilsky, *Transformative Justice*, p. 96.

33. Bilsky, "When Actor and Spectator Meet in the Courtroom," p. 277.

34. Such older "international offense[s]" included "expulsion" (*EJ*, 268). Arendt also argues that the Court's "too eager adherence to the Nuremberg precedent wherever possible" was "part of the failure of the Jerusalem court" (*EJ*, 274), since that precedent collapsed "crimes against humanity" with war crimes.

35. See Robert Cover's *Justice Accused* (New Haven, CT: Yale University Press, 1975) and "Nomos and Narrative," in *Narrative, Violence, and the Law*, ed. Martha Minow, Michael Ryan, and Austin Sarat (Ann Arbor: University of Michigan Press, 1995).

36. Arendt seems to express a similar concern in *The Human Condition* (Chicago: University of Chicago Press, 1958). On the one hand, Arendt seems to approve of the Greek separation between law and politics because it helped to protect the distinctive experience of political freedom. For the Greeks, she writes, law "was quite literally a wall, without which there might have been an agglomeration of houses, a town (*asty*), but not a city, a political community. This wall-like law was sacred, but only the inclosure [*sic*] was political" (1958, p. 64). Yet, on the other hand, Arendt worries in *The Human Condition* about how the strict separation of law and politics can become dangerous. The danger, Arendt says, is the "delusion" that we " 'make' institutions or laws, for instance, as we make tables and chairs" (p. 188). To cast laws as "prepolitical," Arendt says, threatens to portray laws—which she says are properly a part of "the realm of human affairs," of political action and speech (p. 188)—as the work of *homo faber*, who acts instrumentally. This "delusion" is dangerous because of the experience which gives rise to it: it expresses a "conscious despair of all action, political and non-political, coupled with the utopian hope that it may be possible to treat men as one treats other 'material' " (p. 188). In other words—and similarly to her treatment of the Jerusalem Court judges—Arendt is suggesting that when we treat our ability to act politically as dependent on laws that persist independently of that action, we are already despairing of our ability to act.

37. Felman, *The Juridical Unconscious*, p. 121.

38. Ibid., p. 124.

39. Ibid., p. 159.

40. Ibid., pp. 157, 159.

41. Ibid., p. 165.

42. Bilsky suggests that Arendt's reaction to Grynzspan indicates that Arendt was ultimately captured by Hausner's approach to the trial (*Transformative Justice*, p. 150). Perhaps—but why is Arendt captured only by some witnesses and not others? In this chapter, I ask what interpretive possibilities open up if we focus less on how the "architect" of the trial (Hausner) seeks to direct it and more on how the agency present in spectators' responses to the trial may transform it.

43. Arendt, *The Human Condition*, pp. 202–204; and *On Revolution* (New York: Penguin, 1963), p. 167. On this aspect of Arendt's thought, see Patchen Markell's "The Rule of the People: Arendt, *Archê*, and Democracy," *The American Political Science Review* 100(2006), 1–14.

44. Bonnie Honig discusses Arendtian political action *qua* founding in *Political Theory and the Displacement of Politics* (Ithaca, NY: Cornell University Press, 1993); also see Villa's *Arendt and Heidegger*.

45. Arendt, *On Revolution*, p. 166.

46. Arendt, *The Human Condition*, pp. 200, 178, 191.

47. Arendt, *The Human Condition*, p. 200. Also see Honig's *Political Theory and the Displacement of Politics*, p. 78.

48. Markell discusses and reframes this problem in "The Rule of the People."

49. Honig discusses the problem with law/exception frameworks in "Between Decision and Deliberation."

50. Here, my reading draws from and aligns with Honig's reading of Arendt's account as "fabulist" in *Political Theory and the Displacement of Politics*.

51. My conception of agonism here aligns with and builds on Honig's work on agonism in, for example, "Between Decision and Deliberation"; Tully's conception of agonism in *Public Philosophy in a New Key*; and William Connolly's "agonistic respect" in *The Ethos of Pluralization* (Minneapolis: University of Minnesota Press, 1995). Andrew Schaap's edited volume, *Law and Agonistic Politics* (Farnham, UK: Ashgate, 2013), stages a provocative conversation about the relationship between agonism and law.

52. Pp. 80–81.

53. On Arendt's theorization of the relation between law and democratic politics in *On Revolution*, see Jason Frank's chapter on Arendt in *Constituent Moments* (Durham, NC: Duke University Press, 2011) and Jeremy Waldron's "Arendt's Constitutional Politics," in *The Cambridge Companion to Hannah Arendt*, ed. Dana Villa (Cambridge: Cambridge University Press, 2000).

54. Benhabib, *Another Cosmopolitanism*, p. 28.

55. "*Eichmann in Jerusalem*: An Exchange of Letters Between Gershom Scholem and Hannah Arendt," *Encounter* 22 (January 1964):2, 51–54, 52.

56. Ibid., p. 54.

57. In Hannah Arendt, *The Jewish Writings*, ed. Jerome Kohn and Ron Feldman (New York: Schocken Books, 2007). The questions were ostensibly to be used for an article in *Look* magazine—an article that was never written or published. Arendt says, "[T]here is another side to this matter, and in order to discuss it I must refer you to my book *On Revolution* (something I hate to do but it can't be helped). On p. 227 ff. (and in other places as well) I speak of the significance of public opinion, which, in my view, stands in opposition to authentic public spirit. I report there the opinions of the Founding Fathers and say: 'Democracy. . . was abhorred because public opinion was held to rule

where public spirit ought to prevail, and the sign of this perversion was the unanimity of the citizenry; for 'when men exert their reason coolly and freely on a variety of distinct questions, they inevitably fall into different opinions on some of them. When they are governed by a common passion, their opinions, if they are so to be called, will be the same' (James Madison, *The Federalist Papers*, no. 50)" (p. 477).

58. Arendt, *On Revolution*, p. 224.

59. Ibid., p. 93. The American revolutionaries "knew," Arendt says, "that the public realm in a republic was constituted by an exchange of opinion between equals, and that this realm would simply disappear the very moment an exchange became superfluous because all equals happened to be of the same opinion" (p. 93). Consequently, the revolutionaries identified the word "people" not with the "general will" or "unified public opinion" that Arendt argues was characteristic of the French Revolution (p. 245; cf. 76), but with "the meaning of manyness, of the endless variety of a multitude whose majesty resided in its very plurality" (p. 93).

60. Arendt describes "public opinion" as what "remained of" public spirit "after the revolutionary spirit had been forgotten" (Ibid., p. 221). "This transformation corresponds with great precision to the invasion of the public realm by society; it is as thought the originally political principles were translated into social values" (Ibid., p. 221).

61. Ibid., p. 225.

62. Ibid., p. 227.

63. On *On Revolution*, see Honig, *Political Theory and the Displacement of Politics*, and Frank, *Constituent Moments*.

64. Letter from September 20, 1963, in *Between Friends: The Correspondence of Hannah Arendt and Mary McCarthy 1949–1975*, ed. Carol Brightman (New York: Harcourt Brace, 1995), p. 146. In an October 20, 1963, letter to Jaspers, Arendt similarly says: "Nobody on my side dares to publish his views anymore. And with good reason. It's extremely dangerous because a whole very well-organized mob immediately pounces on anyone who dares to say anything. Finally, everyone believes what everyone else believes—as we have often experienced in life" (*Hannah Arendt Karl Jaspers Correspondence 1926–1969*, p. 523).

65. *Hannah Arendt Karl Jaspers Correspondence 1926–1969*, p. 511.

66. Arendt, *Origins of Totalitarianism*, p. 115.

67. Arendt, *The Jewish Writings*, p. 483.

68. This may be why, in contrast to Zola and Burke, she never sought to persuade the public that she was truly on the side of justice, that her book was not the "image" that her detractors made it out to be. As she says in a letter to Mary McCarthy on September 20, 1963, "My position is that I wrote a report and that I am not in politics, either Jewish or otherwise" (*Between Friends*, p. 147). In a later letter, she emphasizes that she will "not answer individual critics" because the "criticism is directed at an 'image' and this image has been substituted for the book I wrote" (p. 151).

69. Although Arendt wrote privately to Mary McCarthy that she thought that really only Sarraute's last two "comic novels," *The Planetarium* and *The Golden Fruits*, were "truly successful" (*Between Friends*, p. 159).

70. Hannah Arendt, "Nathalie Sarraute," in *New York Review of Books*, March 5, 1964. DOI: http://www.nybooks.com/articles/archives/1964/mar/05/nathalie-sarraute. Accessed January 15, 2013.

71. Ibid.

72. Ibid.

73. Ibid.

74. Ibid.

75. Ibid. For Arendt, this companionship achieved through deference to "the they" is ultimately a perversion of the natural kinship individuals actually seek: "This is comedy and like all good comedy concerned with something deadly serious. The falsity of the intellectual 'they' is particularly painful, because it touches one of the most delicate and, at the same time, indispensable elements of human relationships, the element of common taste for which indeed 'no criterion of values' exists" (Ibid.). That is, *The Golden Fruits* addresses how the desire for solidarity—for finding affinity, companionship, and partiality for oneself—becomes perverted in the realm of public opinion. Here, solidarity is only available through abnegating oneself to the opinion of "the they," rather than through the exchange of independent views with others—through acknowledging the independent views of others, and being acknowledged by them.

76. In *The Planetarium*, Sarraute's comedic narrative also reveals a moment when "the they" is revealed as just as gullible and inexpert as the main character in the novel, who aspires to be part of "the they." Arendt depicts, in a long passage, the moment—the "metamorphosis"—in which this reality is revealed:

The story tells how the newly-wed couple-on-the-make obtain the apartment of the young man's aunt (they have an apartment to live in, but they need a new one 'to entertain'), who to her own great grief had installed in it a brand-new door in 'bad taste,' and most of the story's complexities turn about furniture and the unfortunate door. The metamorphosis takes place near the end of the book and, delightfully, concerns the same door: The young man takes the celebrity around for whom he had gone to all the trouble. He is in agony because of the door, but he is saved: While the celebrity is looking around, 'in one second, the most amazing, the most marvelous metamorphosis takes place. As though touched by a fairy wand, the door which, as soon as he had set eyes on it, had been surrounded by the thin papier-mache walls, the hideous cement of suburban houses. . . reverts to its original aspect, when, resplendent with life, it had appeared framed in the walls of an old convent cloister.' Alas, the poor door is not permitted to remain for long in its state of refound grace; there is another embarrassing object in the apartment, a Gothic virgin marred on one side by a restored arm, and the celebrity, oh horror, does not detect it: she 'stares fixedly at the shoulder, the arm, she swallows them stolidly, her stomach digests them easily, her eyes maintain the calm, indifferent impression of a cow's eyes.' *This is the moment of truth when everything comes apart* in 'a breach, a sudden cleavage:' she loses her power to perform miracles and back comes 'the oval door. . . floating, uncertain, suspended in limbo. . . massive old convent door or that of a cheap bungalow. . .' to haunt him forever after (Ibid.).

In this passage, which Arendt says is "one of the most exquisitely funny passages that I know in contemporary literature" (Ibid.), the "truth" about the celebrity is revealed—she does not have the "exquisite taste" to which the young man is supposedly deferring (she "swallows" and "digests. . . easily" the restored arm of the Gothic virgin). Yet rather than this revelation opening up space for his own judgment of reality, the young man is suspended between the two possibilities of the nature of the "exquisite taste" to which he supposedly deferring—the suburban door or the old convent door.

77. Ibid.

78. Hannah Arendt, "Thoughts on Lessing," in *Men in Dark Times* (New York: Houghton Mifflin Harcourt, 1970), p. 6.

79. Ibid.

80. In a 1968 *New Yorker* essay on Isak Dinesen (later included in *Men in Dark Times*), Arendt similarly suggests that the capacity of independent judgment is enabled by laughter and jokes. Arendt notes at the outset of the piece that the first name of Dinesen's

male pseudonym, "Isak," means "the one who laughs" ("Isak Dinesen," *The New Yorker*, November 9, 1968, p. 223) and Arendt frames her discussion of Dinesen's writing in terms of her favorite saying, "God loves a joke." Such jokes consist in ironic deviations from the envisioned story of the life one hoped to, or thought one would, live. For example, it was a "joke" that Dinesen became a writer at all. She only became a story-teller, Arendt says, because she needed to find a way to make a living after her life story (the story she hoped her life would be)—her romance with X and her life in Africa—collapsed (p. 223). Laughter, for Arendt's Dinesen, offered a way to address "traps" of "taking oneself seriously and identifying the woman with the author who has his identity confirmed, inescapably, in public" (p. 223). Through laughter, Dinesen (Blixen) was able to take up the ironical relationship to identity that Lessing's comedies allow one to take up in relation to the world—reconciling oneself to it, but never fully identifying with or being ruled by it. Through such ironic reconciliation, Dinesen was able to tell stories and make judgments about the world as it is, rather than as she wanted or hoped it would be. To return to Arendt's review of Sarraute, we might say that the reader's and author's experience of the "I" and "they" is able to transition to a plural "we" because, through laughter, they have managed to see the supposed unanimity of "the they" as a powerful myth, rather than reality. They have reconciled themselves, as it were, to the power of the myth and its effects, but they have not sold their soul to it. Through laughter, they maintain a distance from it that allows them to see a new possible angle of vision on the world and their place in it. As laughers, together, they already have formed a "we."

81. Hannah Arendt, *Essays in Understanding* (New York: Random House, 2011), p. 16.

82. Ibid.

83. On the very first page of the book, for example, she says that "the German-speaking accused party, like almost everyone else in the audience, follows the Hebrew proceedings through the simultaneous radio transmission, which is excellent in French, bearable in English, and *sheer comedy*, frequently incomprehensible, in German" (my emphasis, *EJ*, 3). The "comedy" here is that this forced speaking in Hebrew ignored what was obvious to everyone: that most people in the courtroom could have under-stood everything if the proceedings had taken place in German (the language of the Nazis). Arendt also calls it "comedy" when the "soul experts"—psychiatrists—certified Eichmann as "normal" (*EJ*, 26). "Behind the comedy of the soul experts lay the hard fact that his was obviously no case of moral let alone legal insanity" (*EJ*, 26). This com-edy—an ironic mismatch between the legal procedures and psychological techniques that attempted to grasp why and how Eichmann committed these crimes and the reality of his person—revealed something very serious, namely, Eichmann's sanity. Arendt suggests in her private notes that her term, "the banality of evil," is meant to reflect this comedic aspect of Eichmann. In her notes for a lecture she was to give at Hofstra University on the Eichmann case on February 18, 1964, next to the typed item #4 in her outline, "Banality of evil," Arendt wrote in the margin, "The comical motto." (in "Speeches/Writings" folder, "Speeches about Eichmann," Hannah Arendt Papers, Manuscript Division, Library of Congress, Washington D.C.) Arendt's narration of the Eichmann trial thus reveals for her audience the comic aspects of the incomprehensibility, or incongruity, of Eichmann that sparked laughter in Arendt, herself.

84. Yasco Horsman, *Theatres of Justice: Judging, Staging, and Working Through in Arendt, Brecht, and Delbo* (Palo Alto, CA: Stanford University Press, 2011), p. 37.

85. Similarly, Arendt says in Volume 1 of *The Life of the Mind* that Eichmann's "cliché-ridden language produced on the stand, as it had evidently done in his official life, a kind of macabre comedy" (New York: Houghton Mifflin Harcourt, 1981, p. 4).

86. Arendt says, referencing this story, that "[n]ow and then, the comedy breaks into the horror itself, and results in stories, presumably true enough, whose macabre humor easily surpasses that of any Surrealist invention" (*EJ*, 50).

87. Horsman, *Theatres of Justice*, p. 42.

88. Ibid.

89. Ibid., p. 43.

90. Ibid., p. 42.

91. Ibid., p. 43.

92. Hannah Arendt, "Introduction" to Bernd Naumann's *Auschwitz: A Report on the Proceedings Against Robert Karl Ludwig Mulka and Others Before the Court at Frankfurt* (New York: Praeger, 1966), p. xi.

93. Ibid., pp. xi–xii.

94. Ibid., my emphasis, p. xii.

95. In this sense, my approach to laughter is sympathetic to, but also departs from John Lombardini's attempt in "Civic Laughter: Aristotle and the Political Virtue of Humor," *Political Theory* 41(2013):2, 203–230, to outline an "ethos of democratic laughter" that "might prepare one to engage with others across lines of difference in a mode of agonistic respect" (p. 222). In contrast, I am interested in how laughter may be a productive way of addressing, but not resolving, democratic failure—a practice that poses its own risks to the democratic goods Lombardini outlines.

Chapter 5

1. Lawrie Balfour, *Democracy's Reconstruction: Thinking Politically with W.E.B. DuBois* (Oxford: Oxford University Press, 2011), p. 16.

2. Ibid.

3. Wendy Brown, *Edgework: Critical Essays on Knowledge and Politics* (Princeton, NJ: Princeton University Press, 2009), p. 6.

4. Ibid., p. 7.

5. Ibid., p. 8

6. Jason Frank *Constituent Moments* (Durham, NC: Duke University Press, 2009), p. 249.

7. "Eric Holder on Terrorist Trials in New York." November 13, 2009. The CSPAN Video Library. http://www.c-spanvideo.org/program/290007-1. Accessed November 5, 2012.

8. Ibid.

9. In contrast to Holder's framing of the trial as a victory for the rule of law over arbitrariness, conservative critics soon lambasted the plan by claiming that federal courts are inappropriate venues for trying terrorists, since the urgency of the "War on Terror" demands that the government use illegal tactics in interrogation, or at least tactics that would keep alleged terrorists' admissions from being admissible in civilian courts. For example, Andrew McCarthy—a former federal prosecutor who led terrorism prosecutions in the 1990s—argued, repudiating the approach in which he himself took part, that the "lawfare" approach of the 1990s mistakenly "regards alien security threats as if they were legal issues to be spotted and adjudicated rather than enemies to be smoked out and defeated before they can kill."McCarthy, *Willful Blindness: A Memoir of the Jihad* (New York: Encounter, 2008). On this point, also see William Shawcross, *Justice and the Enemy: Nuremberg, 9/11, and the Trial of Khalid Sheikh Mohammed* (New York: Public Affairs, 2011).

10. For instance, in *Justice and the Enemy*, William Shawcross defended Bush's categorization of captured alleged Al Qaeda terrorists and associates as "unlawful enemy combatants," who "can be targeted and detained but [are] not entitled to the privileges of a prisoner of war under the Third Geneva Convention" (p. 60). Similarly, McCarthy argues that those "individuals captured or apprehended in connection with armed conflicts and counterterrorism operations'—i.e., jihadists hell-bent on mass-murdering Americans,. . . cannot be tried in either civilian or military courts because the evidence gathered against them is intelligence information (often gathered form foreign agencies on the conditions that it not be exposed)" (*How the Obama Administration has Politicized Justice*, New York: Encounter Books, 2010, p. 22). Shawcross agreed with this claim because, on his reading of the Geneva Conventions (which the majority of the Supreme Court in Hamdan would disagree with)—and on most conservatives' readings of the Convention—those combatants who are not "commanded by a person responsible for his subordinates," who do not "wear a uniform or some other fixed emblem that is recognizable at a distance," do not "carry arms openly," and do not "observe the rules of war" are not entitled to the convention's protections—that is, they are unlawful enemy combatants (p. 61).

11. Shawcross, *Justice and the Enemy*, p. 122.

12. A military court would have been similarly insufficient to address the lawless tactics used against Mohammed because in a traditional court-martial, the same rules of evidence apply as in civilian court (that would keep out evidence obtained through torture) and in a new military commission trial, the rules of evidence are lax enough to admit evidence obtained through torture as legitimate. On this point, see David Cole's "Military Commissions and the Paradigm of Prevention," in *Guantanamo and Beyond: Exceptional Courts and Military Commissions in Comparative Perspective*, eds. Oren Gross and Fionnuala Ni Aolain (Cambridge: Cambridge University Press, 2013).

13. Invoking the law/exigency framework, Cole argues that federal courts are preferable to military commissions in Mohammed's case because military commissions are viewed as "little more than kangaroo courts" and, consequently, "any trial conducted therein will bear a huge presumption of invalidity." While Guantanamo could have been a (perhaps more secure) site of justice and of a fair trial, "our former president squandered that opportunity to conduct the trial in a much safer place by making that place the symbol of American lawlessness." Cole thus suggests that trying Mohammed in a civilian court will keep the trial free of the taint of Guantanamo and its injustices. David Cole, Contribution to a debate on "The Civilian Trial of Khalid Sheikh Mohammed," January 5, 2010. http://www.fed-soc.org/debates/detail/the-civilian-trial-of-khalid-sheikh-mohammed. Accessed May 30, 2013. Of course, Cole here seems to be taking the position that we can quarantine lawless, arbitrary, and coercive treatment of individuals to locations like Guantanamo in such a way that they only secure freedom within the United States, rather than undermining it—a position that he elsewhere rejects. In his 2003 book, *Enemy Aliens*, Cole argues that while there has been "much talk about the need to sacrifice liberty for security," in practice, "the government has most often at least initially sacrificed noncitizens' liberties while retaining basic protections for citizens" (*Enemy Aliens: Double Standards and Constitutional Freedoms in the War on Terror*, New York: The New Press, 2003, 2005). Cole argues that the problem with such policies is not only normative, but also pragmatic: these policies have often, in American history, paved the way for the circumscription of the rights of citizens. In other words, the "enemy alien" is a category that does not remain tethered to the formal constraints with which it is originally associated, but comes to be a category to which we imaginatively assign an "other" (citizen or non-citizen) during a time of crisis, spurred on by the politics of fear (e.g., Japanese internment during World War II). When Cole suggests that a

federal court has the ability to do justice in Mohammed's case in a way that military trials at Guantanamo could not, he is suggesting that federal courts could try Mohammed with the "clean slate" that Holder alluded to in his press conference—that is, because those courts have not symbolically been associated with the lawlessness of Guantanamo. Yet this very aspect of a federal trial threatens to excise the history of the American treatment of Mohammed during the trial and to enshrine a precedent of hiding rather than addressing the illegal and immoral treatment of foreign nationals that Cole critiques in *Enemy Aliens*.

14. David Cole, ed., *The Torture Memos: Rationalizing the Unthinkable* (New York: The New Press, 2009).

15. David Cole, "Guantanamo: The New Challenge to Obama," in *New York Review of Books*, June 9, 2011, http://www.nybooks.com/articles/archives/2011/jun/09/guanta-namo-new-challenge-obama/, Accessed July 11, 2014.

16. Specifically, Cole draws attention to the fact that "when Senator Lindsey Graham in the fall of 2009 sought to bar trying Khalid Sheikh Mohammed in civilian court, the administration succeeded in defeating the proposal by a vote of 55–45. So it can win, but only if it is willing to fight" (Ibid.).

17. Indeed, when he does talk about the public, he invokes the public as having pushed for the policies he supports—for example, by voting for Barack Obama. In the same piece on Guantanamo from the *New York Review of Books* that I discussed above, Cole says, "Most importantly, the President's obligation is to take a stand in support of what he says he believes 'with every fiber of his being,' and not to accept pollsters' predictions as an inevitable reality. That, after all, is what leadership is all about. That is what we elected him for. It is time for President Obama to stand and fight" (Ibid.).

18. Slavoj Zizek. "Knight of the Living Dead," *New York Times*. March 24, 2007. http://www.nytimes.com/2007/03/24/opinion/24zizek.html. Accessed June 20, 2013.

19. Slavoj Zizek, *In Defense of Lost Causes* (New York: Verso), p. 46.

20. Zizek, "Knight of the Living Dead."

21. In contrast to the stagnant "opposition between emancipatory outbursts and the sobering 'day after' when life returns to its pragmatic normal run"—wherein "every attempt to avoid and/or postpone this sobering return to the normal run of things amounts to terror, to the reversal of enthusiasm into monstrosity"—Zizek argues that we should value and affirm precisely attempts to avoid the return to the everyday, even if they have ended historically in failure (Zizek, *In Defense of Lost Causes*, p. 116).

22. Halberstam, *The Queer Art of Failure*, p. 174.

23. For Zizek, the reason we should value these lost causes is because, even if they failed in practice, they contain a core idea on behalf of which we should continue to fight. While Zizek agrees with the "basic Hegelian insight according to which the failure of reality to fully actualize an Idea is simultaneously the failure (limitation) of this Idea," he also suggests that "the gap that separates the Idea from its actualization signals a gap within this Idea itself. This is why the spectral Idea that continues to haunt historical reality signals the falsity of the new historical reality itself, its inadequacy to its own Notion—the failure of the Jacobin utopia, its actualization in utilitarian bourgeois reality, is simultaneously the limitation of this reality itself" (Ibid., p. 209).

24. Steve Johnston. "On the Use and Misuse of Zero Dark Thirty." The Contemporary Condition blog. March 14, 2013. http://contemporarycondition.blogspot.com/2013/03/on-use-and-misuse-of-zero-dark-thirty.html. Accessed June 20, 2013.

25. Ali Soufan with Daniel Freedman, *The Black Banners: The Inside Story of 9/11 and the War Against Al Qaeda* (New York: Norton, 2011). Also see Ali Soufan's "Torture, Lies, and Hollywood," *New York Times*. February 22, 2013. http://www.nytimes.

com/2013/02/24/opinion/sunday/torture-lies-and-hollywood.html. Accessed June 20, 2013.

26. Indeed, the rest of Bigelow's movies, especially *The Hurt Locker*, caution against seeing the lead character in the movie as a conventional "hero." The heroism of the hero in *The Hurt Locker* is enabled not by heroic motives, but by a flight from intimacy.

27. See, for example, Steve Coll's " 'Disturbing' & 'Misleading' " (in *New York Review of Books*, February 7, 2013 , http://www.nybooks.com/articles/archives/2013/feb/07/disturbing-misleading-zero-dark-thirty/, Accessed July 11, 2014.) and Jane Mayer's "Zero Conscience in 'Zero Dark Thirty' " (in a New Yorker blogpost, http://www.newyorker.com/online/blogs/newsdesk/2012/12/torture-in-kathryn-bigelows-zero-dark-thirty.html. Accessed June 20, 2013).

28. Indeed, for Maya, as for the majority of Americans (at least according to opinion polls), all tactics are measured in terms of whether they will help her find bin Laden (or, in the words of her superior, to find targets and kill terrorists). For example, see Amy Zegart's "Controversy Dims as Public Opinion Shifts" (in the *New York Times* online debate about John Brennan's nomination to be CIA Director. http://www.nytimes.com/roomfordebate/2013/01/07/the-right-or-wrong-experience-for-the-job/controversy-dims-as-public-opinion-shifts-5. Accessed June 20, 2013). Zegart shows that public opinion has actually become more pro-torture than even in the Bush years.

29. One review in *Rolling Stone* (Matt Taibbi's " 'Zero Dark Thirty' Is Osama bin Laden's Last Victory over America." January 16, 2013. http://www.rollingstone.com/politics/blogs/taibblog/zero-dark-thirty-is-osama-bin-ladens-last-victory-over-america-20130116. Accessed June 20, 2013) suggested that the film is meant to elicit cheers from the audience (and the reviewer noted that they cheered in the theater where the reviewer saw it), but I do not think the film supports this reading. First, it is clear from the outset in Bigelow's filming that it is an assassination mission (and this is how Maya frames it, as well) and the depiction of this is graphic, without swelling music that gives it any kind of necessarily triumphal feel. Men and women are killed, leaving behind screaming children and blood-streaked floors as the agents gradually find their way to bin Laden. While two of the agents in the movie whoop and holler after killing him, this stands incongruously aside the solemnness of all the other agents and the disgust of others. In other words, the film presents the mission to kill bin Laden as ambivalent—as creating different emotions in different individuals (in the movie theater where I saw the movie, in Manhattan, one person in the audience clapped after the capture of bin Laden; everyone else was silent). Maya's own reaction is not joyous, as described above.

30. See, for example, Marjorie Garber's "Joe Camel: An X-Rated Smoke" (*Baltimore Sun*, April 2, 1992. http://articles.baltimoresun.com/1992-04-02/news/1992093156_1_camel-hamlet-thread-spool. Accessed February 29, 2014) on the recurrence of this motif. Thanks to Bonnie Honig for referring me to this piece.

31. Interestingly, Jessica Chastain—the star who plays Maya—offers a similar analysis of this moment. She says, "I believe that was Kathryn's intention when she made the film—to open a conversation. She ends it with an unanswered question, Where do you want to go? She's asking the audience, Where have we been, and where do we go from here?" (quoted in "Kathryn Bigelow: The Art of Darkness," by Jessica Winter, *Time*, February 4, 2013. http://www.time.com/time/magazine/article/0,9171,2134499,00.html. Accessed June 20, 2013).

32. The public solicited by *Zero Dark Thirty* might be, in other words, the public of plural independent viewpoints, or what Arendt calls "public spirit."

33. Matt Taibbi, " 'Zero Dark Thirty' Is Osama bin Laden's Last Victory over America."

34. On this injustice, see David Cole's "Military Commissions and the Paradigm of Prevention."

35. My turn of phrase, "the art of losing causes," is a nod to the title and subject of Halberstam's *The Queer Art of Failure*. By the queer art of failure, Halberstam refers to the art of understanding, practicing, and becoming attuned to individual failure as a site of promise and social critique rather than just shortcoming. For example, Halberstam argues against treating failure "optimistically," in the terms of norms of success that often place the responsibility of failure on the individual rather than on societal structure, and pursuing "negative think[ing]" instead. Through "negative thinking," "the experience of failure" can show failure not to be the result of insufficient effort, but rather an experience that allows individuals "to confront the gross inequalities of everyday life in the United States" (p. 4).

Halberstam's discussion of the queer art of failure is aimed at attuning us to the promise of failure in a world that portrays failure primarily as the inverse of (rather than a productive challenge to) standards of success. I see such an attunement, and the maxims that Halberstam recommends, as contributing to the art of losing causes. Yet Halberstam's maxims are primarily attuned to the failure of the subject—that is, the failure of an individual to successfully reproduce the norms that constitute successful subjectivity. In contrast, the art of losing causes is the art not only of becoming attuned to the ambiguity of failure, but also of experiencing, naming, and responding to persistent democratic failure without permanently despairing of democracy.

36. In *Worldly Ethics* (Durham, NC: Duke University Press, 2012), Myers argues that "[w]hen 'action in concert' appears to be rare or unlikely, we may be attracted to the notion that democracy can be rescued by something other than itself, namely, the discovery of the proper ethics" (pp. 9–10).

37. As Butler puts the point in *Precarious Life* (New York: Verso, 2004), "Suffering can yield an experience of humility, of vulnerability, of impressionability and dependence, and these can become resources, if we do not 'resolve' them too quickly" (pp. 149–150). Specifically, such experiences could allow us to "imagine and practice another future"—one characterized by an acknowledgment of mutual dependence that "will move beyond the current cycle of revenge" (p. 10) and involve a turn to "non-violent ethics" (p. 139). To put it differently, an experience of suffering can lead us to acknowledge our shared vulnerability to violence and, thus, to value nonviolence—a value that Butler intimates can lead to greater political engagement against violence. Similarly, Stephen White argues in *The Ethos of a Late-Modern Citizen* (Cambridge, MA: Harvard University Press, 2009) that our "common subjection" to our condition of mortality "provides us with a weak ontological illumination of human equality" that should lead us to be skeptical of all forms of inequality (including economic inequality) (p. 94).

38. For example, see Bonnie Honig's *Antigone Interrupted* (Cambridge: Cambridge University Press, 2013) and Simon Stow's "Pericles at Gettysburg and Ground Zero: Tragedy, Patriotism, and Public Mourning," *American Political Science Review* 101(2007):2, 195–208. Of course, both Honig and Stow note that public mourning can serve to shore up dominant national memorial images rather than interrupting them.

39. On the politicality of consciousness-raising groups, see Ch. 2–3 of Sara Evans's *Tidal Wave: How Women Changed America at Century's End* (New York: Free Press, 2003).

40. On the Riot Grrrl movement, see Sara Marcus's *Girls to the Front: The True Story of the Riot Grrrl Revolution* (New York: HarperCollins, 2010).

41. For this distinction, see the Introduction to Bonnie Honig's *Antigone Interrupted* (Cambridge: Cambridge University Press, 2013).

42. Alan Keenan, *Democracy in Question: Democratic Openness in a Time of Political Closure* (Palo Alto, CA: Stanford University Press, 2003).

43. See Michael Warner's *Publics and Counterpublics* (New York: Zone Books, 2005).

INDEX